PRAISE FOR *Myth of Persecution*

"Brilliant and provocative. . . . Drawing on close readings of traditional martyr stories and on deep historical research, [Moss] convincingly demonstrates that little evidence exists for the widespread persecution of Christians by the Romans."

—*Publisher's Weekly*

"Fascinating. . . . One of the most enlightening aspects of *The Myth of Persecution* is Moss's ability to find contemporary analogies that make the ancient world more intelligible to the average reader."

—*Salon.com*

"Like the ancient poets, Moss at once instructs and entertains. She also transgresses the boundary between historian and theologian and calls the church to repentance. She contends that the martyrdom narrative poses grave dangers, having contributed to everything from mild alienation to outright atrocity throughout the church's history."

—*Christian Century*

"Historical argumentation at its most cogent."

—*Booklist*

"Fascinating. . . . Beyond simply recasting ancient stories in a new light, the book provides a hopeful outlook for a world in which modern Christians could drop the myth of their persecuted past."

—*U.S. Catholic*

"Exhaustively researched, yet accessible, . . . Moss's book lays bare that truth and presents us with the opportunity to, instead of retelling myth, begin to explore the actual history of this era."

—*Portland Book Review*

"Compellingly argued and artfully written, [Moss's book] reveals how the popular misconception about martyrdom in the early church still creates real barriers to compassion and dialogue today. An important book and a fascinating read."

—*Archbishop Desmond Tutu*

"This is the best sort of history: delightfully accessible yet based on prodigious scholarship, deeply serious, yet entertaining and enlightening. Above all, it shows the reader the importance of sweeping away myth in order that we do not behave badly in the present, using the past as our excuse."

—Diarmaid MacCulloch, Professor of the History of the
Church at Oxford University and author of *Christianity:
The First Three Thousand Years*

"A tour de force addition to the literature of sacred violence; a case study in how bold scholarship can dismantle it. Candida Moss's religious history will change religion, and, if Christians heed it, history, too."

—James Carroll, author of *Jerusalem, Jerusalem*

"Moss compellingly dismantles the wall of righteousness that some Christians erect in order to justify both their own certitude and conflict with others. Without this persecution narrative, we will be better equipped to work together in our complex and pluralistic world to resolve differences and perhaps even live the Gospel value of loving all."

—Sister Simone Campbell, executive director of NETWORK

"This is a timely and eye-opening book. Moss's carefully researched and readable account corrects and clarifies an important feature of a history that has been fictionalized for too long."

—Harvey Cox, Hollis Research Professor of Divinity at
Harvard and author of *The Future of Faith*

"In engaging prose and with scholarly acumen, Moss pulls back the curtain on one of Western history's best-kept secrets—that Christians were never subjects of sustained persecution. Read this book and rejoice as Moss turns history on its head and points the way beyond religious violence."

—Diana Butler Bass, author of *Christianity After Religion*

"This remarkable book is certain to spark an intense debate over yet another myth of early Christianity, namely that the persecution of Christians was widespread and continues to this day. Not only has Candida Moss reminded us that much of what we accept uncritically is pious legend, but that such myths poison the religious and political rhetoric of our time. There is something here to offend everyone, which is the first sign of groundbreaking work."

—Rev. Dr. Robin R. Meyers, UCC Minister and author of *The
Underground Church: Reclaiming the Subversive Way of Jesus*

The

MYTH

of

Persecution

The
MYTH
of
Persecution

HOW EARLY CHRISTIANS INVENTED
A STORY OF MARTYRDOM

CANDIDA MOSS

HarperOne
An Imprint of HarperCollinsPublishers

HarperOne

HarperCollins books may be purchased for educational, business, or sales promotional use. For information please e-mail the Special Markets Department at SPsales@harpercollins.com.

HarperCollins website: http://www.harpercollins.com
HarperCollins®, ≡®, and HarperOne™ are trademarks of HarperCollins Publishers.

FIRST HARPERCOLLINS PAPERBACK EDITION PUBLISHED IN 2014

Library of Congress Cataloging-in-Publication Data

Moss, Candida R.
    The myth of persecution : how early Christians invented a story of martyrdom / Candida R. Moss.
        p. cm.
    ISBN 978–0–06–210455–7
    1. Martyrdom—Christianity. 2. Persecution. 3. Christianity—Relations. I. Title.
BR1601.3.M67   2013
272—dc23   2012028405

14 15 16 17 18   RRD(H)   10 9 8 7 6 5 4 3 2 1

This book is dedicated to my grandmother, the glamorous and utterly singular Rosamund Fisher. I aspire to be to others the kind of unforgettable heroine that she has been to me.

Contents

Contents

INTRODUCTION

SHORTLY BEFORE MIDNIGHT ON December 31, 2010, a young woman named Mariam Fekry paused at her computer to share her thoughts on the expiring year with her friends and Facebook acquaintances. She happily wrote, "2010 is over. This year has the best memories of my life. Really enjoyed this year. I hope that 2011 is much better. Please God stay beside me and help make it all true."[1] Mariam's dreams for the coming year lasted a little more than a quarter of an hour. At twenty minutes past midnight, January 1, 2011, a car bomb exploded across the street from al-Qiddissin ("The Saints") Church in Alexandria, Egypt. Mariam, her mother, aunt, and sister Martina were among the more than twenty Coptic Christians killed in the blast. After a long day of preparing food, the four women were attending midnight Mass in celebration of the New Year. Young and beautiful, Mariam was, by all accounts, full of life. She attended university, taught Sunday school, and had high hopes of that year finding the elusive man of her dreams and settling down. She was only twenty-two when she died.

The explosion sparked clashes between police and locals in Alexandria. People filled the streets protesting the lack of government action and the mistreatment of Christians in Egypt. Copts, a minority in Egypt, angrily hurled stones at the authorities, stormed a nearby mosque, and threw religious books into the streets. That the source of the carnage was unknown only made the situation worse. Conflicting newspaper reports attributed the bombing to the terrorist group al-Qaeda and to local Egyptian Muslims. While both the head of the Coptic Church and the Egyptian president called for peace, protestors defiantly chanted, "We will not be afraid" and "With soul and blood we will redeem the cross."

In the media and on the Internet, Mariam and the other Christians who died in the New Year's Day attack were hailed as something more than innocent victims of terrorism—they were acclaimed as martyrs. Mariam became the face of martyrdom in the cyber age: her Facebook wall, the site of her final message to God and the world, was flooded with messages from people she had never met. People were drawn to this beautiful young woman, attracted to her innocence, and inspired by the tragedy of her story. Christian bloggers asked Mariam to pray for them. Virtual support carried none of the risks of in-person protest, of course, but thousands joined online groups dedicated to her memory and posted homemade video tributes to the modern-day martyr. Even the president of Egypt talked about "the blood of the martyrs" killed in the attack. Many of the virtual memorials dedicated to Mariam connect her to the heroes of the early church—to St. Polycarp, to Sts. Perpetua and Felicity, and to the host of Christian saints that preceded her. The form of her celebration is modern, but the ideas behind it are ancient. Contrary to what people might have imagined, the admiration for and love of the martyrs is as alive as ever.

In the blink of an eye the terrorist attack on the church in Alexandria changed from an unjust act of violence to a cause for religious martyrdom. There is no doubt that the church in Alexandria was targeted precisely because it was a place where Christians met, but the moment that Mariam and her relatives started to be called martyrs, the popular perception of the event changed. No longer was the attack simply an act of horrifying violence perpetrated by a terrorist group. Nor was it the unfortunate result of local religious, political, and social tensions. It became a direct and outright attack on Christianity as a whole. Rather than "turning the other cheek," the

Christian community was militarized. What happened to the Coptic Christians was barbaric, horrifying, and wrong. They were victims of an act of terrorism. Once Mariam became a martyr, she and the other Christian victims were seen as soldiers in a two-thousand-year-old religious conflict: a conflict between Christianity and the world, a battle between good and evil.

The perception that the events in Alexandria were part of a larger struggle between Christianity and the world fueled the retaliation that followed. The violent Christian responses to the bombing were grounded in a sense of religious self-preservation and self-righteousness. Even though it was unclear who was responsible for the bombing, the protestors targeted specifically Muslim institutions. Their slogans show just how intimately their acts of violence were related to their Christian identity: the protestors saw the attack on the church as one more entry in a history of unjust violence against Christians. By resisting this persecution, even with violence, they were actively assisting Jesus: they shouted that their blood would *redeem the cross*. Under ordinary circumstances no Christian would presume to play such an important role in the world. By using this language, the protestors aligned their actions with the death of Jesus. The introduction of religious language and the theologizing of violence made the deaths of the victims of the New Year's Day bombing meaningful and intelligible to a traumatized Christian community. But it also had the unintended effect of encouraging people to fight in defense of their faith.

Ironically, it is the belief that Christians are persecuted that empowered the protestors to attack others. Against the objections of church leaders that the violence should end with Mariam and the other victims, the Christian protestors replied that they were unjustly persecuted and that their actions were sanctioned by God. The rhetoric of persecution legitimates and condones retributive violence. Violence committed by the persecuted is an act of divinely approved self-defense. In attacking others they are not only defending themselves; they are defending all Christians. This idea isn't simply the by-product of strained twenty-first-century Christian-Muslim relations. The view that Christians are by their very nature at odds with the world is an ancient one. Its roots lie in the history of Christianity and, more specifically, in the way Christians think of themselves as the successors of the early church.

The Age of the Martyrs

SINCE THE DEATH OF Jesus, hundreds of thousands of Christians have been hailed as martyrs. A recent study estimates that over the course of the past two thousand years as many as *seventy million* Christians have died for their beliefs—more than the total number of fatalities in World War II.[2] Some of these individuals are household names—Joan of Arc, Martin Luther King Jr., Sir Thomas More, and Oscar Romero—while others are just anonymous Christians executed en masse, not even leaving their names behind. These martyrs are held up as models for all kinds of Christian conduct. Churches, schools, and infants are named after them. Their stories are taught to children in Sunday school, and their deaths are remembered as glorious examples of lives lived in obedience to God. But why?

Considered from a modern secular perspective, martyrdom is a very strange concept. Today, people work hard to stay alive: we vaccinate our children, get annual checkups with doctors, take antibiotics, avoid antibiotics, look both ways when we cross the street, drink green tea, and wear seat belts, all as part of an effort to avoid dying a moment before we have to. Given that we expend so much effort staying alive, it might seem strange to think that anyone would choose to die. And yet, even today, people are still willing to give up their lives for a cause they believe in. Even if they are reluctant to take the plunge themselves, many more respect those who have sacrificed their lives for others. Where did this idea of martyrdom come from? Why would someone die for his or her religious beliefs? How is it that people can see violence and death as something good and holy?

The valorization of martyrs, in fact even the title "martyr," can be traced back to the early church. According to the Bible, persecution has been a part of Christianity from the very beginning. In many ways, this persecution began with Jesus himself, for, although they differ in numerous important details, the Gospel writers are in agreement that Jesus was unjustly sentenced to death. In the Gospel of John, Pilate actually declares Jesus innocent (19:4), and in the Gospel of Matthew he reluctantly washes his hands of Jesus's blood before condemning him to die (27:24). Historians have noted that some of Jesus's sayings and his disruption of Temple affairs were dramatic enough to warrant his arrest and execution.[3] Yet to readers, the death of Jesus seems unwarranted. This sense of injustice sits unexpectedly comfortably with the idea that Jesus's death was purposeful. He died for our sins, after all. Yet even though Jesus gave up his life for humanity, no one reading the Gospels would come away with the impression that he deserved it.

At the time, most Jews expected a victorious military messiah who would liberate them from the tyrannical Romans. But for the followers of Jesus, the death of their leader changed the way they thought about conquest and death. Although some Christians argued that the crucifixion was an elaborate magic trick and that Christ never really died, the majority started to see the suffering of the innocent as a good thing. The fact that the Son of God willingly embraced death for the salvation of others necessarily meant that death for God must be good—otherwise why would he have done it? The death of Jesus and the promise of the resurrection became a model for Christians. In times of persecution, the answer to the question "What would Jesus do?" is that Jesus would die.

The idea that Jesus's death should be an example for Christians is not an inference made by careful readers attempting to decipher the opaque meaning of the Bible. Jesus actually *tells* his followers that they should expect to find themselves arrested. Even more pointedly, Jesus insists that his followers should "take up their cross" and follow him (Mark 8:34–38). Later generations of interpreters have worked hard to read this passage figuratively, but for early Christians this was an unambiguous call to martyrdom.

Jesus was the first to die, but his death quickly became a model for his followers. In the New Testament book of the Acts of the Apostles (chaps. 6–7), an articulate young man named Stephen attracts the attention of the Jewish authorities. He is brought before the Jewish high council, where he is charged with predicting the destruction of the Temple and invited to defend himself. Stephen offers what is possibly the least effective speech of defense in recorded history. Rather than repudiate the charges, he delivers a passionate speech in which he indicts the Jewish people for always rejecting and persecuting their prophets. He calls the Jews betrayers and murderers and accuses them of killing the messiah. The people are enraged; they drag Stephen out of the city and stone him to death. Stephen's execution actually proves his point: he argued that the Jews had always rejected and persecuted the prophets of God, and they promptly killed him. With Stephen's speech and the story of Stephen's death, the author of Acts creates a tradition in which the true people of God—the followers of Jesus— are constantly under attack.

Stephen stands at the head of a long line of early Christian martyrs. According to tradition, all but one of Jesus's apostles met gory, untimely ends. Peter was crucified upside down in Rome, Matthias and Barnabas were stoned, James the Just (the brother of Jesus) was thrown from a precipice and then beaten to death with clubs, and— perhaps most horrendous of all—Bartholomew was flayed alive. The drama of these stories made them wildly appealing; they were the campfire stories and bestselling novels of their day.

The persecution only began with the apostles. In 64 CE a great fire ravaged Rome, devastating the city in a mere five days. The emperor Nero, who may well have been responsible for starting the fire himself, used the Christians as scapegoats for the disaster.[4] As a punishment, Nero apparently devised grotesque executions for the Christians: he covered them in animal skins and had them torn apart by dogs, and he doused them in tar and used them as human torches to light the night sky. Christians weren't ordinary criminals, and they didn't die ordinary deaths.

As Christianity grew, so did the ranks of the martyrs. According to the fourth-century historian Eusebius, first- and second-century Christians were racked, beaten, and scourged. They were condemned to the amphitheaters to face wild animals, forced to fight gladiators, beheaded or strangled quietly in jail, and burned publicly as a mark of shame. Tens of thousands were arrested and executed, but despite these and other tortures, the martyrs stood strong and resolute. Even in periods of fierce persecution and faced with threats of rape and torture, they refused to recant their beliefs, preferring martyrdom and unity with God in heaven to long life with their families on earth. Even though the night sky was lit with the pyres of Christian martyrs and the streets ran red with the blood of the saints, Christianity ultimately emerged victorious over the Roman Empire and became the powerful world religion that we know today.

We might expect that continual persecution and the desire to achieve martyrdom were a threat to Christian survival. After all, if everyone is killed for the faith, who is left to practice it? Paradoxically, we learn, for Christianity the reverse was true. When early Christians described the growth of the faith during this period, they credited martyrdom with its success. Writing around the turn of the third century, a North African lawyer named Tertullian famously wrote that "the blood of the martyrs is the seed" of the church.[5] The way the early Christians tell it, martyrdom was a necessary part of Christian existence and fostered the survival of Christianity. The deaths of Christians fueled the growth of the church and were an integral part of its success; the popularity of the stories of the early martyrs played an important part in both disseminating the Christian message and converting people to Christianity.

For the first three hundred years of its existence, the tradition maintains, Christianity was a persecuted and suffering religion. During this period—the so-called Age of the Martyrs—its members were hunted down and executed, and their property and books were burned by crusading emperors. Women and children were thrown to the lions and boiled alive in cauldrons, as maddened crowds bayed for blood. The history of early Christianity, as we have received it, is a history of victimization and pain. Yet despite these overwhelming odds, Christianity survived, and with the ascension of the Roman emperor Constantine in 313 CE Christians at last had the freedom to practice their religion in peace.

Modern Stories of Persecution

DURING THE SEVENTEEN HUNDRED years since Constantine's acceptance of Christianity, Christians have not forgotten their persecuted roots or the importance of martyrdom. Whenever Christians have felt threatened, they have returned to the New Testament and to the martyrs of the early church for consolation and inspiration. During the Reformation, an English Protestant named John Foxe wrote a Protestant history of martyrdom entitled the *Acts and Monuments of the Christian Church*.[6] Foxe lived and wrote during a dangerous, turbulent time, full of religious conflict and uncertainty. In 1553 Mary Tudor, the daughter of the frequently married Henry VIII, became queen of England, and England was restored to Roman Catholicism until her death in 1558. Her religious reforms were met with resistance from devout Protestants, and nearly three hundred people were burned at the stake for heresy. Foxe's book told the stories of these English martyrs as part of a grand history of martyrdom, beginning with the martyrs of the early church, moving through the medieval period, and concluding with the events of his own time. His book cast the Protestant martyrs as the heirs of the apostles and the early church and their opponents as agents of Satan. There were two sides in Foxe's world—the true church and the devil-led Papists—and they were engaged in a battle to the death. The book was an instant success; it was reprinted in multiple editions and turned Foxe into a literary celebrity.[7]

Modern Christians often interpret their experiences in the world and interactions with others as part of this history of persecution and the struggle between good and evil. Sometimes this idea inspires great courage and heroism and provides comfort to the sick or dying. And there are places in the world where Christians face real violence. This violence often goes unpublicized and unnoticed. The fact is, though, that the influence of these stories isn't limited just to situations where the oppressed or suffering need help. It is not only the suffering and oppressed who think of themselves as persecuted. Martyrdom is easily adapted by the powerful as a way of casting themselves as victims and justifying their polemical and vitriolic attacks on others. When disagreement is viewed as persecution, then these innocent sufferers must fight—rhetorically and literally—to defend themselves. In this polarized view of the world, disagreement and conflict—even entirely nonviolent conflict—is not just a difference of opinion; it is religious persecution. The source of the persecution is often explicitly demonized, labeled "evil," or cast as warfare. From Rick Santorum's statement during a speech in 2008 that "Satan is attacking the great institutions of America"[8] to Rick Perry's campaign promise to "end Obama's war on religion,"[9] the idea that Christians are under attack is pervasive.

On April 14, 2012, Daniel R. Jenky, the bishop of Peoria, Illinois, delivered one of the most controversial sermons in recent American memory. During his sermon at the Mass for the "Call to Catholic Men of Faith" rally, he challenged his audience to practice "heroic Catholicism." Heroic Catholicism, in this case, meant standing—and voting—against the Obama administration and opposing the U.S. Department of Health and Human Services mandate. There's nothing surprising about a Catholic bishop opposing abortion and contraception, but what drew heated responses and fervent debate was the implicit comparison that Jenky made between President Obama, Adolf Hitler, and Joseph Stalin. Jenky stated, "Barack Obama—with his radical, pro-abortion and extreme secularist agenda—now seems intent on following a similar path" as other governments throughout history who "have tried to force Christians to huddle and hide only within the confines of their churches." Jenky singled out the Nazi and

Stalinist regimes as antecedents to Obama's health-care reforms.

Bishop Jenky's homily immediately highlighted the divisions among the already polarized Catholic laity. His comments about Hitler and Stalin in particular were met with public declarations of support, horror, and outrage. They serve as code words for genocide and, whether Bishop Jenky intended this or not, they implied that Obama's policies might set us on the road to another Holocaust. Although some defended Jenky's right to free speech and the content of his sermon, others called the comparison morally reprehensible and rhetorically suspect.

Yet Jenky's repeated exhortations to Catholics to "fight" drew upon a much lengthier history of the church. This was not just about Obama, Stalin, and Hitler; this was about the history of the church in the world. Jenky said:

> For 2,000 years the enemies of Christ have certainly tried their best. But think about it. The Church survived and even flourished during centuries of terrible persecution, during the days of the Roman Empire. The Church survived barbarian invasions. The Church survived wave after wave of Jihads. The Church survived the age of revolution. The Church survived Nazism and Communism. And in the power of the resurrection, the Church will survive the hatred of Hollywood, the malice of the media, and the mendacious wickedness of the abortion industry.[10]

Jenky here invokes the now standard Christian idea that the church has always been persecuted. The position in which the church finds itself is nothing new. Catholics should not fear opposition, he says, because "the devil will always love their own, and will always hate us." If you are not with us, he implies, you are with the devil, Judas Iscariot, Hitler, and Stalin.

Similar uses of the rhetoric of persecution in discussions of American society are not limited to clergy. It spills over into political commentary and reform. In 2003, David Limbaugh, the younger brother of celebrity talk-show host Rush Limbaugh, published *Persecution: How Liberals Are Waging War Against Christianity*.[11] The book describes itself as a "call to action" for modern Christians who, like Christianity's founders, should stand up and defend their right to religious freedom. The basic thrust of the book is that, although Christians are no longer thrown to the lions, they suffer other forms of oppression. As Christians and as patriots they must defend themselves. By linking his assessment of the Christian experience to both the founding fathers and conservative politics, Limbaugh implies that being an American and being a Christian are the same. Moreover, being an American Christian means being persecuted by others. The dust jacket of the book even depicts a prowling lion poised to strike the unsuspecting reader. In other contexts, we would not consider those whose civil rights and political liberties are firmly protected to be persecuted, but Limbaugh interprets his situation within this framework. He claims that contemporary American Christians are *persecuted*, and in so doing he links the modern world to the early church.

The connection between patriotism, Christianity, and political issues is still at the forefront of modern politics. In August 2011 Republican presidential candidate Rick Santorum publicly complained that the "gay community . . . [had] gone out on a jihad" against him.[12] The issue at stake was gay marriage and comments Santorum had made about homosexuality in general. By repeatedly stating that his position was rooted in the Bible and characterizing the position of his critics as holy war, Santorum claimed that he was the victim of religious persecution. Even though Santorum is a political figure whose words and actions have ramifications for others and, thus, invite scrutiny and criticism from the public, he cast his critics as persecutors. In doing so he implied that he was the victim of hatred, that this was not a matter of differing opinions, and that his opponents had no reason for criticizing him. It wasn't even a question of whether their arguments were good or bad; in Santorum's view they were attacking him because he is Christian and, as such, he is part of a long tradition of the Christian persecuted.

But Santorum went much further than this. By using the hot-button term "jihad" Santorum grouped his critics with suicide bombers and terrorists. He could have used Christian language like "holy war" or "crusade," but instead he invoked the horrifying specter of 9/11 in order to suggest not only that gay-rights activists are unchristian, but also that they are un-American. They are like the outsiders seeking to attack America. As a true patriot and true Christian, he is just defending himself. Whatever a person's opinion on gay marriage, it is clear that gay-rights activists are not, in reality, in league with al-Qaeda, but this is exactly what Santorum implied. At this point the issues themselves had completely vanished. For Santorum, it had become a case of "us versus them," and they're with the terrorists.

The use of this kind of polemical rhetoric is not limited only to the writings of conservative politicians. On June 5, 2012, *New York Times* columnist Maureen Dowd published an editorial called "Is Pleasure a Sin?," the subtitle of which is "In Its Jihad on Nuns, the Vatican Shows No Mercy to a Sister of Mercy."[13] The subject of the piece was the response by the Vatican's Congregation for the Doctrine of the Faith to an academic book by Yale Divinity School's emerita professor Margaret Farley. The subtitle of the article and the selection of the strikingly evocative term "jihad" implicitly serve to highlight the apparently unchristian nature of the Vatican's decision. The characterization of the Vatican's actions as persecution continued into the body of the article, as Dowd went on to describe the event as a "thuggish crusade." However we might regard the decision made by the Vatican's Congregation for the Doctrine of the Faith or the content of Dowd's argument, the rhetoric of persecution is no less damning and polarizing than in Santorum's case. Only the target and content of the politics are different. The rhetoric reinforces the divisions in the Catholic Church by characterizing the hierarchy as persecutors, and it automatically designates the actions of that hierarchy as hateful, irrational, and of the very worst kind.

In these contexts, the use of this language of persecution is discursive napalm. It obliterates any sense of scale or moderation. This stymieing, dialogue-ending language is disastrous for public discourse, disastrous for politics, and results in a more deeply poisoned public well for everyone. When all areas of modern society and politics are recast as a battle between God and Satan, good and evil, "us" and "them," then people are compelled to fight. Evil must be identified, resisted, and uprooted. Resisting this "evil" might mean resorting to physical violence or outright war, but if Christians are being "attacked" and "persecuted," then what else can they do? Just as in the early church, today's innocent, victimized Christians should stand their ground rather than seek compromise or resolution. It's what the martyrs would have done. It's what Jesus would have done. Persecution has always been a part of being Christian, and it always demands the same response.

The Myth of Christian Martyrdom

IN THIS UNDERSTANDING OF what it means to be a Christian, a lot of weight rests on the history of the early church. Bishop Jenky's speech cites only Jesus and the early Christians before moving to the modern period. If there was no persecuted early church, he could not claim that Christians should expect persecution. Even though Jesus predicted the suffering of his followers, it is the belief that Jesus's statements were proven in the persecution of the early church that gives force to the idea that Christians are always persecuted. It is this idea, the idea that Christians are *always* persecuted, that authenticates modern Christian appropriations of martyrdom. It provides the interpretative lens through which to view all kinds of Christian experiences in the world as a struggle between "us" and "them." Without this history and interpretative lens, each situation would have to be judged on its own merits. Disagreement and oppression might be the result of differing opinions, injustice, and conflict, not a cosmic battle between good and evil.

What if Christians weren't continually persecuted by the Romans? If there had never been an Age of Martyrs, would Christians automatically see themselves as engaged in a war with their critics? Would Christians still see themselves as persecuted, or would they try to understand their opponents? Would the response to violence be to fight back or to address the causes of misunderstanding? Would we be more compassionate? Would we be less self-righteous? The history of Christianity is steeped in the blood of the martyrs and set as a battle between good and evil.[14] How would we think about ourselves if that history were not true? The language of martyrdom and persecution is often the language of war. It forces a rupture between "us" and "them" and perpetuates and legitimizes an aggressive posture toward "the other" and "our enemies," so that we can "defend the faith." Without this posture and the polarized view of the world upon which it relies, we might—without compromising our religious or political convictions—be able to reach common ground and engage in productive government, and we might focus on real examples of actual suffering and actual oppression.

As we will see, the traditional history of Christian martyrdom is mistaken. Christians were not constantly persecuted, hounded, or targeted by the Romans. Very few Christians died, and when they did, they were often executed for what we in the modern world would call political reasons. There is a difference between persecution and prosecution. A persecutor targets representatives of a specific group for undeserved punishment merely because of their participation in that group. An individual is prosecuted because that person has broken a law. The issue is complicated with respect to the ancient world, both because religion and politics were not neatly divided and because religious freedom was not an inalienable human right. But there is something different about being prosecuted under a law—however unjust—that is not designed to target or rout out any particular group. It may be unfortunate, it may be unfair, but it is not persecution, and it is very far from the myth of how Christians were treated by the Romans. This is not an inconsequential detail. The myth of persecution assumes that the other demonically inspired party is deliberately and continually trying to attack the church. But, as we will see, although prejudice against Christians was fairly widespread, the prosecution of Christians was rare, and the persecution of Christians was limited to no more than a handful of years.

The evidence for Christian martyrdom is of three basic types: evidence for persecution from Roman sources and archaeology, stories about martyrs, and descriptions of Christian martyrdom in the writings of church historians. On the Roman side, there is very little historical or archaeological evidence for the widespread persecution of Christians. Where we do have evidence for persecution, in the middle of the third century, it is not clear that the Romans were specifically targeting Christians at all. Even the so-called Decian persecution in 250 CE was about political uniformity, not religious persecution. Nothing in our evidence for Decius's legislation mentions targeting Christians. Before Decius, the prosecution of Christians was occasional and prompted by local officials, petty jealousies, and regional concerns. That Christians saw themselves as persecuted and interpreted prosecution in this way is understandable, but it does not mean that the Romans were persecuting them. This interpretation does not match up with the political and social realities: Christians were ridiculed and viewed with contempt, and they were even sometimes executed, but they weren't the subjects of continual persecution.

Then there are the stories about early Christian martyrs, commonly known as "martyr acts" or martyrdom stories. Most of these stories have been handed down from generation to generation and accepted as authentic on the basis of tradition. The vast majority of these stories, however, were written long after the events they purport to describe. There are literally hundreds of stories describing the deaths of thousands of early Christian martyrs, but almost every one of these stories is legendary. There are many pious reasons why someone might choose to fabricate a story about a martyr, and there are plenty of examples of genuine errors, but for those interested in the history of martyrdom, fabrication causes a problem. In some of these cases, scholars are not sure that the people described in these stories even existed, much less that they were martyred.

The problem with forged martyr stories was so widespread that in the seventeenth century a Dutch Jesuit priest named Héribert Rosweyde began to sort through the European manuscripts that preserved the earliest stories of the martyrs. The size of the task of cataloging thousands of manuscripts proved to be too much for Rosweyde alone, and the project was eventually taken over by a group of scholars led by an ambitious priest named John Bolland. The Society of Bollandists, as they came to be known, spent the next three centuries culling the corpus of hagiographical literature (literature pertaining to the saints) into a huge sixty-eight volume collection of texts about the saints. Of these sixty-eight volumes of texts and commentary, they decided that only a handful of stories were historically reliable. The rest—the vast majority—had been thoroughly edited or had simply been made up.

Scholars of early Christianity agree that there is very little evidence for the persecution of Christians. Although there are references to the deaths of Christians in the writings of the early church, these are vague and often exaggerated. For the first two hundred and fifty years of the Christian era there are only six martyrdom accounts that can be treated as reliable. These stories describe the deaths of Christianity's oldest and most beloved saints: the elderly bishop Polycarp, the young mothers Perpetua and Felicity, the teacher Ptolemy, the philosopher Justin Martyr, the martyrs of Scillium, and the brave members of the churches of Lyons and Vienne in ancient Gaul, modern-day France, who endured unspeakable tortures at the hands of the Romans. Even today some of these martyrs are mentioned in the religious services of the Catholic Church.

When we look closely at even these stories, however, it becomes clear that they have been significantly edited and changed. They refer to theological ideas that didn't exist in the period described in the stories and contain elements borrowed from other ancient sources. Details like these suggest that even the earliest stories have been tampered with. This difficulty isn't limited to just stories about martyrs. Early Christians, like many others in the ancient world, constantly updated and rewrote their sacred texts. The fact of the matter is that there are no stories about the deaths of martyrs that have not been purposely recast by later generations of Christians in order to further their own theological agendas.

The problem becomes even more acute when we look at the ancient evidence for martyrdom. Christians, and early Christians in particular, like to think of their martyrs as unique. The fact that early Christians were willing to die for their beliefs has been seen as a sign of the inherent truth of the Christian message. Why would the apostles have been willing to suffer and die for Jesus if he hadn't really been resurrected from the dead? Why would early Christians have been martyred if Christianity weren't true? Today, we are pointedly aware that martyrdom is not an exclusively Christian practice; virtually every religious group holds the deaths of their heroes in high esteem, and many people have died for religions that no longer exist. Yet many still declare that there is something special about the character and nature of Christian martyrs.

Even in the ancient world, Christianity wasn't alone in respecting those people who were willing to die for their beliefs. In fact, Christianity adopted the martyrdom idea from non-Christians. Long before the birth of Jesus, the ancient Greeks told stories about the deaths of their fallen heroes and the noble deaths of the philosophers, the Romans saw the self-sacrifice of generals as a good thing, and Jews in ancient Palestine accepted death before apostasy. The idea of sacrificing oneself for one's religious principles, country, or philosophical ideals was remarkably common. An ancient Greek or Roman would have expected an honorable person to prefer death to dishonor, shame, or failure. This kind of conduct wasn't even seen as heroic; it was expected.

Many people would argue that even if Christians aren't the only ones to respect martyrdom, Christian martyrs are in some way different or special. This isn't just because one's own martyrs are always good, while other people's martyrs are crazy; this is because there is a general perception that Christian martyrs are somehow intrinsically better. They are thought of as peaceful, passive, kind, and humble. And yet not all ancient martyrs were portrayed as pacifists. Some martyrs were, by modern standards, suicidal. The second-century teacher Justin Martyr describes how at the execution of a Christian named Ptolemy two Christian bystanders volunteered to die.[15] Many martyrs were prepared to accept death in exchange for rewards in heaven. Some looked forward gleefully to the Day of Judgment, when they would be able to watch their persecutors condemned to eternal torment.[16] This is hardly the kind of irenic behavior that people think of when they imagine Christian martyrs.

If the historical evidence does not support the theory that Christians were constantly persecuted, then why do we think they were? The answer lies in the writings and interests of the historians of the early church and the hagiographers (writers of saints' lives) from the fourth century on. I have already referred to the fourth-century historian Eusebius, who wrote predominantly during the reign of the emperor Constantine. Eusebius's selection of persecution as one of the enduring currents in the history of Christianity has deeply affected not just our knowledge about martyrdom, but also the extent to which we see it as a central part of Christian history and identity.

There's almost no evidence from the period before Constantine, or the Age of the Martyrs, to support the idea that Christians were continually persecuted. Most of this information comes from later writers, especially from the anonymous hagiographers who edited, reworked, and even forged stories about martyrs during periods of peace. The stories of beloved martyrs like St. Valentine, St. Christopher, and St. George were written long after the time in which these people supposedly lived, by authors who were preserving folklore, not facts.

The reason these Christians invented martyrdom stories and saw their history as a history of persecution is because then, as now, martyrdom was a powerful tool. Early Christians respected saints as holy people with a special connection to God. And, as already noted, there was no better argument for the sincerity of an individual's belief than the fact that he or she was prepared to die for it. As such, in later times martyrs were powerful spokespersons for the church. When early Christians wanted to prove the antiquity and orthodoxy of their own opinions, they would edit or compose a story attributing their own views to an early Christian orthodox martyr. An anecdote in which a martyr denounced a heretic was worth a hundred rational arguments about why that heretical position was wrong. Martyrs became mouthpieces for later religious positions.

At the same time, martyrs were deeply cherished by the Christian laity. Martyrs were ordinary people—slaves, women, and children—as well as bishops and soldiers who had risen above the constraints of their circumstances to display exceptional courage. For those who experienced hardship and heard stories of the sufferings of martyrs, these Christian heroes were deeply personal sources of inspiration. They were part superhero and part celebrity and, according to Christians, they now enjoyed rewards that were, literally, out of this world. In a world in which social mobility did not exist, they lived a dream that many dared not imagine.

This attraction to and love of holy persons was harnessed in the cult of the saints—in the construction of martyr shrines to house the remains of saints. These centers of worship attracted pilgrims and thus revenue. This led to competition between pilgrimage sites, as various towns tried to attract visitors to the graves of their saints. The institutionalization of martyrs and competition between religious centers required ever more exciting and dramatic stories. Thus, from the fourth century on, there was a veritable explosion in the production of stories about martyrs. These stories were then supplemented with descriptions of miracles and visions associated with specific churches and shrines. They drew the Christian faithful to obscure towns and out-of-the-way shrines, and in exchange they offered them the opportunity to commune with the memory of their heroes. Stories were an integral part of this connection. It was said that when martyrdom stories were read aloud, the saints were truly present, sweet smelling fragrances would fill the air, and the world of the martyr and the world of the pilgrim would meet.[17] With so much at stake, martyrdom stories multiplied in order to meet this demand. Martyrdom mattered to people, and the love people felt for the martyrs led to pious exaggeration and well-intentioned forgery.

The same is true even today. Martyrdom continues to matter. Persecution remains an integral part of how Christians think and talk about their history and themselves. It endures in the claims of Christian politicians and commentators that they are persecuted and under attack, and it is powerful precisely because it refuses to acknowledge its own power. Everyone agrees that a country that is invaded by enemy forces is morally justified in defending itself. In the same way, when the powerful and politically secure claim that they are persecuted, oppressed, and attacked, then they can claim that all of their actions are born out of self-defense. They can act aggressively and even violently and maintain the moral high ground in the knowledge that they are the victims.

The purpose of this book is to show that the foundations for this idea are imaginary. The traditional history of martyrdom is a myth, a myth that gives Christians who deploy it in the sorts of examples adduced here the rhetorical high ground, but a myth that makes dialogue impossible. The recognition that the idea of the Christian martyr is based in legend and rhetoric, rather than history and truth, reveals that many Christians have been and remain committed to conflict and opposition in their interactions with others, but also that they don't have to be. Christians can choose to embrace the virtues that martyrs embody without embracing the false history of persecution that has grown up around them. Correcting the misunderstandings that surround martyrdom in the early church is not a question of tidying up some ancient facts or revising our understanding of events that happened in the distant past. This point is not merely academic. The view that the history of Christianity is a history of unrelenting persecution persists in modern religious and political debate about what it means to be Christian. It creates a world in which Christians are under attack; it endorses political warfare rather than encouraging political discourse; and it legitimizes seeing those who disagree with us as our enemies. It is precisely because the myth of persecution continues to be so influential that it is imperative that we get the history right.

CHAPTER ONE
Martyrdom Before Christianity

WHEN I WAS GROWING UP IN England we had a religious studies class—rather piously called "divinity class"—in my school. It was
something of a throwaway class that involved drawing illustrations of
biblical concepts as much as it did learning about the Bible or anything
that could strictly speaking be called "divine." I was, then as now, a history nerd, and my enthusiasm for the subject irritated both my teacher,
who preferred not to answer tough questions, and my classmates, who
preferred that class end on time. One day I asked the teacher how we
knew that Christianity was true, given that the Bible contradicts itself
and there are all these other religions that also claim to be true. She
thought for a minute and responded, "Why would Jesus's followers
have been prepared to suffer and die for him, if he had not, in fact, risen
from the dead and if Christianity was not, in fact, true?"

That stumped me, I must confess. This was before the advent of
suicide bombers, and we had skipped over martyrdom in other religions altogether. So instead of pointing out that *lots* of religions have
martyrs, I found myself convinced, enamored with these early Christians, and greatly admiring the dedication and courage of the early
church. How could I question a religion founded and fed by such
heroes? Everyone breathed a sigh of relief and filed out of class.

My divinity teacher is in good company. The claim that Christians and Christians alone are martyred has its roots in the earliest days of the church. It was a point of pride among ancient Christian teachers and writers. Justin Martyr, a second-century Christian teacher who taught and died in Rome, wrote in his defense of Christianity that in his own time only Christians were persecuted for their name, "Christian"; that heretics were not persecuted; and that the only ones the Jews ever persecuted were the Christians.[1] Justin's declaration is slightly nuanced and has clear rhetorical aims—he skewers his intellectual opponents and the Jews with one thrust—but his claims have been rehearsed by generations of Christians from antiquity to the present day. Even modern Christians will assert that real martyrdom is unique to Christianity and serves as proof of the authenticity and truth of the Christian message.

This view is not unique to believers; many scholars argue something similar. The majority of biblical scholars and early church historians acknowledge that Christians used ancient stories of heroic death to develop their own understanding of martyrdom, but they *at the same time* argue that martyrdom was peculiar to Christianity. Glen Bowersock, a noted classicist and historian of religion, is typical when he says:

> Martyrdom was not something that the ancient world had seen from the beginning. What we can observe in the second, third, and fourth centuries of our era is something entirely new. Of course, in earlier ages principled and courageous persons, such as Socrates at Athens or the three Jews in the fiery furnace of Nebuchadnezzar, had provided glorious examples of resistance to tyrannical authority and painful suffering before unjust judges. But never before had such courage been absorbed into a conceptual system of posthumous recognition and anticipated reward, nor had the very word martyrdom existed as the name for this system.[2]

Prior to the rise of Christianity, Bowersock and others argue, there was no such thing as martyrdom. He admits that there are precedents for martyrdom in the ancient world, but says that, because there was no system of posthumous rewards (heaven, hell, etc.) and no concrete word for this kind of death ("martyrdom"), these were not martyrs in some true sense. The argument goes that those individuals who died for king, country, nation, God, or on principle died what scholars call "noble deaths," but these deaths are not martyrdom. It's truly this idea—the notion that martyrdom is unique and special to Christianity—that forms the centerpiece of martyrdom's power in Christianity today.

But is it true that there were no martyrs before Christianity? Did Christians invent the idea of martyrdom?

In order to get at why people think that martyrdom is limited to or different in Christianity, we have to first establish a working definition of "martyrdom." It's really only once we know what we're looking for that we can ascertain to what extent Christianity is or is not unique with regard to it.

Definitions

WHEN PEOPLE USE THE term "martyr" today, they do so to refer to lots of different ideas and concepts. Even the straightforward use of the title is applied not just to saints like Joan of Arc, who died (at least on the surface) for religious causes, but also to political or activist heroes like Martin Luther King Jr., Mahatma Gandhi, Yitzhak Rabin, and Matthew Shepard. The application of the term "martyr," which carries religious overtones, to an assassinated civil rights activist or a political figure colors either death with a touch of the religious. For example, although Martin Luther King Jr. was ordained and utilized religious imagery and language in his speeches and self-understanding, he was assassinated not because he was Christian, but rather because he was a rallying point and leader in the civil rights movement. Calling Dr. King a martyr blurs the line between his religious vocation and his political activism. This blurring is probably an accurate description of how Dr. King saw his own work, but it also demonstrates how using the title "martyr" changes the character of a person's actions. When it comes to dying a meaningful death, the distinction between religious and political principles is not clear-cut.

It's not even the case that the application of the title "martyr" is always a positive thing. The title is sarcastically applied to those who seem to delight in and seek attention for rather mundane forms of suffering. The phrase "She's such a martyr" is often unflatteringly used of women who are perceived as wallowing in the sacrifices they make (or think they make) for others. In a similar vein the term is humorously applied to marriage. Many people I meet, upon learning that I study martyrs, jokingly inquire if their marriages "count" as acts of martyrdom. Even in English, then, the word has a great deal of fluidity. It can be a religious title, a political rallying point, or a derogatory insult. This fluidity isn't limited just to the word "martyr"; there are lots of titles that can be used technically, metaphorically, or sarcastically depending on the context. The weightier the word, the more susceptible it is to these multiple interpretations.

The ambiguity surrounding the use of the term in the modern world is matched by its changing use in antiquity. The English term "martyr" comes from and is a direct transliteration of the Greek word *martys*. The original, pre-Christian meaning of this Greek word was simply "witness" in the sense of a legal witness, someone who presents evidence in a trial.[3] In its pre-Christian use, therefore, the term carried connotations of courtrooms, truth, and formal testimony. Just like today, people could give true or false witness, and there was some discussion about how to tell the difference between them.

When Christians were arrested and tried, they acted as witnesses at their trials; they were asked to state whether they were or were not Christian. Initially, then, they were legal witnesses in the original technical sense because, much like today when a defendant testifies at his or her own trial, they gave testimony. When Christians did admit to being Christian, they could be executed as a result. The fact that giving accurate testimony in court meant that Christians could be executed resulted in a gradual shift in the meaning of the word *martys*. In Christian circles, *martys* first came to mean a Christian who admitted to being a follower of Jesus and was executed as a result and, then, a person who was executed for being Christian. This process of changing terminology took place over several hundred years. Some scholars have tried to argue that there was a radical shift in the meaning of the term in the middle of the second century, but this is difficult to prove. The problem is that even if some Christians started to use the term differently during the second century, there was no uniform shift in the meaning of the word. Moreover, the older meaning of "providing testimony in a courtroom" continued to be accurate (as Christians still were witnesses in courtrooms) and thus continued to resonate in the minds of people in the ancient world.

It's much the same with the change and spread of terminology in the modern world. The launch of the social networking application Twitter in 2006 led to a change in the way that the term "tweet" is used. The recognition of the new use and supplementary terms like "retweet" or "tweeter" was gradual and grew with the number of Twitter users and cultural awareness about the phenomenon. Nonetheless, the term "tweet" can still be used to refer to the sound birds make, and there are undoubtedly lots of people who are completely unaware of any other meaning.

In scholarship on martyrdom a great deal of the argument that Christianity invented martyrdom is related to the origins of the word "martyr" and this shift in the meaning of the term *martys*, as is evident from the Bowersock quote above. Bowersock argues that because there was no term for martyrdom before Christianity, there was no such thing as martyrdom. In 1956 Norbert Brox, a German Catholic Bible scholar, published an influential book called *Zeuge und Märtyrer* [Witness and Martyr], in which he argued that it was in the middle of the second century, with the publication of a story called the *Martyrdom of Polycarp*, that the meaning of the term changed from simple witness to martyr.[4] The book was essentially an enormous word study of the term *martys* in the ancient world. He tried to show that, gradually and through use, the meaning of the word shifted, so that it came to mean someone who died for Christ. Christianity, in other words, redefined the term. From this, Brox, and many modern scholars since, concluded that it was Christians who developed the language of martyrdom and thus Christians who are responsible for martyrdom in the modern sense of the word.

It is certainly true that Christians should be credited for coining the word "martyr" as we now use it. Moreover, it doesn't seem to have been the case that ancient Jews, Greeks, or Romans had their own technical terms for people who died for their religious beliefs. They were heroes who died good deaths. In creating or, perhaps better, developing terminology to describe people who died for Jesus, Christians were doing something new. The development in the meaning of this particular term is not due to some self-conscious effort on the part of Christians. It is tied to the fact that Christians acted as legal witnesses (the original sense of *martys*) and were subsequently sentenced in actual courtrooms.

At the same time, however, we have to ask whether the existence of pre-Christian martyrdom hinges on ancient people having words for things. I would argue that it does not. There are lots of concepts for which there aren't English technical terms that have meaning for English speakers. Take, for example, the French phrase *déjà vu*. There is no English equivalent for the sense of having already experienced something before, but everyone, from an early age, knows the feeling. Or take the German word *Schadenfreude*, which generally refers to the satisfaction one experiences in the failure of others. We don't need to know German or even the word itself to be familiar with the concept. Concepts can exist even if one's native language doesn't provide a single definitive word for them. It's a mistake to say that because Christians adapted the term "martyr," they also get credit for coming up with the idea.

Another way to think about the origins of the concept of martyrdom is to think in terms of ideas rather than words. The *Oxford English Dictionary* describes someone who dies as a martyr in the Christian church as someone who "chooses to suffer death rather than renounce faith in Christ or obedience to his teachings, a Christian way of life or adherence to a law or tenet of the church." If we take this widely held definition of a martyr, rather than the word itself, as our starting point, then the evidence starts to look different. Embedded in this definition are certain principles: (1) that individuals have a choice to either live or die, and (2) they prefer to die, because they value either a way of life, a law, a person, or a principle more highly than their own life. In order to find out whether the origins of martyrdom do lie in Christianity, we have to look at the evidence for these principles both prior to the advent of Christianity and among Christianity's religious contemporaries.

Death in the Ancient World

IN COMPARISON TO TODAY, the ancient world was saturated with death. The vast majority of serious diseases and medical ailments were fatal, because ancient medicine was unable to provide antibiotics or antiseptics. More than one-third of infants died before the age of five. The realities of battle meant that almost all of the injured died of their wounds or subsequent infection. For those unable to go to war themselves, gladiatorial conflict and dramatic reenactments brought the bloodshed to them. Capital punishment was administered publicly for a wide variety of crimes. No one in the Roman world—young or old, aristocratic or plebian—would have been personally unacquainted with death.

One of the results of this dangerous death-filled world was that, unlike today, death was not pushed to the margins of the ancient consciousness. Instead of death being placed out of mind or considered taboo, ancient philosophers, orators, politicians, and poets theorized about it on a regular basis. This wasn't just an aristocratic pastime, however. Given the realities of the human condition and the fact that death was so pervasive, every corner of ancient society paid a great deal of attention to questions of how to die well, with honor, with purpose, and for causes outside of and greater than oneself.

The Heroes of the Trojan War

THE WESTERN LITERARY TRADITION traces itself back to Homer's *Iliad*, and it is in the myths that surround the Trojan War that we find our first characterizations of noble death and how to die well. Homer's poetry describes neither the beginning of the war nor its conclusion, but focuses instead on the heated conflicts of the battlefield and the personal journey of Achilles. In an epic poem about duels between sword-wielding young soldiers, there is ample opportunity to contrast the courageous and the weak, the good soldiers and the cowards.

Throughout the poem, assumptions about death and what constitutes a good or honorable death linger close beneath the surface of the rhyme, only to puncture the veneer of the story as each hero falls. The Homeric heroes, it is clear, fight for glory, honor, and everlasting fame. Death is a fact of human existence; the important part is how you choose to die. Death should be taken like a man, with head held high, steady resolve, and manly courage. In an encounter with one of the less remarkable Trojan princes, the easy victor Achilles is disgusted by the defeated prince's desperation. As the Trojan begs for his life and promises Achilles that he will fetch a hefty ransom if spared, Achilles dismisses him as sniveling and girlish. He instructs the prince to "face" his death and not to be so "piteous about it"; they must both bravely greet the death that comes to all.[5] Those who do not embrace glory and death are elsewhere called "women, not men."[6] This view is typical in a text and world in which courage and manliness are essentially the same word—*andreia*. The problem here is not death, which is natural and expected; the problem is failing to secure glory and conducting oneself in a manner that is womanly and shameful.

The narrative pretext for the *Iliad*, the whole reason for the poem, is Achilles's clash of wills with King Agamemnon, the leader of the allied Greek forces. A somewhat petulant Achilles refuses to fight and returns to the field of battle only after the death of his beloved friend Patroclus. Achilles's willingness to swallow his pride and reenter the fray is an act of humility born out of heartache. Yet in returning to war more was at stake than merely his bruised ego and pride, for in rejoining the battle Achilles chooses an early death. Achilles tells Odysseus of a prophecy of his own eventual fate:

> For my mother the goddess, silver-footed Thetis, tells me that twofold fates are bearing me toward the doom of death: if I abide here and play my part in the siege of Troy, then lost is my home-return, but my renown shall be imperishable; but if I return home to my dear native land, lost is my glorious renown, yet shall my life long endure, neither shall the doom of death come soon upon me.[7]

The prophecy presents Achilles with a choice—a glorious but brief life that will be rewarded with immortal fame or a long comfortable life in anonymity. The already weighty choice is further burdened with the ramifications of his decision for the outcome of the war: if Achilles fights, then Troy will fall; if he leaves for his homeland, the Greeks will be defeated. Achilles's death is intricately interwoven with the fate of his people. Death *pro patria* ("for country") was the ultimate act of patriotism. At the same time, the choice, as set by Achilles, is not just between victory and defeat, life and death, but between immortal glory and mundane existence. There is personal advantage for Achilles in dying young in that he will have glory and an immortal name. Even if Achilles does not weigh present life against future reward in terms of a heavenly afterlife, he still has in mind a different kind of immortality—the manner in which he will live on (or not) in the memories of others.

For people well versed in Christian ideas of the afterlife and the rewards that await the faithful—heaven, banquets, crowns, harps, and angels—the promise of fame and memorialization may not seem like much, but for Achilles and for many in the ancient world, being remembered and spoken well of was of great importance. This is about much more than a person's reputation. A persistent and pressing anxiety in the ancient world was the fear of being forgotten, that when you died no one would remember that you had ever lived. In a world of Google searches, Social Security numbers, and embarrassingly permanent Facebook photos, it's difficult for us to wrap our minds around how strong this fear would have been, but this was a world in which only 5 percent of people were literate.[8] Immortality meant being kept alive in the memories of others, and for that you had to be extraordinary. In trading long life for eternal renown Achilles is choosing a kind of immortality for himself. People will remember him and admire his courage long after he dies. And they do.

Achilles's pride and fate form the centerpiece of Homer's epic. Yet subsequent authors fleshed out the gaps in Homer's story, supplying additional plot details about the background to the war and the biographies of its heroes. Narratively speaking, the first example of death for a cause greater than oneself begins before the war has even started, with the death of the young princess Iphigenia. Iphigenia was the favorite daughter of Agamemnon, the king of Sparta, leader of the Greeks, and Achilles's rival. As they wait on the coast at Aulis for troops to arrive, Agamemnon hunts for sport and angers the goddess Artemis by killing one of her sacred deer. Agamemnon should have known better. Artemis punishes Agamemnon by stranding the Greek fleet in port without so much as a breeze to nudge them out of the harbor.

Appeasing the goddess means a considerable personal sacrifice, and Agamemnon agrees to sacrifice his beloved daughter to Artemis. He lures Iphigenia to the port with promises of marriage to handsome Achilles, who is without a doubt the finest warrior of the combined Greek forces. According to the playwright Euripides's version of the story, Iphigenia arrives at the Greek encampment on the coast flushed with excitement, her head filled with adolescent dreams of marriage and children. It is only then that she and her mother,

Clytemnestra, learn the real reason for their presence. The scene is heartbreaking, and the situation is hopeless; the army's appetite for war means that Iphigenia can never escape alive. Even if Agamemnon changes his mind and tries to smuggle her out of the camp, the mass of soldiers will see to it that she dies.

At first, Iphigenia, still a young girl, clasps her father's leg and begs him to spare her life. Then, as she accepts the reality of the situation, her desire to live turns to courage and resolve. In a lengthy monologue, Euripides has her describe her death not as tragic or meaningless, but as a critically important part of the war effort and larger destiny of her people. Toward the end of the play Iphigenia turns to her bereft mother, Clytemnestra, and reshapes her death as a sacrifice on behalf of Greece, called here Hellas:

> Listen, mother, to what I have been thinking. I have decided to die. I want to do this gloriously, by yielding and doing away with my low-mindedness. Come, mother, look at it with my eyes and see how nobly I speak. All of majestic Hellas looks upon me now. It is through me that the ships will be able to sail and the Phrygians [that is, the Trojans] will find their grave. And if barbarians do something to women in the future, it is through me that they will be prevented from seizing them from happy Hellas. . . . All this I will secure by dying, and mine will be the blissful glory that I brought Hellas freedom. . . . I offer my body for Hellas. Sacrifice me and destroy Troy. That will be my monument for ages to come. That will be my children, my husband, my glory.[9]

Iphigenia's death here serves multiple purposes. As a sacrifice, she appeases the anger of the goddess Artemis, but as a willing and noble sacrificial victim, she undergoes a death that has more potency and power. There is a blending of martial and marital imagery in Iphigenia's speech. She will become the liberator of her country, Hellas, and an instrumental part in the destruction of Troy. For this she will be remembered and praised, as would a good soldier.

At the same time her role in this military victory stands in the place of the family she had been promised: the destruction of Troy will be her husband and her offspring. If children were the traditional way of ensuring one's legacy in the world, she acquires a lineage for herself by dying well. Like Achilles's, Iphigenia's death is effective— she contributes to the destruction of the Trojans—and, again like Achilles, she is remembered for her self-sacrifice. She achieves glory and lives in the memories of others as a result. It's not just that she dies, but that she chooses to die and dies with honor that makes Iphigenia legendary. The parallel to Christian martyrdom is striking. She gives up her life for a cause greater than herself. Arguably, she didn't have much of a choice, but neither did followers of Jesus once they had admitted to being Christian. The difference is that instead of a harp and wings, Iphigenia received eternal renown.

Funeral Orations

EVEN IF THE TROJAN War was regarded in antiquity as the greatest of wars and the touchstone for Greek culture, it was only the first of several important conflicts both between the Greek city-states and invaders from the east and between the Greek cities themselves. During wartime the fallen dead were habitually remembered in the form of funeral orations, or *epitaphios logos*, which were performed by city-appointed orators during the annual state funeral. These speeches offered the opportunity to remember the dead, to propagandize for the military cause, and to boost morale.

Although the funeral oration was a performance, it also became a whole literary genre of its own. From antiquity six classical funeral orations survive, including, most famously, Thucydides's version of Pericles's funeral oration at the end of the first year of the Peloponnesian War. This speech inspired not only ancient Athenians, but generations of people since. Even Abraham Lincoln is rumored to have based his Gettysburg Address on Thucydides's text.[10] A less well known but equally paradigmatic example is Demosthenes's *Funeral Oration*, which he delivered in memory of the Greek soldiers defeated in 338 BCE by the Macedonian Philip II, Alexander the Great's father. The defeat of the Greek tribes at this battle marked the beginning of Macedonian supremacy in the region. In the funeral oration, Demosthenes lauds specific examples of self-sacrifice from the individual Greek tribes, those men and groups whose losses were especially severe.

Among them he praises the descendants of Erechtheus, who had famously sacrificed his own daughters in order to secure the safety of their individual peoples:

> All Erechthidae knew Erechtheus, who has given his name to their tribe. They were well aware that he, in order to save this land, had offered his own daughters, who are called Hyacinthides, to be killed publicly. They thought it a disgrace that while the one begotten by the immortals sacrificed everything to liberate his fatherland, they should appear to consider their mortal body more important than immortal glory.[11]

The historical data about the sacrifice of Erechtheus's daughters are shaky at best. Various versions of the story disagree on how many daughters he fathered and executed. Regardless, the legend inherited by his descendants was that he sacrificed his beloved daughters in order to protect Athens from attack. Whether or not the original story was true, it is clear that in Demosthenes's time people thought of themselves as participating in this tradition. In fact, they identified with it to such a great extent that they were willing to lay down their own lives to honor it.

In this speech the daughters of Erechtheus serve as a kind of cultural shorthand for self-sacrifice for the greater good. Their deaths are a foundational moment in the consciousness of the Erechthidae. Narratives of communal origins were important points of reference in the ancient world just as they are today. Just as Americans will refer to the intentions, actions, and principles of the founding fathers in discussions of political issues, Demosthenes uses the original virgin sacrifices by Erechtheus to account for and promote self-sacrifice in times of war. He turns the myth of origins into military propaganda.

The Erechthidae weren't the only group whose founding myths involved tales of death and human sacrifice. Arguably, in locating their origins in the crucifixion of their messiah, the followers of Jesus did the same thing. That a group was founded on the principle of meaningful self-sacrificial death not only meant that they valorized that kind of death, but that other members of the group would be expected to make the same kind of sacrifice. Both the Erechthidae and, later, early Christian martyrs thought that the values embodied by their founders were worth reproducing in their own lives. Both groups were willing to die out of loyalty to and in imitation of the sacrifice of their heroes.

Socrates

ROMAN WRITERS, EARLY CHRISTIANS, medieval theologians, and Renaissance thinkers all trumpeted Socrates as a model of conduct for their audiences. There's no doubt that Socrates was influential, not least in the work of his student Plato. It's ironic, though, that for all of his notoriety and reputation as the world's wisest man, Socrates is famous largely for the manner in which he died. The Stoic philosopher Epictetus, for instance, alludes to Socrates's death when he describes him as an ideal philosopher, a witness to truth, and one who refused to betray his principles.[12] For Epictetus, Socrates's death tells us something important about his character. To us, it is entirely unclear whether Socrates would have been as well respected by later generations if he had not died nobly. During his lifetime he was ridiculed as a pedant and a morally ambiguous sophist. Aristophanes's depiction in *The Clouds* (ca. 423 BCE) of Socrates debating arcane details, such as how far a flea can jump, paints a very unflattering picture of the great philosopher. Perhaps, if he had not accepted death, Socrates would have been remembered in this way rather than as an ideal philosophical martyr.

The circumstances of Socrates's death—his trial and imprisonment—are narrated by his students and in some ways constitute a larger portion of his legacy than his actual teachings. In fact, much like Jesus, nothing that we know of Socrates comes from the man himself; everything comes from a succession of students and admirers interspersed with the occasional critic. Plato's *Apology* relays the details of Socrates's trial in Athens; the *Crito* describes a conversation between Socrates and a student about whether it was ethical for Socrates to flee into exile; and the *Phaedo* describes Socrates's final hours, his final words, and his suicide by drinking the poison hemlock. Xenophon, another student of Socrates, wrote a slightly different version of Socrates's trial, in which he argued that Socrates could have escaped death, but deliberately chose to die. Xenophon was answering the question, also faced by the Gospel writers, "If he's so great, how did he let himself get into this situation?" We also know that there were other, now lost, documents about the death of Socrates. A pamphlet by Polycrates (ca. 393 BCE) entitled the *Prosecution of Socrates* apparently included a speech denouncing Socrates as an enemy of democracy, and the biographer Diogenes Laertius cites a number of other lost sources about Socrates's death.[13]

The mushrooming legends surrounding the demise of Socrates demonstrate the enduring popularity of this aspect of his legacy. They provide evidence that his death captivated the imagination of ancient readers. Those accounts that do remain are concerned not just with outlining the legal basis for Socrates's conviction or the historical causes for his death, but with establishing Socrates's demise as an example of noble death for successive generations.

In the course of the Platonic dialogues about Socrates's death, the hero makes a number of statements about death and its aftermath. He is adamant that death should not be feared. In fact, "a man who has really devoted his life to philosophy should be cheerful in the face of death."[14] According to Plato, Socrates was unfairly charged with atheism and corrupting the youth of Athens. He was a noble person who refused to flee death in order to go into exile on the basis that it would be a bad example to others and a betrayal of the social contract he had made with Athens.[15]

In the hours leading up to his death, Socrates appeared calm and detached. He scolded his wife and friends for mourning and behaving emotionally and in his last moments even insisted on silence.[16] His final gestures and words were poised and measured; in what was perhaps an ironic play on religious piety he poured out a libation to the gods, prayed as he drank the poison, and instructed his disciples that after his death they should offer a sacrifice to Asclepius, the god of healing, on his behalf.[17] Socrates even had a good sense of timing: he orchestrated the events so well that he even had time to take a bath before imbibing the poison.

Socrates's conduct may seem emotionally detached, but in his passive and dispassionate acceptance of death he embodies the classical understanding of masculine self-control. While others—his wife, his friends, even his jailer—weep, Socrates is poised. If he does feel something here, it is joy, but even this joy is rational. It is based on his argument that death is the liberation of the soul from the body.[18] All in all, Socrates's death is a triumph of self-control over fear, irrationality, and emotion. By dying in this way Socrates puts his proverbial money where his mouth is; he is willing to defend his principles even to death. His belief that the body is contemptible is nowhere better demonstrated than in his willingness to see it annihilated. His axiomatic statement, "The really important thing is not to live, but to live nobly," is proved in his acceptance of an unjust sentence for the sake of democracy.[19]

Just because Socrates dies on philosophical principle doesn't mean that he thinks death is without advantage. An unexpected and often overlooked aspect of Socrates's final musings is his discussion of the fate of the soul after death.[20] Socrates describes a quasi-mythical view of the cosmos in which human beings currently live in hollows in the earth. After death, souls proceed to the mythical lakes of Tartarus and Acheron for punishment; or, if their souls are purified by philosophy, they have the opportunity to ascend to the true earth above. This heavenly true earth is a region in which there is no sickness, and it is filled with jewels brighter than gold and innumerable fruits and flowers. It has an idyllic flavor to it, as it is here that people will converse with the gods.

The fairy-tale-like quality of this description has caused embarrassment for some scholars, who find the interest in plants and jewels a little superficial, but the interesting part—for our purposes—is how this vision of the afterlife fits with Socrates's understanding of his own death. Socrates says that it is by exercising "self-restraint, justice, courage, freedom, and truth" that he hopes to acquire this better afterlife.[21] In other words, by dying well in the manner befitting a good masculine philosopher, Socrates hopes to ascend to the "real earth." Whether Socrates himself really believed in a region of sparkling jewels and hypersanitary air, we can imagine that readers of the *Phaedo* took this story at face value and connected the idea of dying a noble death in defense of truth with postmortem rewards. Even for the rational philosopher, dying nobly conferred great benefits. Christians thought much the same. If we went through Socrates's words and replaced "democracy" with "Jesus" and "philosopher" with "Christian," we would think that Socrates was a Christian martyr.

The Deaths of the Philosophers

SOCRATES HAS BEEN CALLED by some the "world's first recorded martyr," and his manner of embracing death for principle provided a model for subsequent generations of well-educated Greeks and Romans. One is hard-pressed to identify a philosopher who didn't exit the world dramatically and with a clever parting quip. From Diogenes of Sinope, the Cynic philosopher who, according to some sources, improbably held his breath until he died, to Zeno, who bit off his own tongue and spat it at the tyrannical king interrogating him, philosophers liked to go out in style. It's difficult to know how seriously to take such stories. You don't have to be a doctor to know that it's physically impossible to hold your breath until you die. Whether these stories accurately portray the manner in which a particular philosopher died, they were wildly popular and formed a central part of the memorialization of famous intellectuals.

In his third-century BCE collection of *Lives and Opinions of Eminent Philosophers*, the Greek writer Diogenes Laertius is keen to include in his biographies stories about how his protagonists died. A number of these stories emphasize the resolute stubbornness of the philosophers, who, far from fitting the shy academic stereotype we have today, were robust and courageous models of bold, forthright speech. They were professors who actually professed something—and boldly. One such example is Anaxarchus, a philosopher companion of Alexander the Great. One of Anaxarchus's intellectual achievements was developing an ancient "atoms theory" that hypothesized that a vacuum must exist in order to separate beings (or atoms) from one another.

On one occasion during a trip to the east with Alexander, Anaxarchus met Nicocreon, the king of Cyprus, at a dinner party and made a snide remark at Nicocreon's expense. The incident clearly left a lasting impression on the king, because some years later, after the death of Alexander, when Anaxarchus inadvertently found himself on Cyprus again, Nicocreon promptly had him arrested and threw him into a large mortar, where he was beaten with pestles. Anaxarchus responded to this treatment with the now famous remark: "Just pound the bag of Anaxarchus. You do not pound himself."[22] The philosophical idea that the torture of the body is not equivalent to the torture of the self is at once frustrating to the philosopher's opponent, humorous to the audience, and a serious statement about the relationship between body and soul. When an enraged Nicocreon ordered that Anaxarchus's tongue be cut out, Anaxarchus, like Zeno, bit off his own tongue and spat it at the tyrant.

This is but one of many lively tales about the death of philosophers in the Greek world. Throughout these stories there is a common thread: the philosopher dies with courage, on principle, and with a dismissive, almost nonchalant attitude toward both his torturers and death. The philosophers cannot be conquered with torture or pain and are silenced only of their own volition when sheer contempt prompts them to preemptively bite off their own tongues. These defiant acts of self-mutilation and self-destruction are really acts of resistance. If the aim of torture is to force the philosopher into submission, then the almost casual way in which the philosopher coolly amplifies the torture frustrates this objective. Rather than allow the torturer to have power over them, Anaxarchus and Zeno bit off their tongues to spite their enemies.

These stories tell us something about the kinds of things that ancient audiences liked to hear, and they tell us a great deal about the kinds of deaths people admired and valued. Today, when we talk about someone dying well, we generally mean that they died comfortably, without feeling any pain, at an advanced age, and ideally surrounded by their families. According to a 2011 poll commissioned in the United Kingdom by the charitable organization Dying Well, 83 percent of people fear dying in pain, and more people are afraid of dying in hospital than they are of divorce or bankruptcy.[23] A similar study by Demos in 2010 found that two out of three people describe dying peacefully at home surrounded by their family as the ideal way to die.[24] One incarnation of this concern, manifested by advocates of euthanasia, is the preoccupation with dying with dignity. This is often taken to mean dying comfortably and in full possession of one's mental and physical faculties.

If our modern concern is to die without pain, Greek and Roman authors were interested in a person's conduct toward and at the moment of his or her death. Nobility and self-control—often demonstrated through a voluntary increase of pain—reigned over comfort. The seemingly ridiculous manner in which Diogenes holds his breath until he dies articulates the expanse of his self-control. The point of this part of the story is that Diogenes has absolute control over his own body and physical reactions. The moral for audiences listening to stories of the deaths of philosophers is that this controlled, dismissive attitude toward death should be admired and emulated.

Lucretia

IT WAS NOT ONLY men who were willing to die for noble causes. In the Roman period noble death was domesticated and brought into the home. Women were willing to die, not now just in defense of their country, but for virtue and chastity. Of these the most famous is Lucretia, one of the founding heroines of the Roman Republic. Lucretia was married to the aristocrat Collatinus, son of a former governor. One evening after a long night's hard drinking and eating, Collatinus made a wager with Sextus Tarquinius, the son of the Etruscan king of Rome, as to which of their wives was the more virtuous. They returned to their homes on horseback to find Tarquinius's wife nearly passed out from booze and Lucretia demurely overseeing weaving on the looms.

Tarquinius, who was quite clearly bested in the contest and embarrassed by his wife's behavior, was seized with desire for Lucretia. He stole into her bedroom at night and, creeping around the sleeping servants, alternated between threats and declarations of love. In the end he threatened that if she did not submit to his sexual advances, he would kill her and a male servant, place their bodies in a compromising position, and claim that he had caught them in flagrante.

After she was raped, Lucretia threw herself at the mercy of her father and husband. Even though she declared herself to be innocent because it was against her will, she withdrew a dagger from the folds in her clothing and plunged it into her heart. Her death provoked a rebellion, and her relatives drove the Tarquins from the city. Her body was then placed on display in the forum of her hometown as a symbol of the oppressive rule of the former monarchs. In many ways the death of Lucretia set in motion the events that led to the founding of the Roman Republic. Her violation became a symbol for Tarquinian oppression, and her suicide the catalyst for rebellion. The conceptual cornerstones of Rome were laid with Lucretia's death.

Given that, in the other examples we've looked at, dying nobly is associated with masculinity, it is interesting to note that commentators on Lucretia's death use masculine language to describe her accomplishment. The Roman poet Ovid calls her a lady of "masculine spirit" as well as a model of feminine chastity.[25] Another Roman historian, Valerius Maximus, describes her as a military leader for virtue. The inference seems to be that, in dying nobly for virtue, Lucretia proves herself to be as virtuous as a man, in the terms proper to a man, while simultaneously embodying feminine virtues. Noble suicide was one venue in which a woman could outdo herself.

To us the idea that Lucretia's suicide is what proves her virtue is nothing short of horrifying. The notion that a woman is better off dead than raped is the stuff of misogynistic nightmares. Her suicide is all the more tragic in light of the fact that her family believed her story and had no intention of punishing her. Her death seems futile and pointless, but her final words may hold the key to understanding her actions, at least from an ancient perspective. Before she died, Lucretia declared, "Death shall be my witness." In the story, her death serves as a kind of legal proof of her innocence. No one will be able to doubt the veracity of her claim or use her example as an excuse if she dies. The notion that her innocence is proved by her death is uncomfortable to us, but it is the same idea that we saw with Socrates: individuals' worth and the truth of their claims are irrefutably proved by their deaths.

Ironically, this is precisely the same idea that my divinity teacher proposed to me in middle school; namely, if someone is willing to die for it, then it must be true. Many aspects of these stories seem just like Christian martyrdom. The idea that death is a witness to truth, the belief that death for country, principle, or virtue is a good and honorable thing, and the notion that by dying a person secures a permanent personal reward (glory, fame, a better kind of immortality) are all elements of Christian martyrdom. The fact that these heroes were held up as models for emulation and imitation means that they also serve the same function as Christian martyrs. We are supposed to admire their courage, their virtue, and their deaths.

Noble Death and Martyrdom in Second Temple Judaism

ALTHOUGH GREEKS AND ROMANS wrote extensively about the glory of dying for a cause, they were not unique in this; the same principle can be found in the Hebrew scriptures and in ancient Jewish literature. Although hints of the idea can be found earlier, the idealization of dying for God or the law really began to take shape in the second century BCE, when the Jews lived under foreign rule.

In 167 BCE the Hellenistic monarch Antiochus IV, king of the Seleucid Empire, put down a rebellion in Jerusalem and issued a decree outlawing many Jewish religious and ethnic practices. As part of this decree he outlawed sacrificial offerings in the Temple and circumcision, and he ordered the desecration of the sanctuary, the profaning of the Sabbath and religious festivals, the placement of idols in the Temple, the erection of an altar to Zeus on the Temple grounds, and the sacrifice of traditionally unclean animals such as swine in religious rituals (1 Macc. 1:41–50). Some have argued that Antiochus was trying to establish himself as a divine king like the Egyptian pharaohs. There's no doubt that Antiochus had a fairly elevated view of himself. He assumed the divine epithet *theos epiphanes*, meaning "manifest god," but the objective of this decree appears to have been a desire to bring about a unity and to foster a common identity among his subjects. By eradicating the particularly Jewish elements of Temple worship and prohibiting circumcision, Antiochus was trying to draw the members of his diverse constituencies together. Although this decree had dire consequences for the Jews, it was part of a larger program of reform that concerned all of his subjects.

Whatever his intentions, Antiochus underestimated the importance of these religious customs to the Jews. His actions elicited a revolt and a succession of military uprisings, the details of which are described in 1 and 2 Maccabees. After considerable back and forth, this conflict eventually resulted in Jewish independence in 142 BCE. It was out of this struggle to create and preserve Jewish identity that the first solid articulations of the idea that Jews should die for God emerged. A number of texts, both canonical and noncanonical, that came out of this context espouse the view that Jews should prefer the law to life. We'll focus here on the book of Daniel and the texts ascribed to the Maccabees.

Daniel

Written in the second century BCE, the biblical book of Daniel may not appear, at first glance, to have much to say about martyrdom. After all, it does not include the actual deaths of any heroes. Yet Shadrach, Meshach, and Abednego in the fiery furnace (Dan. 3) and Daniel in the lions' den (Dan. 6) became important stories for later generations of Christians. These biblical characters' resolve to hold fast to the principles of monotheism and the commandments of the law became paradigmatic for both Jews and Christians. When commanded to worship King Nebuchadnezzar's statue, the three young men respond:

> If our God whom we serve is able to deliver us from the furnace of blazing fire and out of your hand, O king, let him deliver us. But if not, be it known to you, O king, that we will not serve your gods and we will not worship the golden statue that you have set up. (3:17–18)

As it turns out, the three young men are delivered from the fiery furnace. They saunter about in the flames with another mysterious fourth figure as a companion, or perhaps protector, before being retrieved alive and unharmed. A similar situation arises with Daniel, who is sealed in a den of lions overnight. The way Daniel explains it, he is delivered from the lions because he was found blameless before God (6:22). Daniel's accusers are thrown with their wives and children into the lions' den, where their bodies are torn apart even before they reach the ground (6:24). When Christians ruminated on these stories, they saw them as hopeful symbols and prefigurations of the general resurrection at the end of the world. Both stories encapsulate the idea that God will deliver the faithful from seemingly hopeless situations. For Christians thinking about the fate of their deceased loved ones or facing the reality that faithful members of their communities were being executed, the stories of the three young men and Daniel gleamed with promise.

Even though the protagonists are rescued from danger, the author of Daniel knows that not everyone will be so lucky. Righteous sufferers should not fear, however, because their reward will come after death. Daniel describes a heavenly book in which the names of the righteous are inscribed and says that, in the future, those whose names are written in the book will receive eternal reward:

> Your people shall be delivered, everyone who is found written in the book. Many of those who sleep in the dust of the earth shall awake, some to everlasting life, and some to shame and everlasting contempt. Those who are wise will shine like the brightness of the sky, and those who lead many to righteousness, like the stars forever and ever. (12:1–3)

It is not the case, says Daniel, that the righteous who suffer and die have been abandoned by God. They will awake to everlasting life in the future. Their names have been recorded in an unalterable heavenly book, and they will be rewarded for their good deeds.

Here in Daniel, we find something new. Prior to this, the prophets had promised people that if they kept God's commandments they would be rewarded in the here and now with prosperity, family, and success. God promised the patriarch Jacob, for example, "Your offspring shall be like the dust of the earth, and you shall spread abroad to the west and to the east and to the north and to the south; and all the families of the earth shall be blessed in you and in your offspring" (Gen. 28:14). Notions of the afterlife in this period were still amorphous and imprecise, because justice could be found in the present and God could be trusted to make good on his promises. We can find intimations of immortality in the prophets and Psalms, but the majority of people saw offspring as the means of achieving eternal life.

Scholars hypothesize that this idea of delayed judgment and eschatological reward developed because these promises of immediate reward were constantly unfulfilled. As a result and in order to avoid the conclusion that God was either notoriously unreliable or fundamentally incompetent, the idea of future eschatological reward and punishment emerged. Injustices that were not righted in one's lifetime would be settled at the end of time. Within the context of persecution and martyrdom, this promise proved particularly potent. It diffused larger questions about suffering and divine power. That a righteous person died for God was no longer a potential threat to the omnipotence of God; it was a means of securing eternal reward.

Perhaps the last element we should note here is the hint of eschatological vengeance. In the story of Daniel in the lions' den, Daniel's accusers and their families are eaten alive. To put this in ancient terms, it is not only Daniel's enemies who are destroyed, but also their offspring and thus the means by which they will live forever. In one fell swoop their legacies are destroyed. And it seems that the persecutors will not be left alone at the end of the world either. They will be resurrected to "shame and everlasting contempt." It is not enough for the author that the righteous be resurrected for heavenly rewards; their enemies must be around to see it. In Daniel, persecution and martyrdom are linked to the idea of postmortem reward and justice.

Apart from the fact that Daniel and the three young men don't die, these are exactly like Christian martyrdom stories. A pious individual refuses to perform some action because it goes against religious law and is condemned to death. This idea is linked to the expectation that the person will be rewarded for piety and the opponents will be punished. Everything we need for martyrdom we can find in Daniel.

The Maccabees

The books of the Maccabees are a medley of literary genres and sources. They blend together history, philosophy, letters, and theology in order to tell the story of the triumph of the Maccabees and their liberation of the Jews from Hellenistic rule. Although not a part of the canonical Hebrew scriptures, 1 and 2 Maccabees are well-respected historical documents that chart the history of the Jewish people in a period in which Jewish identity was being forged in fire. For some Christians—Orthodox, Roman Catholic, and Coptic—1 and 2 Maccabees are part of the canon, while for Protestants they are noncanonical and are placed in the Apocrypha.

There are many interesting examples of death in this body of literature, but we will focus here on 2 Maccabees, which contains the earliest stories of suffering and martyrdom in the Maccabean corpus. These examples should sufficiently demonstrate the existence of martyrdom in the Hellenistic period when the Jews lived under Seleucid rule. In 2 Maccabees the most notable instances of special death are those of the elderly scribe Eleazar and an unnamed Jewish mother and her seven sons. The Christian adoption of these individuals, commonly referred to by scholars and believers as the "(Holy) Maccabean martyrs," is a remarkable example of religious revisionism. Although they are regarded to this day as saints in the Roman Catholic and Orthodox Churches and visitors to St. Andrew's Church in Cologne, Germany, can venerate a gold reliquary believed to contain the relics of the mother and her seven sons, the Maccabean martyrs were quite adamantly Jews. In fact that was the whole point. It was in defense of their Jewish ancestral customs that they willingly embraced death.

In 2 Maccabees the stories of these martyrs follow closely on the heels of more general narratives of persecution and death. After crushing an attempted uprising led by the high priest Jason (5:5–16), King Antiochus decreed that the Jews must abandon their ancestral traditions. The treatment of those who resisted was strikingly brutal: women who had had their sons circumcised were thrown off the city ramparts with their infants hung around their necks (6:10), and Sabbath observers who were discovered worshipping secretly in caves were walled up and burned, unable to defend themselves because the Sabbath laws prohibited labor (6:11).

From this general picture of quiet resistance and vicious punishment, the account moves to a personal level with the introduction of Eleazar. Eleazar was a well-respected elderly scribe who was brought before the king in order to set an example for the rest of the people. His mouth was pried open by the guards, so they could force-feed him pork sacrificed to idols. But Eleazar spat the meat out, preferring to die rather than contaminate himself with the polluting effects of the meat. The sight of the frail old man being manhandled was a source of discomfort to the onlookers. In an effort to help him, some of the people in charge of the sacrifices took him aside and proposed that they substitute something else for the pork, so that it merely appeared that Eleazar was cooperating with the Greeks. Even though Eleazar had the opportunity to escape on a technicality, he refused:

> "Such pretense is not worthy of our time of life," he said, "for many of the young might suppose that Eleazar in his ninetieth year had gone over to an alien religion, and through my pretense, for the sake of living a brief moment longer, they would be led astray because of me, while I defile and disgrace my old age. Even if for the present I would avoid the punishment of mortals, yet whether I live or die I will not escape the hands of the Almighty. Therefore, by bravely giving up my life now, I

will show myself worthy of my old age and leave to the young
a noble example of how to die a good death willingly and nobly
for the revered and holy laws." (6:24–28)

Having made this statement, Eleazar moved nimbly toward the
rack and invited the torture to begin. His final words, as his body was
wrenched apart, were that his soul was glad that he suffered on account of his fear of the Lord (6:30). His death, the narrator remarks,
leaves behind it an example of "nobility" and a "memorial of courage"
(6:31).

There are a number of similarities between the depiction of Eleazar in 2 Maccabees and the accounts of the death of Socrates in Plato.
Both individuals are described as "noble" and are well advanced in
age. Both refuse to use deception in order to save their lives on the
grounds that to do so would set a bad example for and harm the youth.
And both die in a manner that is self-composed, explicitly exemplary,
and unequivocally virtuous. Given that Plato lived and wrote approximately two hundred years before the persecutions of Antiochus, we
have to conclude that the Maccabean account is borrowing from earlier philosophical traditions.

There's a sort of intriguing irony to the similarities between Eleazar and Socrates. Second Maccabees is a text about Jewish efforts to
reject and resist Greek cultural oppression, and yet here the author is
drinking from the same intellectual well as Plato. There is insufficient
evidence to prove, as some have suggested, that the author of 2 Maccabees actually possessed copies of Plato's writings and used them to
compose his own treatise, but the two vignettes are so similar to one
another that some kind of cultural dependence seems likely.[26] At a
minimum, the author of 2 Maccabees shares Plato's values and ideas
about how to die heroically. The reuse of Greek death stories may be
slightly subversive: Eleazar rejects everything that Hellenism stands
for, and yet he plays the role of the unjustly persecuted philosopher
very effectively. As readers, we see Eleazar compared to the heroes
of Greek society and recognize that he embodies their principles

better than Antiochus does. Even if this was not the author's intention, he still shares the same view of death as his oppressors. What these shared cultural values show us is just how widespread idealized noble death was in the ancient world. The overwhelming majority of people—whether Jewish or Greek—would have agreed that dying for the law, for God, or on principle was a good thing.

If the idea of a frail old man racked to death tugs at the heartstrings, then the author of 2 Maccabees ups the ante in the next story. In 2 Maccabees 7, seven brothers and their mother are brought before the king and also commanded to eat pork. The immediate response of one of the brothers, who acts as a spokesperson for the whole family, is that they are ready to die rather than breach their ancestral customs. The king flies into a rage and immediately has the young man butchered: the boy's tongue is cut out, he is scalped, his hands and feet are cut off, and he is placed into a frying pan and sautéed. The culinary undertones of the scene invoke the ideas of barbarism and cannibalism—a taboo in the ancient world as today. The implication is that the people forcing others to eat pork have other, darker appetites. One by one each of the brothers is interrogated and executed. Each says that he must adhere to the laws of their ancestors. As the final and youngest son's time for interrogation arrives, Antiochus thinks that he can persuade him and the mother to submit to his demands. He encourages her to persuade her youngest to participate in the sacrifice. She does not. Instead she speaks to her son using the "ancestral language" and encourages him to stand fast. Finally, with the bodies of her murdered children around her, the noble mother also dies.

The Maccabean martyrs are presented as examples of courage and moral fortitude, but they are—like the author of Daniel—absolutely confident that in the future they will be vindicated and rewarded for their behavior. The young men and their mother are certain that their bodies will be returned to them in the resurrection (2 Macc. 7:11, 14, 23, 29, 36). This posthumous restoration of the body is connected to the biblical idea of divine creation. One brother declares that he received his hands from heaven and can expect them back again (7:11). Apparently he is convinced that at some point in the future his body will be pieced back together by God. If God created his body originally, the argument goes, surely he can put it back together. What we find here, once again, is a connection between martyrdom and ideas about the afterlife. Contrary to Bowersock's argument about the uniqueness of Christian martyrdom, expectations of immortality play a prominent role in Jewish ideas about martyrdom. It's even more striking that the idea of the afterlife that the martyrs describe is bodily restitution. This is remarkably similar to the idea of the resurrection of the body for which Christians became famous.

Conclusion

THE EXAMPLES DISCUSSED IN this chapter are just some of the numerous instances of martyrdom in the ancient world. In the course of the past two thousand years, many people, including many scholars, have argued that there's something special and unique about martyrdom in Christianity and that prior to Christianity martyrdom didn't really exist. As we've seen, however, this isn't true. There was a great variety of opinion about the value of this kind of death, but at one time or another Jews, Greeks, and Romans respected, revered, and valorized their fallen heroes.

The argument made by Glen Bowersock discussed at the beginning of this chapter is that these individuals were not martyrs because (1) the term "martyr" was not applied to them and (2) there was no system of posthumous rewards. We've seen that this simply does not match the historical record. Just because the Greek term *martys* was not used to describe these individuals does not mean that they do not meet our modern definition of a martyr. It just means that they weren't *called* martyrs. In some important ways Christians are just like these other groups. Death for Christ is just a variant in an ancient worldview that thought that dying for something greater than oneself was the best way to die.

Neither is it true that non-Christian groups did not have a system of rewards for those who died for country, law, God, or king. The manner in which martyrdom was rewarded may have varied from group to group, but it was rewarded. Whether through glory, fame, ascent of the soul, or resurrection of the body, many groups connected the good death to rewards of one form or another.

Even if dying well was a commonly held belief in the ancient world, Christians have still claimed that there was something distinctive about the Christian experience. It is that Christians died *for Christ* and presumably for truth that is supposed to make their deaths different and special. It's true that only Christians modeled their conduct on the example set by Jesus in the Gospels, but as we have seen they were not the only group who treated the deaths of their literary and cultural heroes as exemplary. Figures like the Maccabees, Achilles, Lucretia, and Socrates loomed large in the cultural imagination of the ancient world. That Christians imitated Christ hardly made them unique in a world in which Jews imitated the Maccabees and Greeks imitated Socrates.

Part of the argument for the uniqueness of Christian martyrdom has rested on the assumption that Christian ideas were uniquely different and utterly separate from those of these other traditions. It might be argued that just because other groups had ideas about martyrdom doesn't necessarily mean that Christians knew about them. But in fact, they did. In the next chapter we'll see that Christians adapted, borrowed, and even directly copied from these other traditions.

CHAPTER TWO

Christian Borrowing of Jewish and Pagan Martyrdom Traditions

IN THE PREVIOUS CHAPTER WE saw that the *idea* of martyrdom predates Christianity by hundreds of years. It's to be expected, therefore, that Christians were influenced by legends of the Trojan heroes, examples of philosophers' good deaths, and stories of their Jewish forebears. We might even say that it's understandable that the values that led Christians to embrace death in preference to apostasy were inherited from Judaism and Greek and Roman mythology, philosophy, and history. After all, we all think and express ourselves using ideas from contemporary culture, and isn't imitation said to be the sincerest form of flattery?

The relationship of Christian martyrdom to pre-Christian martyrdom consists of a lot more than just superficial similarities, an amorphous influence, or a vague reiteration of a general principle or idea. One of the striking things about early Christian stories of executed heroes is just how similar they are to some of the stories discussed in the previous chapter. A little too similar, some might say. When we look at stories about early Christian martyrs from Jesus on, we can see that early Christians borrowed the myths of earlier generations. This is particularly noteworthy in the earliest martyrdom stories, the documents credited with inventing the concept of martyrdom.

To try to catalog every instance in which early Christians borrowed or adapted ideas about noble death would take hundreds of pages. A few select examples here will demonstrate that early Christian martyrdom stories are actually highly stylized rewritings of earlier traditions.

The Deaths of Jesus and Socrates

MOST THINGS IN CHRISTIANITY go back to, or claim to go back to, Jesus himself. And when it comes to martyrdom, the death of Jesus becomes the model for later Christians. Dying for Christ in the manner in which Christ himself died becomes an ideal for subsequent generations. Ignatius of Antioch says that he "longs" to be an imitator of the suffering of his God.[1] In a similar vein the author of the *Martyrdom of Polycarp* writes that Christians love martyrs, because they are disciples and imitators of Christ. There's something more than a little ironic about this idea. Christians long to be like Jesus, but the stories about the death of Jesus in the Gospels were shaped by non-Christian examples. Behind the theater of the crucifixion was a whole cast of Greek tragic heroes.

The story of the death of Jesus is told in each of the four Gospels—Matthew, Mark, Luke, and John—and yet each version of this story is different from the others. Many people have noted the inconsistencies in the passion narratives. For example, in the synoptic Gospels—Matthew, Mark, and Luke—Jesus dies on the Passover. In the Gospel of John, Jesus dies on the eve of the Passover, on the Day of Preparation, at the same time as the sacrifice of the Passover lambs (19:17–37). All four Gospels agree that Jesus died on a Friday, but they cannot agree on the religious significance of the day. These sorts of discrepancies can be quite alarming for anyone who views the Bible as inerrant, but this inconsistency is relatively inconsequential when we compare the various portrayals of the character of Jesus as he faces death in these Gospels. The evangelists present radically different pictures of how Jesus approached and faced his death.

In the earliest version of the life and death of Jesus, the Gospel of Mark, Jesus is portrayed as emotional and lost. The night before his death, after the Last Supper, Jesus and his disciples go out of the city to the Garden of Gethsemane. This incident is known as the Gethsemane agony, because it is here that Jesus prays mournfully, alone, before his death. In Mark's version Jesus is unsteady and passionate and grieves over his imminent death. He asks his disciples to stay awake with him to keep him company, and he begs God, his Father, that "this cup" (that is, death) might pass from him (14:36).

Jesus's desperation only grows more fevered as he dies. On the cross his final words are words of abandonment; he cries out, "My God, my God, why have you forsaken me?" (Mark 15:34). The cumulative image is one of a man broken and betrayed, desperately grasping at life, and mournfully accepting death. To paraphrase the words of biblical scholar and Nobel Prize winner Albert Schweitzer, Jesus appears crushed by the wheel of history.[2] The very world that he had hoped to influence has trampled him, and at the very end, he is alone and disillusioned. It's a poignant scene, full of emotion.

As modern readers, we might be overwhelmed with empathy for Jesus. But if we were to imagine ourselves as ancient audience members, we can almost hear Achilles sneer.

Christian interpretations of the death of Jesus in Mark have sought to downplay this problem. Since the early church, patristic authors have argued that the apparent weakness of Jesus is highlighted in Mark to show his "human side." Jesus appears weak, so that no one could mistakenly think that he's *only* divine. Biblical scholars have pointed out that Jesus's words of despair are citations of psalms that begin despondently but end with promises of restoration. Psalm 22, from which the words "My God, my God, why have you forsaken me?" are taken, concludes on a much more hopeful note. It is likely that Mark invokes echoes of the whole psalm in order to imply—to those who catch the allusions—that Jesus's death, though tragic, will in the end turn out for the good.

At the same time, however, there were those who found Jesus's agony and emotional turmoil crushingly embarrassing. Certainly, Christianity's enemies seized on this incident as evidence of Christianity's flaws. Celsus, a well-educated second-century pagan critic of Christianity, sums up the problem when he says, "Why does [Jesus] howl, lament, and pray to escape the fear of destruction, expressing himself in a manner like this: Oh father, if it be possible, let this cup pass?"[3] For some Christian readers, too, Jesus appears a little *too* human. It's human to die, but to many it seemed a little weak to whine about it ahead of time. One of these readers was the evangelist Luke, who, writing some years later, radically edited Mark's version of the death of Jesus. Luke, like Matthew, had a copy of Mark's Gospel in front of him and based his own version on this source. Yet he often departs from Mark, either to correct what he sees as mistakes in Mark's Gospel or to advance his own theological vision.

In Luke's version of the passion narrative, all superfluous traces of human suffering are stripped away.[4] If we compare Mark's and Luke's versions of Jesus praying in the Garden of Gethsemane, the difference is immediately apparent:

Mark 14:32–36: They went to a place called Gethsemane; and he said to his disciples, "Sit here while I pray." He took with him Peter and James and John, and began to be distressed and agitated. And he said to them, "I am deeply grieved, even to death; remain here, and keep awake." And going a little farther, he threw himself on the ground and prayed that, if it were possible, the hour might pass from him. He said, "Abba, Father, for you all things are possible; remove this cup from me; yet, not what I want, but what you want."

Luke 22:39–42, 45: He came out and went, as was his custom, to the Mount of Olives; and the disciples followed him. When he reached the place, he said to them, "Pray that you may not come into the time of trial." Then he withdrew from them about a stone's throw, knelt down, and prayed, "Father, if you are willing, remove this cup from me; yet, not my will but yours be done." When he got up from prayer, he came to the disciples and found them sleeping because of grief.[5]

In Mark's version Jesus is desperate and in need of comfort. He asks the disciples to stay awake with him, because he is grieving. He is described as distressed and agitated and begs God, as his son, using the familial, childlike term "Abba." In Luke, Jesus feels no distress at all. He instructs the disciples to pray for themselves and, although he still asks God to remove the cup, the whole scene has an almost businesslike feel to it. What was once a story about the struggle of Jesus has now become something of a test for his disciples. All references to the idea that Jesus suffered emotional anguish, was "grieved," "agitated," or "distressed," have been removed. In Mark, Jesus's distress is apparent even in his comportment: he "threw himself on the ground and prayed" (14:35). Compare this to Luke's more sturdy and precise "knelt down, and prayed" (22:41).

The same editorial program continues throughout Luke's passion narrative. Instead of Mark's cry of despair and dereliction ("My God, my God, why have you forsaken me?" 15:34), Luke has the more reserved and controlled "Father, into your hands I commend my spirit" (23:46). Both Mark and Luke cite Psalms. Mark uses the Aramaic of Psalm 22:2, and Luke refers to Psalm 31:6. Luke has selected a psalm that conveys Jesus's control, rather than his anguish. In Luke only the disciples feel grief, and Jesus himself appears calm and self-possessed.

Luke's changes to Mark's Gospel revolutionize our picture of Jesus. In his version of the passion narrative Luke has radically altered not just the events, but Jesus's character and conduct. Luke's Jesus appears resolutely self-controlled. While his followers mourn, he is calm. He continues to instruct them just as he did throughout his ministry. We can see how Luke dodges some uncomfortable questions about Jesus's behavior, but we still have to ask why and under what influences Luke would do this.

One explanation is that Luke was attempting to portray Jesus as a kind of second Socrates.[6] The Roman Stoic philosopher Seneca, for instance, writes that imprisonment and impending death "changed Socrates's soul so little that they did not even change his expression" and that Socrates was an example of "how to die if it is necessary."[7] The same observations can be made of Jesus in Luke. He is unperturbed and accepting. Their combination of exemplarity, calmness, innocence, and acceptance of death make Jesus and Socrates all the more similar.

It is difficult to know if Luke really used the example of Socrates from the writings of Plato and Xenophon to edit Mark's version of the passion narrative. There are similarities between the Lukan Jesus and Plato's Socrates, but many of these similarities can be found in other descriptions of the deaths of other philosophers or ancient ideas about death in general. Regardless of whether Luke has Socrates in particular in mind, it is clear that Luke has edited the passion narrative to make Jesus's death reminiscent of the death of a philosopher and consonant with ancient views of death in general. He knows that his audience might find Jesus weak, unmanly, or contemptible, and he reconfigures the portrait of Jesus to make him more controlled and, thus, more virtuous. The effect is that the death of Jesus appears as a kind of philosophical martyrdom. Luke's audience would understand the death of Jesus as the heroic death of an emboldened philosopher. The fortified Lukan Jesus was now much more appealing to Greco-Roman audiences, and this helped Luke win converts for Christ.

Scholars generally assume that Mark's account, as the earliest and simplest Gospel, is the closest to the events, but that Luke was more interested in making Jesus die well than in telling the events as they happened. This was probably rather earnest editorial work. It is not the case that Luke found Jesus himself wanting, but rather that he found Mark's version of events deeply unsatisfying. For Luke, Jesus really was a philosopher like Socrates, and in editing the details of the passion narrative in this way, he was just showing Jesus off to his best advantage. He shifts the paradigm and intellectual frame in which to understand the significance of Jesus's death and identity. The effects of Luke's heavy-handed editorial work have been devastating for our knowledge of what actually happened at the time. The historical facts of what occurred during Jesus's last days were overwritten with a theology of noble death and martyrdom, but this theology wasn't originally Christian; it drew on widely held ancient beliefs about what constituted the good death.

Luke isn't the only early Christian to view Jesus in this way. This particular vision of Jesus's death was influential in early Christian circles, and *especially* among those interested in martyrdom. In the late antique *Acts of Apollonius*, the second-century martyr Apollonius says:

> Just as the Athenian informers convinced the people and then unjustly condemned Socrates, so too our Savior and teacher was condemned by a few malefactors after being bound.[8]

Putting aside the fact that Jesus was only briefly bound, it's interesting that Apollonius compares Jesus to Socrates. It seems that early Christians themselves consciously thought of Jesus as a Socrates figure and his death as comparable to that of Socrates. Evidence like this suggests that Christians not only used the death of Socrates to tell the story of Jesus; they were proud of the comparison.

Now, someone might argue that Apollonius is speaking using the terms of the Roman audience in the courtroom where he was being tried and invokes Socrates just in order to win them over. The difficulty with this theory is that, according to most scholars, this is not an accurate report of the trial of Apollonius.[9] If it isn't historically accurate, and Apollonius himself didn't actually say this, then the audience for this statement is not the people trying Apollonius in the story, but the Christians listening to the account being read. We have to conclude, then, that the Christians in the audience would have approved of the comparison.

Martyrs Imitating Icons

FROM THE VERY BEGINNING Christian authors used the deaths of other, non-Christian heroes to tell their own stories. Interest in behaving as Jesus did actually go all the way back to the dawn of Christianity and to the earliest Christian martyrs. To this day millions of Christians appeal to the example set by Jesus as a guideline for their ethical conduct. Catholics call this *imitatio Christi*, or the "imitation of Christ." Protestants ask themselves, "What would Jesus do?" The problem is that, as we have received it in the Gospel of Luke, the model embodied by Jesus was itself partly based on other non-Christian examples. This means that every time someone is referred to or described as dying like Christ they are actually dying like Socrates and the Maccabees.

The tendency to emphasize similarities between the deaths of Christians and death of Christ began very early, with the account of the death of Stephen in Acts 7. Given that the same author was likely responsible for writing the Gospel of Luke and Acts, perhaps we can forgive him for copying his own work. By portraying Stephen's death as like that of Jesus the author is able to show continuity between the ministry of Jesus and ministry of the church. But it's not only the author of Acts who uses the death of Jesus as a narrative template. Early Christian authors, who were already engaged in the project of reading the death of Jesus in dialogue with the deaths of ancient philosophers and heroes, presented their martyrs as iconic hybrids. In crafting narratives of defiance and suffering, these authors wove together the manifold canonical and noncanonical portraits of Jesus with memories of Socrates refracted through generations of emboldened philosophers and echoes of the Maccabean martyrs. The result is that it is sometimes difficult to parse one biblical or cultural allusion from another. These are creative reimaginings of Jesus, Socrates, and Eleazar, but they are nonetheless contingent on and derive their power from the pre-Christian icons that supply the heroic script.

Polycarp

Sometime in the middle of the second century, an elderly man was brought before the Roman proconsul in Smyrna, Izmir, in modern-day Turkey.[10] He had been betrayed by someone close to him, hunted down to a dwelling outside the city, and dragged to the center of the town for a public trial and brutal execution at the stake. His name was Polycarp, and he was Smyrna's most famous bishop. According to the statement made at his trial, Polycarp had served Christ for eighty-six years prior to his arrest. According to the legends that swirl around him, he had learned Christianity from the example of the evangelist-apostle John and had always and everywhere eschewed heresy in his travels and comportment. As a correspondent of the bishop and martyr Ignatius of Antioch, Polycarp is a bridge between the apostles and the early church and, for generations of later Christians, a mouthpiece for orthodoxy.[11]

The details of his arrest, trial, and execution are described in the *Martyrdom of Polycarp*, an account saturated with allusions to the passion of Jesus and carefully crafted statements about the value of martyrdom. The entire narrative labors deliberately toward this goal; Polycarp is three times described as performing a kind of martyrdom "in accordance with Gospel." Even if the author were less forthcoming with his agenda, the parallels between Jesus and Polycarp are too obvious to miss. Before his arrest, hearing rumors of persecution, Polycarp goes outside the city. There he prophesies his own death and awaits his arrest. He is betrayed by someone close to him and prays when the captain of the police, who is fortuitously named Herod, comes to arrest him. He is arrested at night and acquiesces out of a sense of obedience to the will of God, and when he enters the city, he does so on the back of a donkey. While the bloodthirsty crowd chomps at the bit to execute Polycarp, the Romans equivocate over the death sentence by attempting to reason with Polycarp. Polycarp is instructed by a heavenly voice, and finally, when he is executed around Passover, a stream of blood gushes from his side.[12]

There's no doubt that the author of this account wants to portray Polycarp as being just like Jesus or, to use religious terminology, an "imitator of Christ." At the same time, however, there are parallels with other important ancient literary traditions. Both Polycarp and Socrates are described as "noble" and charged with atheism.[13] Neither was willing to persuade others in order to save his life.[14] Socrates took control of his death by requesting the hemlock rather than waiting for it to be administered to him.[15] Polycarp took control of his death by removing his own clothes and standing on the pyre without being nailed to a stake.[16] Both Socrates and Polycarp prayed before dying, and the accounts of both of their deaths explicitly interpret their deaths as sacrifices.[17] Socrates refers to Asclepius and pours out the hemlock as a libation offering, and Polycarp is described as being like a ram bound for sacrifice.[18] With regard to the image conjured up in the minds of the audience, both men are elderly. Socrates was in his seventies when he died, and Polycarp was at least eighty-six.[19] Finally, their deaths are described as being models for others.[20]

The parallels between Jesus and Polycarp are much more obvious than the parallels between Socrates and Polycarp. We have to bear in mind, however, that in the second century, when these events were supposed to have taken place and been written down, Socrates was much better known than Jesus. The stories of Socrates's death were also much better known than the passion narrative. Not only were there multiple accounts of Socrates's death; the admirable qualities of Socrates's death were rehearsed by later generations of philosophers and writers. More strikingly, when people actually committed suicide, they did so with a gesture toward Socrates. For instance, in the first century, two Roman senators, Thrasea and Seneca, staged Socratic suicides for themselves after being condemned unjustly by the emperor Nero.[21] What this shows us is that even in the common era the philosophical death of Socrates continued to be the model for those wanting to die the good death. For an audience member familiar with the stories about Socrates and other philosophers from coins, statues, campfire stories, and school, the image of another old man dying unjustly on the charge of atheism was likely to sound familiar. Even if the allusions to the philosophical tradition appear more strained to us, at the time they were likely as obvious as the allusions to Jesus.

One of the interesting things about the allusions to philosophical death in the *Martyrdom of Polycarp* is the way in which the combination of biblical echoes and philosophical allusions improves the quality of Polycarp's death. When Polycarp comes to the place of execution, he calmly removes his own clothes, clambers onto the pyre, and demands that he not be nailed to the stake, saying, "Leave me as I am; for he who enables me to endure the fire will also enable me to remain on the pyre without moving, even without the sense of security which you get from the nails."[22] Polycarp's confidence that he can stand without flinching as the flames burn the skin off his body is in keeping with the self-controlled confidence of the philosophers we have examined. Like Zeno and Anaxarchus, Polycarp takes control of the torture and demonstrates with his words that he is both manly and self-controlled. With regard to biblical allusions, Polycarp's request that he not be nailed results in his being bound to the stake and compared to a ram, a description that evokes comparisons with the binding and near sacrifice of Isaac in Genesis 22. At the same time, however, the fact that he is not nailed subtly alters his imitation of Christ. Jesus was nailed to the cross. That Polycarp does not need nails in some respects "one-ups" Jesus.[23] An ancient Christian hearing the story read for the first time might imagine that Polycarp dies a nobler death than Jesus. By portraying Polycarp as stoic and using ideas from philosophical martyrdom, the author has run the risk of making Polycarp better than Jesus. Mixing cultural allusions inadvertently improves on and endangers the status of the model.

All of this goes to show how important influences other than Jesus were on the composition of the *Martyrdom of Polycarp*. The author wants to make Polycarp into the kind of hero any Greek or Roman might admire, and in order to do so he uses the literary conventions of the death of the philosopher. What this means, ultimately, is that one of the most famous and important Christian martyrdom accounts was dependent on pagan martyrdom for its substance. Martyrdom is not unique to Christianity, nor did early Christians think it was. Christian martyrdom stories were completely at home among the ancient accounts of noble death, and this familiarity made these stories popular and contributed to Christianity's success.

Ptolemy

Ptolemy is one of the hidden martyrs of early Christianity. Next to the dramatic Polycarp or the adventurous and dynamic Perpetua, he seems staid and boring. Even the story of his death is tucked away in a larger, less auspicious work: Justin Martyr's *Second Apology*. Ptolemy was a Christian teacher in Rome who had come to the attention of a wealthy, hedonistic woman. He persuaded her that her lifestyle was morally unacceptable, and in her adoption of Christianity, she ended up suing her husband for divorce. Her husband, being the licentious type, was understandably upset and blamed Ptolemy. He complained to the authorities, and Ptolemy was arrested. After Ptolemy was convicted, Lucius, an otherwise unknown bystander at the trial, piped up and complained about the sentencing, only to find himself subject to interrogation and summarily sentenced to death. Finally a third, unnamed individual came forward and was punished.

The title the *Acts of Ptolemy and Lucius* is a slightly misleading one. In its current form the story is a part of Justin's defense of Christianity, which is styled as an "apology," the literary genre that Plato and Xenophon used to exculpate Socrates. This literary presentation is actually the key for understanding Justin's motivation. There are subtle allusions to Socrates throughout the *Second Apology*, suggesting that Justin wants us to think of Christians in general and Ptolemy in particular as being just like the famous doomed philosopher. This fits into Justin's overarching goal of presenting Christianity as a philosophy to his primarily Greek- and Roman-educated audience.

The idea that Ptolemy is just like Socrates is confirmed by the peculiarity of the story itself. We have almost no information about Ptolemy or what he actually taught. There's no reason to doubt that Ptolemy and Lucius were actually executed as Justin says, but there's something a little curious about the story. There are very few overt references to Christianity at all. We have to infer from Justin's description of the woman's new convictions exactly what it was that Ptolemy had taught her. Apparently she had previously been intemperate and self-indulgent, participating with her husband in all sorts of actions that were not in accordance with nature or befitting a person of self-control. She has now, it seems, come around to something like the opinion that

> the unjust and undisciplined shall be corrected by eternal fire, but that the virtuous and those who lived like Christ shall dwell with God in a state that is free from passions—we mean, those who have become Christians.[24]

At first blush, the references to eternal fire might seem like the proverbial hellfires that kept our hands out of the cookie jar as children. Dwelling with God might similarly conjure up images of clouds and harps. Certainly in Justin's time there were some, like the author of the Gospel of Matthew, who were on their way to thinking of the afterlife in these terms. It doesn't seem likely, though, that Ptolemy was one of them. There's a great deal of technical philosophical language underlying the English translation. The text speaks of being *persuaded* to think something, not of "believing" it. The eternal fire is contrasted with living in a manner like that of Christ and in a state "without passion." The Greek term for being without passion is *apatheia*, which was a technical term that Stoics used to describe the ideal state of the philosopher.

When we put the language of self-control, temperance, and living free from passion together, the description has a very philosophical ring to it. Ptolemy seems to be teaching the woman something like Stoicism—Stoicism grounded in the exemplary conduct of Christ. The idea of imitating the ethical behavior of one's philosophical instructor was very common in antiquity, and this seems to be what is happening here: Justin is presenting Jesus as an example of how to live a good life. This good life is further defined as a life of temperance, self-control, righteousness, and so on. It's a concept of virtue that resonated with both Christians and Stoics.

To put this in modern terms, Justin describes Ptolemy's teachings as general morality in which you treat other people with respect, or there will be repercussions. This could be Christianity, but it could be any number of ancient philosophies. That seems to be Justin's point here. His argument is that Christianity is an ancient philosophy and should be treated just like any other philosophy. The emperor Marcus Aurelius was himself a Stoic, so by presenting Christianity as a kind of mild Stoicism Justin is making the case that Christians are socially acceptable.

The allusions to Socrates work in the same way. The Romans respected Socrates as a philosophical defender of virtue. By borrowing from legends about Socrates, Justin is able to make the case that Christians are unfairly treated. What this means for us, then, is that Christian martyrs were deliberately portrayed as being like Socrates. This may have been expedient and pragmatic, but the fact of the matter is that Justin's idea of Christian martyrdom is taken in part from ancient philosophy. Ancient readers might have thought that Christianity was just a new form of philosophy and that Ptolemy was just another heroic philosopher like Socrates or Zeno. That Justin would not only allow but even encourage us to think this shows just how comfortable Christians were with borrowing the pagan understanding of martyrdom.

The Martyrs of Lyons and Vienne

In 177 in Lyons, France, a group of Christians from the town and neighboring Vienne were rounded up and tried as Christians. The account of their deaths is an ensemble piece featuring Christians from various socioeconomic backgrounds: a lawyer, at least one Roman citizen, a wealthy slave owner, a soldier, a young boy, an aging bishop, and a slave girl. Narratively, these characters are refashioned using biblical molds, so that they take on the roles of a cast of scriptural actors. At certain points, the assimilation is overt: the lawyer Vettius Epagathus, who unexpectedly speaks up on behalf of the arrested Christians at the beginning of the accounts, is explicitly compared to Zechariah, the father of John the Baptist.[25] The use of the Maccabean literature is comparatively subtle, but the discretion and ambiguity in its presentation render the allusions all the more potent.

The characterization of these martyrs as being like the Maccabees begins with Pothinus, the aging bishop of Lyons. Here is the description of Pothinus:

> The blessed Pothinus, who had been entrusted with the bishopric of Lyons, was dragged to the judgment seat. He was more than ninety years of age, and very infirm, scarcely indeed able to breathe because of physical weakness; but he was strengthened by spiritual zeal through his earnest desire for martyrdom. Though his body was worn out by old age and disease, his life was preserved that Christ might triumph in it.[26]

Compare this description of Pothinus with that of Eleazar:

> Eleazar, one of the scribes in high position, a man now advanced in age and of noble presence, was being forced to open his mouth to eat swine's flesh. But he, welcoming death with honor rather than life with pollution, went up to the rack of his own accord. . . . "Such pretense is not worthy of our time

of life," he said, "for many of the young might suppose that Eleazar in his ninetieth year had gone over to an alien religion. . . . In my soul I am glad to suffer these things because I fear [God]." (2 Macc. 6:18–30)

Like Eleazar, Pothinus is energized by the possibility of martyrdom. Though he felt the weariness of aging, the prospect of death brought him renewed vigor. The similar status of Pothinus and Eleazar, both of whom were leaders in their respective communities, their advanced age, and their rush of energy as they embrace death make it likely that the author of the *Martyrs of Lyons* had Eleazar in mind when he sketched the contours of Pothinus's martyrdom. If anything, there is a touch of one-upmanship at work. Eleazar is merely ninety, but Pothinus is *more* than ninety years old and very infirm. Eleazar is glad in his soul, but Pothinus is strengthened by spiritual zeal. There is something of a clever wordplay at work here. Pothinus was scarcely able to breathe (*empneô*, from *pneiô*, meaning "to breathe"), but spiritual zeal (*prothumias pneumatos*) provides supernatural life-support. That the root terms for "breath" and "spirit" are identical here shows the extent to which Pothinus's actions are enabled through divine assistance.

Pothinus is not the only Maccabean-styled martyr in the story. The allusions reappear toward the end of the narrative where Blandina is described as a "noble mother," who encourages and sends her children on to God before finally accepting death herself.[27] This is akin to the "noble mother" of 2 Maccabees 7, who dispatches her seven sons to God before joining them in death. The allusion might be relatively banal, were it not for the fact that Blandina does not actually have any children. Even within the world of the text the only candidate for her "child" is the youth Ponticus, with whom she is paired in death. Although Blandina certainly encourages the young man to embrace martyrdom, the text refers to her having children, in the plural. The narrative incongruity of the plural noun (*tekna*) points us to the scriptural subtext.[28] Blandina, though not biologically or legally a mother to the other Christians, plays the part of the brave martyr's mother with great aplomb.

Blandina and Pothinus are not the only Christian martyrs compared to the Maccabees. Explicit references are found in the late-third-century forgeries the *Martyrdom of Marian and James* and the *Martyrdom of Montanus and Lucius*. In the former, the mother of Marian, "now sure of her son once his passion was finished, rejoiced like the mother of the Maccabees, congratulating not only Marian but also herself that she had borne such a son."[29] In the same way in the *Martyrdom of Montanus and Lucius* the mother of the martyr Flavian is described as "a mother of the Maccabees."[30] All of this goes to show that early Christian authors deliberately and self-consciously utilized Maccabean literature in their depictions of the torture and deaths of martyrs in Gaul and North Africa.

In the *Martyrs of Lyons*, however, the use of Maccabean motifs is tempered by the presence of other biblical figures. Blandina is not only the mother of the Maccabees; she is an imitator of the death of Jesus. When she is led into the arena for public execution, she is strung up like a carcass for the animals:

> Blandina was hung on a stake and set as food before the beasts driven in the arena. Because she was seen hanging in the form of a cross and on account of her energetic and unceasing prayer, she stirred up great enthusiasm among the contestants. During the contest they looked with their eyes through their sister to the one who was crucified for them so that [s]he convinced those who believe in him that everyone who suffers for the glory of Christ will have eternal fellowship with the living God.[31]

Though she is introduced as one of the dregs of society, she is in this scene transformed into the embodiment of divine power. She is able to perform the crucifixion for her fellow martyrs and the audience. This is more than just a trick of the light; she plays Christ so well that she disappears, the audience sees only Christ, and the martyrs are compelled to follow her into death. The illustrious role she plays and identity she takes on in this scene contrast with the earlier description of her as cheap and worthless. In Blandina a cluster of biblical allusions coalesce and mingle. She is both the Maccabean martyr and Christ crucified.

The biblical allusions in the *Martyrs of Lyons* are unambiguous, constructive, and theologically significant. This is not the plagiarism of a simple hack. The author creates a new vision of the world in which scripture blends into the present and the actors in the texts and listeners in the audience can participate. That the author is creative and imaginative does not mean, however, that he is not utilizing the rhetorical power of the Maccabean heroes. In histories of or homilies on martyrdom, the similarities between biblical heroes and Christian martyrs are dismissed as unproblematic. The Maccabees have been so completely integrated into Christian histories of martyrs that their resolutely Jewish identities are brushed aside. Either the authors are seen merely as plumping up the characters with Maccabean charisma, or the Maccabees are seen as prophecies of the later martyrs. Just because the author is an articulate and engaging writer, however, should not keep us from reflecting upon the repackaging of Maccabean traditions.

The use of the Maccabees *is* problematic if we want to pretend that only Christians have martyrs. Not only does the author know the Maccabean stories and use them in presenting his own characters; he utilizes their power in order to further his own agenda. As creative as the author is, he is also parasitic, turning the religious potency of ancient non-Christian heroes to his own advantage. Just because Christians believe that the Maccabees were also Christian doesn't mean that they actually were. In their own minds, they died as Jews. This is nothing other than the deliberate and strategic borrowing of earlier martyrdom traditions.

Perpetua

Of all the martyrs from the early church, Vibia Perpetua is one of the most well known and most beloved. Perpetua was a well-educated young Roman woman who most likely lived in Carthage (modern-day Tunis) at the turn of the third century. At the time of her arrest she was not yet baptized; she was a catechumen in the process of receiving instruction before her initiation into Christianity. Although her husband is never mentioned in the account, she was apparently married and had a young son whom she was still nursing for part of her imprisonment. The story of her trial, a diary written during her confinement, and an account of her execution along with a group of other Christians are contained in a document called the *Passion of Perpetua and Felicity*. We will deal with the authenticity and historicity of this famous story in the next chapter, but for now we will focus on those elements that seem borrowed from Greek and Roman literature.

The editor of the account was a highly skilled writer. The vividness of his descriptions have led some to conclude that he must have been an eyewitness to the Christians' deaths in the arena. It's possible that he was. I have visited the amphitheater in Carthage in which Perpetua and her companions were executed, and providing the author sat in the front row and Perpetua was on his side of the arena, it's possible that he really could have seen the whites of her eyes, as he claims. On the other hand, perhaps he was just a good writer.

There are elements that seem familiar to readers of ancient mythology, and it's possible that the editor deliberately invoked these stories in order to give his story a sophisticated literary veneer. Of particular interest is Perpetua's modesty. When Perpetua's attire becomes disheveled in the arena, she modestly tugs at the hem of her clothing. The scene is reminiscent of one in Euripides's play *Hecuba*. In the play the virgin princess Polyxena modestly arranges her dress to cover herself as Achilles's son Neoptolemus slits her throat.[32] Perpetua takes things further, one-upping Polyxena by asking for a comb so she can rearrange her hair, but the basic idea of the modest young woman virtuously covering herself seems to have been plucked from Greek drama.

The Genre of Christian Martyrdom Stories

ONE OF THE DISTINCTIVE things about early Christian martyrdom stories is the form they take. Stories about the deaths of early Christian martyrs seem to have circulated separately from and prior to other legends about their lives before death. As stories that describe only the trial, torture, and execution of their protagonists, they are neither biographies nor histories. In this respect their structure corresponds to the original form of the passion narrative, which many New Testament scholars believe circulated separately from the rest of the Gospels.[33] The distinctiveness of this literary form led some to conclude that the genre of the martyrdom story as well as the term "martyr" and the concept of martyrdom itself were the products of the Christian imagination. Scholars of early Christianity Edgar Goodspeed and Robert Grant exemplify this view when they write, "With the *Martyrdom of Polycarp* and the *Martyrdom of Justin* begins a new form of Christian literature that became immensely popular, the 'acts of martyrdom.'"[34]

The "Acts of the Pagan Martyrs"

We have been talking about martyrdom stories that conform to the "passion" genre and describe the tortures, sufferings, and execution of the martyrs in some detail. Some of the earliest Christian accounts of martyrdom, however, are concerned exclusively with the events that take place in the courtroom. These unembellished trial-style reports are called *acta*, or "acts," as they appear to conform to the generic conventions of court proceedings.

These early Christian martyrdom stories appear to be pure records of the trials of the martyrs. They are simple reports, unencumbered by lurid descriptions of torture or execution. This makes these stories very distinctive and generically different. Unlike Greco-Roman stories of noble death, which are excerpted from poetry about the Trojan War or philosophical treatises about noble death, the courtroom stories are brief vignettes of a few hours of a person's life. Instead of forming part of larger historical, poetic, or philosophical works, these stories begin and often end in the courtroom. The content of these stories is mostly the dialogue between the Roman judge—usually a governor or proconsul, but sometimes an emperor—and those individuals on trial. The stories resemble court transcripts similar to those produced by stenographers today.

The distinctiveness and simplicity of this writing style have led many scholars to argue that these Christian martyrdom accounts were based on actual court documents. They are transcripts of what actually happened in the courtroom. Ironically, this scholarly position is incompatible with the view that Christians created their own new genre. It cannot be the case that an early Christian *acta*-style martyrdom account is both a copy of a historically accurate authentic court transcript *and* a completely new Christian genre. Either they are copies of court documents, of which there are thousands of examples about all kinds of crimes, or they are a whole new genre. We will return to the question of the historicity of these stories in the following chapters; our focus for the moment is the assertion that Christians' stories were generically distinct and, thus, special.

In 1896 young British archaeologists Bernard P. Grenfell and Arthur S. Hunt traveled to Egypt to excavate the town of Oxyrhynchus. They were very much latecomers to the excavations. By the time Grenfell and Hunt arrived, other archaeologists had already raced through the site, uncovering the most interesting finds, with the result that all that remained for them were a few graves and the town trash heap. What was, literally, garbage to ancient Romans was a mine of information for modern scholars. They discovered portions of Christian texts, receipts, letters, fragments of Homer, and many other important literary finds. Among these documents was a cluster of fragmentary court documents describing the trials of various Alexandrians in the first century BCE. They appeared at first glance just to be records of the trials of citizens there, but upon further inspection some of these texts went beyond the courtroom and bore some striking similarities to Christian acts.

In these documents, as in Christian stories, the protagonists are unjustly sentenced to die and are willing to do so out of loyalty to their native city. Patriotism, it seems, is a just and worthy cause for self-sacrifice and something that should not cause distress.[35] To give but one example, a piece of papyrus known as the *Acts of Appianus* relays the events surrounding the execution of Appianus, a prominent citizen in Alexandria. Apparently, although this portion of the account is not preserved, Appianus had accused the emperor of profiting at the expense of local merchants who had been tasked with the supply of grain. The account of his trial describes the lively encounter between Appianus and the emperor. In it Appianus speaks confidently against the emperor, gladly embraces death for his city, and goes to his death dressed in the trappings of the upper classes and proclaiming the injustice of the emperor Commodus's actions.

What is interesting about these stories is that, like Christian martyrdom accounts, they seem to have an interest in the righteousness of their protagonists and the injustice of the events. They aren't simple descriptions of events; they have a message for the audience. This combination of courtroom-style document and ethical agenda makes them valuable comparative material for Christian texts. It seems that even the barest of the literary genres within which early Christians worked was not distinctively Christian or invented by Christians themselves.

Apocryphal Acts of the Apostles and the Romance Novel

Some stories about martyrs are staidly legalistic, but others have something of the feel of an adventure novel. These other stories include biographical information, background stories about the imprisonment and torture of the saints, and exquisitely detailed descriptions of the martyr's deaths. In the case of the apostles the background information is quite lengthy. The canonical Acts of the Apostles ends before Paul dies in Rome, and we hear nothing about the fate of Peter, Andrew, Barnabas, or the rest of the Twelve. In many ways the audience is on tenterhooks wondering what happened next. As Christianity spread, legends about the work and eventual fate of the apostles began to circulate. Congregations in major cities began to develop myths of origins for themselves in which this or that apostle founded their church or that could account for how the physical remains of an apostle had found their final resting place in their town. Everyone wanted a piece of the apostles, as it were. These stories have a sensational dramatic character to them: they include miracles, shipwrecks, talking animals, prodigious infants, Harry Potter–like battles of wits with powerful magicians, and flying, talking, and walking crosses. The Gospels look dry and plodding by comparison.

These dramatic stories of beloved characters tossed about by the winds of fate and surrounded by the marvelous, the horrifying, and the miraculous were familiar to ancient audiences from ancient fiction in general. The popularity of the apocryphal acts resulted from the rise of a new genre in ancient Greek literature, the Greek novel. Stories had always been an important part of Greek literature, but the rise of the novel—tales filled with adventure, star-crossed lovers, travel, and intrigue—was something distinct in the ancient world. These Greek novels, of which about twenty survive, are as formulaic as modern romantic comedies.[36] They always feature a central pair of young, attractive, well-bred lovers who are torn apart by fate, miscommunication, or familial interference and who spend the course of the plot faithfully attempting to reunite with one another. Throughout their harried adventures the fidelity of the young lovers is always threatened by the lust of other characters, both male and female. In the end, though, the couple are reunited to live happily ever after. These stories were not merely for entertainment; they inculcated certain values in their audiences. Just as modern romances privilege an idea of love that overcomes unfair social divides, ancient romances idealized hellenization and love between aristocrats.

In many ways the apocryphal acts of the apostles replicate the narrative motifs and plotlines of the Greek novels.[37] Travel, pirates, shipwrecks, aristocrats, important and alluring young women, and adventure all play a prominent role in the apocryphal acts. In particular, the *Acts of Paul and Thecla* reproduces elements of the Greek novel in the description of Paul's involvement with Thecla. Thecla, like the heroines of the Greek novels, is a beautiful young aristocrat who was engaged to be married. She one day overhears Paul preaching and converts, abandoning her family and fiancé in pursuit of and fidelity to her new beloved. She preserves her chastity through a series of trials and tribulations during which she is nearly killed yet miraculously escapes. She is delivered from the clutches of not one, but two vicious suitors (Thamyris and Alexander) in a manner akin to the heroine of a Greek novel rejecting the advances of other men. The difference between Thecla and a heroine from a Greek romance is that Thecla preserves her chastity permanently. Her devotion to God and to Paul, though, and her desire to follow and be reunited with Paul echo the romantic heroine's quest to be reunited with her beloved.

At the same time, however, the eroticism and happy endings of the Greek novels are subverted.[38] Thecla rejects her family, traditional feminine dress, and patriarchy in pursuit of Paul and out of devotion to God. The message of sexual continence ultimately trumps the eroticism of the Greek novels. Even as the story of Thecla appears to be modeled directly on Greek romance novels, it is an antagonistic relationship. This denial of conjugal rights and subversion of sexual consummation reconfigure the genre so that the "happy ending" of the apostolic novel is now not marriage, but asceticism or death. The *Acts of Paul and Thecla* modifies the genre, but it is nonetheless dependent upon the genre for its own existence. Once again, Christian martyrdom is woven from the fabric of the ancient world.

Conclusion

EVEN A BRIEF STUDY of early Christian martyrdom literature reveals that Christians were influenced by ancient Greek, Roman, and Jewish traditions about death. The heroes of the classical world were reshaped into soldiers for Christ. When people admit that Christians were heirs to this legacy, they do so selectively. Many acknowledge that Christian martyrs inherit or at least claim to inherit the mantle of martyrdom from ancient Judaism. The references to and comparisons with the Maccabees provide incontrovertible evidence that Christians saw their martyrs as part of this tradition. This much is acknowledged or at least implicitly acknowledged in most scholarly and religious treatments of the subject.

When it comes to Greek and Roman influences, however, things are very different. We would be hard-pressed to find any modern denomination of Christianity that admits Greek and Roman heroes and heroines into their canon of martyrs, even if Christians like Justin Martyr were willing to revere Socrates as a Christian before Christ. Why the difference? The distinction is not based on the evidence, but on the way that people think about the relationship between Christians and Jews. For Christians, the Old Testament is believed to contain a series of prophecies about Jesus and the church. If Christian martyrs seem to be like figures from the Old and New Testaments, it is because their deaths are the fulfillment of prophecies. They are seen as being part of a single unbroken tradition, a single witness to truth.

In the case of Greek and Roman examples, the connection between Christian and pagan martyrs is more problematic. There is no prophetic or divine tie between Christianity and Greek and Roman religion and philosophy. On the contrary, the adaptation of paganism into Christianity threatens the idea that Christianity alone has the truth. Those who reject the classical tradition for religious reasons and hold Christian martyrs in high esteem tend to ignore Greek and Roman antecedents to martyrdom.

This is a game of cultural favorites. There's a theological explanation for the fact that Christian martyrdom stories are similar to biblical narratives of persecution, but there is no such explanation for the similarities with pagan traditions. That Christianity might have borrowed from pluralistic, polytheistic religious traditions is difficult for those who conceive of themselves as part of an unbroken singular tradition. The problem is exacerbated by the fact that Greek and Roman religious practices no longer exist. The idea that Christianity borrowed from or was dependent upon morally questionable failed religions ruffles feathers and prayer books.

The truth of the matter is that as we have seen, Christians adapted their ideas about martyrdom and sometimes *even the stories about the martyrs themselves* from both ancient Jewish and pagan writers. We cannot help but note the irony here. Christians are thought to be unique because they die for Christ, but the stories by which they communicate their uniqueness are borrowed from other cultures. Clearly Christian martyrdom is one of a number of ancient varieties of martyrdom. Even though early Christians adapted, augmented, and otherwise contorted ancient models in their own stories, they were nonetheless dependent upon earlier literature. To be sure, Christian martyrdom stories depart from classical examples of noble death, but toying with, trumping, reversing, and usurping are not the same as inventing. Early Christians consciously and deliberately harnessed the cultural power of Greek, Roman, and Jewish heroes for their own ends.

Moreover, when the argument is made that martyrdom is unique to Christianity, it ignores *what ancient Christians themselves* had to say about the matter. Of course, Christians want to have it both ways—

they claim that they are both utterly unique and just like the heroes of the past—but the idea that Christian martyrs were just like the Maccabees or Socrates was an important part of what Christians themselves said about their heroes.

Recognizing this fact should not unsettle the claims of Christians, ancient or modern. It is to be expected that, when early Christians sat down to write the stories of their own heroes and heroines, they did not start afresh. They drank deeply from the well of the noble-death tradition. Many cherished Christian ideas and practices, not only martyrdom, were borrowed or adapted from their ancient contemporaries. We moderns might see this as intellectual property theft or lying, but in an ancient context such borrowing doesn't have to have a negative valence. If I were to explain the game of rugby to an American, I would use the language and rules of American football to do so. This doesn't mean that rugby is American football, just that they are similar enough to be useful in illuminating one another.

In the same way, we could see Christian reuse of contemporary traditions about noble death as the use of a commonly held ancient cultural vocabulary. Even if we are generous and say that reworking stories was very common in the ancient world, we would still have to admit that this kind of storytelling is in no way unique to Christianity. Christians may have been the first to use the term "martyr," but valuing this kind of death is just one of the aspects of Christianity that make it at home among the ancient religions.

The problem is that this isn't what Christians have said about martyrdom. They have said that it is unique to Christianity, thoroughly new, and a mark of Christianity's sole possession of the truth. Christianity is true, it is said, because only Christians have martyrs. The inaccuracy of these kinds of statements becomes more pointed when we recognize that early Christian authors are criticizing the very people from whom they are borrowing. We can understand why and how Christians borrowed other stories of noble death, but we cannot pretend that they didn't do it.

This kind of literary and cultural borrowing raises a bigger problem. Can we really trust that these martyrdom stories are giving us the whole story? What does it mean that the literature is preserving theology and interpretation rather than facts and history? How many of the stories about martyrs can really be deemed accurate? In the next chapter we look at the evidence for the historicity and authenticity of these stories. Do we know what actually happened?

CHAPTER THREE

Inventing Martyrs in Early Christianity

IN THE WANING DECADES OF the third century, during the reign of the emperor Numerian, a young Christian couple was buried alive for refusing to have sex. Their names were Chrysanthus and Daria, and things didn't have to end this way. Chrysanthus was the only son of an Egyptian patrician named Polemius, who was raised in Alexandria. Polemius, like most parents, had high hopes for his son. Perhaps he nurtured aspirations that his son would have a career in politics or oratory. In pursuit of his dream of social advancement, he moved the family from Egypt to Rome and placed his son in the hands of Rome's finest tutors. Chrysanthus, however, was something of a free spirit. He was quickly and easily disenchanted with the superficialities of life in Rome, and it was in this period of teenage existential crisis that he ran across a copy of the Acts of the Apostles, encountered a Christian priest named Carpophorus, and ended up converting to Christianity.

Polemius was understandably annoyed by his son's conversion. Chrysanthus was his only son and his hope for the future. So far as Polemius was concerned, his son had joined an embarrassing cult. Having taken advice from his friends, he attempted to lure his son away from his new religion. He organized a dinner party attended exclusively by prostitutes. Upon realizing that he had been tricked, a horrified Chrysanthus retreated to a corner to pray, and miraculously all the women fell asleep. When he left the room they would wake up, and when he reentered they would fall asleep. The dinner party ruse was a failure.

Convinced that he had been looking for distractions in the wrong place, Polemius approached a young vestal virgin named Daria. As a vestal, Daria was from one of the finest families in Rome. She was a local celebrity, virtuous, and in perfect physical condition. Polemius convinced Daria to marry Chrysanthus and arranged a meeting between the two at his home. Chrysanthus was not impressed. He berated Daria for her ostentatious jewelry and engaged her in a debate about God and virtue. By the end of this first meeting, Chrysanthus had converted Daria to Christianity, and they planned to marry and live lives of perpetual virginity together.

Following their marriage, Chrysanthus and Daria took to the streets of Rome, where they converted thousands of people not just to Christianity, but to lives of chastity. It was at this point that they attracted the attention of the authorities. The couple was arrested by the tribune, Claudius, who had Chrysanthus tortured. Chrysanthus's endurance under torture compelled Claudius, his wife and sons, and seventy of his soldiers to convert to Christianity. Upon discovering Claudius's betrayal, the emperor had him executed. Chrysanthus was imprisoned in a dank, putrid prison that was miraculously transformed so that it smelled of flowers. Daria was sent to a brothel to be subjected to rape as a prostitute. She was protected, however, by an escaped lion, which pinned the first would-be rapist to the ground until Daria signaled for his release. This man too was converted to Christianity. After unsuccessful attempts were made to capture the lion, the authorities set fire to Daria's cell. Once again, however, Daria was delivered, and after a brief conversation with his mistress, the lion roared his good-bye and escaped. Finally, after these unsuccessful attempts to degrade the martyrs, the emperor sentenced them to be buried alive.

This is the story of the martyrdom of Chrysanthus and Daria, respected saints in the Roman Catholic and Orthodox Churches.

There are hundreds of martyrdom stories like this. They're romantic, exciting, interesting, and completely untrue. Many elements of the story are early Christian literary clichés. The studious young man searching for more and stumbling across Christianity could be Justin Martyr. And a protective lion springs to the defense of an inviolate virgin in the *Acts of Paul and Thecla*. This isn't a surprise; lions had been leaving God's righteous ones alone since the time of the biblical Daniel. And almost all the Christian virgins sentenced to brothels escape with their virtue miraculously intact. These plot details are Christian equivalents of a heroine opening the basement door in a horror movie.

Just because a story is clichéd does not, of course, mean that it is necessarily untrue. But the story of Chrysanthus and Daria has some other, more fundamental problems. Daria is a vestal virgin, meaning that she had been placed in service to the goddess Vesta as a young girl and was required to tend the hearth of Rome for no less than thirty years thereafter. A condition of a vestal's service was that she would remain a virgin for the entire period of her priesthood. If she broke her vows of virginity, she would dishonor and sully the hearth of Rome, throwing the stability of the city and empire into jeopardy. The only way to right this affair and cleanse the city of this kind of religious pollution was to take the vestal outside the city and bury her alive.

With all this in mind, we have to wonder how Polemius persuaded Daria to leave her post as vestal to marry his son. How did he even get close enough to a vestal virgin to proposition her in this way without being arrested? And why on earth would she risk certain death to marry someone she had never even met? The account does not say if Polemius brought a portrait of Chrysanthus with him, but it's difficult to imagine that even the prospect of a young Adonis would have swayed her.

Perhaps Daria was a former vestal who had served her time and was now at liberty to marry as she chose? Well, maybe, but this would make her at least thirty-seven years old and hardly the ideal temptress Polemius was looking for. Although it was not unheard of in ancient

Rome for younger men to marry older women for money, we do not get the impression from the story that she is supposed to be past her prime. Middle-aged or not, it's still peculiar that Daria goes to Chrysanthus's house alone to meet him. No respectable woman, much less a former vestal, would have thrown herself at a man in this fashion. We cannot help but wonder where her fellow vestals, bodyguards, or (if she is retired) family members are throughout the whole affair. Why doesn't her family try to secure her release? She is apparently from one of the most important families in Rome, but they are content to see her dispatched to a brothel. And what about the brothel? Sentencing a vestal to rape within the walls of Rome would have been an unthinkable crime. If Romans thought an impure virgin brought disaster on the city, we can only imagine the ramifications of forcing a vestal into prostitution. Historically, it makes no sense. This simply could not have happened. From a literary perspective, however, it's quite clever—a vestal virgin, buried alive for *not* having sex after the Romans themselves tried to defile her. How ironic. How very damning.

To what is already an impossible story we can add other historical problems. Numerian was not in Rome at the time when Chrysanthus and Daria died, so he could not have been the one to sentence them. Chaste marriages only really became de rigueur in the late fourth century when aristocratic Romans became enamored of the idea of urban monasticism. If Chrysanthus and Daria had converted thousands to this practice a hundred years earlier, surely there would be some trace of the idea in other third-century Christian literature. Finally, we have no record of either thousands of people converting to Christianity or, more important, the execution of a vestal virgin in Rome at this time. Scandals involving vestals are well documented. It is almost unthinkable that a vestal could have been sent to a brothel and publicly executed without some ancient writer mentioning it. We have to conclude not only that the story was invented, but that whoever composed this story lived during a period when people no longer understood how important vestals were.

As fantastic and unbelievable as stories like the *Martyrdom of Chrysanthus and Daria* are, they are remarkably common. The majority of saints' lives have the qualities we find here. They are elaborate, ornate, entertaining, and very far from the truth. And for centuries people believed these stories. Many people still do. The names of these saints are memorialized as part of the calendars of the Roman Catholic and Eastern Orthodox Churches, and the saints themselves are venerated as part of local tradition. In Reggio Emilia in Italy, where the relics of Chrysanthus and Daria are said to be housed, people had and still have strong connections to these saints. If a woman was infertile, profits were low, a family member was sick, or an individual was unlucky, then the local saints were the first port of call. Unlike God, who might be a little busy and important, saints offered a personal connection and a friend in heaven. That you could make a pilgrimage to the site where a saint was buried only made the relationship more intimate.

But it doesn't make the story historically true.

Fraud and Error in the Lives of the Saints

THE CLOSE RELATIONSHIP THAT Christians develop with martyrs has a dark side too. During the Reformation, one of Martin Luther's chief complaints about the Catholic Church was that it was full of corruption and fraud. He argued that the cult of the saints, in particular, was riddled with forged relics and superstitious practices. It is rumored that Luther's epiphany about the Catholic Church came as he ascended the legendary *Scala Sancta* in Rome in 1510. These "Holy Stairs" are believed to have been the very steps on which Jesus ascended to be tried by Pilate in Jerusalem. To this day pilgrims who ascend the stairs on their knees are granted an indulgence that knocks nine years off their time in purgatory for each of the twenty-eight steps. Luther purportedly became so disillusioned with indulgences and relics after this event that he famously complained, "What lies there are about relics! . . . How does it happen that eighteen apostles are buried in Germany when Christ had only twelve?"[1]

The problem was not limited to relics but spread to the legends and literature surrounding the saints, as we have seen. Some of the stories are positively sensational. Take Marina, a pious woman who abandons her family, dresses like a boy, and secludes herself in a monastery, only to be accused of misconduct and outed as a woman after her death. It's a great story, but the events are practically identical to those in the lives of Sts. Pelagia, Eugenia, Euphrosyne, Theodora, Margaret, and Apollinaria. How many cross-dressing women have to hide in monasteries before priests grow wise to the problem? The fact of the matter is that these aren't historical accounts; they are religious romances written and intended to be read for moral instruction and entertainment.

In the case of Sts. Chrysanthus and Daria, there may well be a kernel of truth buried deep in the story—perhaps there really were martyrs with these names—but there are many other legends about saints that have no basis in fact at all. One particularly embarrassing example of this is the story of St. Josaphat. According to the religious romance *Barlaam and Josaphat*, Josaphat was an Indian prince who was converted to Christianity by the hermit Barlaam. Astrologers had predicted at his birth that he would rule over a great kingdom, the kingdom of glory, a prediction that led his father to shut the boy away in seclusion. Despite his father's best efforts to keep him from the world, Josaphat realized the horror of the human predicament through encounters with a leper, a blind man, and a dying man. His view of the world thrown into jeopardy, he then met Barlaam the hermit, converted, and spent the remainder of his life in quiet contemplation of the divine.[2]

If this story sounds familiar, it should. It's nothing but a Christianized version of the life of Siddhartha Gautama, the Indian prince who became the Buddha. This is no secret, but it's not common knowledge either. Since the nineteenth century scholars have recognized the similarities and acknowledged that this story is simply the legend of Siddhartha thinly covered in a Christian glaze.[3] It isn't just the broad plot details that are similar; minute plot details and even phraseology are identical. Even the name Josaphat is just a corruption of the word Bodisat or Bodhisattva (the letters y/j and b are easily mistaken for each other in Arabic), a title for the Buddha or an enlightened person. The transformation of the Buddha into a Christian saint took many generations; the roots of the story can be traced back to a Sanskrit Mahayana Buddhist version of the tale, which was filtered through Manichaean and Arabic sources.

The invention of Josaphat was not a deliberate forgery; it was the result of human error. The story grew and spread, moved from one region to another, and was translated and retranslated until Christian hagiographers mistakenly set it in literary stone. It is impossible to ascertain when Josaphat was canonized, but by the time Cardinal Caesar Baronio sat down to revise the official church calendar in the late sixteenth century, Barlaam and Josaphat were included under November 27. In a cruelly ironic twist Barlaam and Josaphat became wildly popular. Their story was translated into every European language, and it even makes a cameo in Shakespeare's *Merchant of Venice*.

Some historians have sought to soothe religious anxieties about this mistake, even arguing (no doubt correctly) that the Buddha was very saintly.[4] But the inclusion of this narrative in the Catholic calendar is a gross error. No medieval Christian hagiographer worth his salt would have knowingly turned the figurehead of a different—and thus false—religion into a saint. Others have used the story to rail against the notion of papal infallibility.[5] Whatever our opinion about the wider ramifications of these mistakes, they are very common. They're the consequences of expanding oral traditions and the spread of folklore across continents and from one language to another.

The Society of Bollandists and the Birth of Critical Hagiography

THE PROBLEMS WITH THE legends surrounding saints and saints' remains have not been lost on Catholics themselves. They recognized and appreciated Protestant criticisms of excesses and fraud in the veneration of saints and were eager to uncover the truth. As mentioned in the introduction of this book, in the opening decades of the seventeenth century a small group of scholars dedicated to the critical study of saints' lives was formed in Belgium. The work was begun by a Jesuit priest named Héribert Rosweyde, who in 1607 published a pamphlet entitled the *Fasti Sanctorum*, an outline for an eighteen-volume collection of ancient and medieval saints' lives compiled using historical and linguistic criteria.[6] Rosweyde never got around to writing his magnum opus (he died in 1629), but he was the intellectual father of critical hagiography.

After Rosweyde's death, John Bolland, another Jesuit, was summoned to Antwerp by his Jesuit superior to sort through Rosweyde's papers. Bolland was more savvy than Rosweyde. Realizing the importance and huge size of the task before him, he asked for exclusive use of Rosweyde's papers and requested two assistants to aid him in his work. In 1643 Bolland and his two students, Godefroid Henskens and Daniel Papebroch, the founding members of the Société des Bollandistes, published the first two volumes of the *Acta Sanctorum*. His students spread out, scouring the libraries and monasteries of Europe for copies of stories about the saints. From this they set about compiling the definitive work on the historicity of the saints' lives.

The Bollandists, as they are commonly referred to in English, exist to this day. Despite their ecclesiastical origins and the fact that the Bollandists themselves were until very recently composed exclusively of Jesuit priests, their work has not always been appreciated by the Catholic Church. Quite the contrary. From the beginning they faced staunch opposition. Rosweyde's work was opposed by a certain Cardinal Robert Bellarmine.[7] Bellarmine had participated in the Counter-Reformation and was wary about the potentially damaging results of the Bollandists' work.

As it turned out, Bellarmine was right to be concerned. In the 1670s the Bollandists discredited the cherished idea that the Carmelites, a beloved order of monks, had been founded by the prophet Elijah.[8] At the time the Carmelites were at their most popular and their most powerful. The fallout from the affair was that three of the Bollandists' chief works were placed on the Roman Index of Prohibited Books, the list of books banned by the Vatican. It was the Bollandists who demonstrated that St. George, the patron saint of England, never met a dragon, much less slew one.[9] Even now, some three hundred years after their founding, the Bollandists' scythe remains well sharpened. It was Bollandist methodology that revealed that the legend of St. Christopher, the patron saint of travelers, was of dubious origin, thereby turning, in one fell swoop, a hundred thousand religious medals into mere jewelry.[10]

The Authentic Accounts

IN THE NEARLY FOUR centuries since the Bollandists were founded, they and subsequent generations of Dutch, German, Italian, and French scholars have whittled away at the canon of saints' lives. If the saints are supposed to participate in the heavenly banquet, what was once a crowded buffet now resembles an intimate dinner party. Once scholars had stripped away the pious frauds, entertaining forgeries, and well-intentioned legends, they were left with only a small handful of martyrdom stories from before 250 that they judged to be historically reliable.

The remaining accounts were either greatly edited and expanded or composed long after the events by people who hadn't met an eyewitness to the events they described, much less witnessed them themselves. Many of the discarded accounts were religious romances long on adventure and intrigue and short on probability and accuracy. Others were implausibly anachronistic and referred to institutions, ideas, and concepts that didn't exist at the time their protagonists lived. Others still were forgeries that copied the form, style, and sometimes words of earlier martyrdom accounts. Some, like the legend of Barlaam and Josaphat, turned out to be literary houses built on sand; their protagonists never existed. A few were more slippery and presented themselves as simple transcriptions of court affairs, when in fact they were written long after the events.[11]

Once the pious chaff had been separated and the forged weeds cut, out of the hundreds of martyrdom stories only six accounts remained from the earliest church.[12] These so-called authentic accounts are as follows:

1. *Martyrdom of Polycarp*

2. *Acts of Ptolemy and Lucius*

3. *Acts of Justin and Companions*

4. *Martyrs of Lyons*

5. *Acts of the Scillitan Martyrs*

6. *Passion of Perpetua and Felicity*

The martyrs named in these stories, because of their status as the "earliest martyrs" and the supposed antiquity of these accounts, have been extremely influential. Perpetua and Felicity are among the few martyrs named in the Roman Catholic Mass as part of the intercession of saints. Perpetua even has her own word-processing font, graphic novel, and animated movie. There are other martyrdom tales from the third and fourth centuries that some scholars claim are historically accurate, but we will focus on these early stories, because they are the bridge between the world of the New Testament and the history of the church.[13] They are used to demonstrate the fulfillment of Jesus's prophecies about persecution and to form the backbone of the argument that Christians have always been persecuted. The supposed reliability and antiquity of these martyrs, verified by the careful Bollandists and their successors, have made their words all the more powerful.

We saw in the previous chapter that even these, the earliest stories about the martyrs, borrowed ideas from their non-Christian contemporaries. We have to wonder whether we can trust Christian documents that borrow from ancient myth and philosophy. Can we be sure that the events described in these texts actually happened? In the remainder of this chapter we will examine this small group of martyrs and ask: Can any of the stories of early Christian martyrs be considered precise historical reports of what actually happened?

The stories that we are going to examine here are the most historically reliable texts. Unlike the story of Chrysanthus and Daria, they are not easily dismissed as entertaining romance. They are edited stories, not outright fictions. Perhaps heavy editing or later theological interpretation does not seem too serious. After all, it's unfair to hold ancient writers to modern standards of history writing—surely a little sparkle and some theological gloss aren't too serious. But we have to remember that these six accounts are as good as it is going to get. The texts looked at here are considered by scholars to be the *most* historically reliable and the *most* authentic. These are the stories believed to preserve the actual words of the martyrs. They are the first martyrs, the cornerstones upon which an edifice of thousands of martyred saints is built. If we cannot trust that these stories preserve the events precisely, then we cannot trust that any martyrdom stories do.

The same uncertainty surrounds almost all ancient texts, and in some ways it is anachronistic to hold stories from antiquity up to our modern standards. But there is more at stake when it comes to martyrs, and there is something especially problematic about not knowing what the martyrs actually said. For many people, it is important that Christian martyrs confessed to being Christian and that they maintained that confession up until their deaths. A martyr who initially confessed and then, under torture or at the last minute, recanted and begged to be spared would be looked at very differently than would someone who resolutely refused to abandon Christ.[14]

Martyrdom texts were used and continue to be used to inspire people. The martyrs themselves are sources of consolation, inspiration, and spiritual guidance. These stories are meaningful for what the martyrs said and did. For many people there is a difference between murder and martyrdom. Once we realize that the texts are edited, then we have to ask what, if anything, we can say about the historical martyrs. A death without our knowing the circumstances and what was said is just another ancient death. We can still read these stories as inspirational literature, but if we cannot be sure of what the martyrs said, then we cannot use them to construct a history that we use to define ourselves.

Even today the words of the martyrs and their conduct in their final moments matter. Take Cassie Bernall, one of the victims of the Columbine High School shootings in 1999. Initial reports after the shootings suggested that, moments before she died, her attacker asked if she believed in God. She replied, "Yes, I believe."[15] Cassie was hailed as a martyr. Her mother, Misty, even published a book entitled *She Said Yes: The Unlikely Martyrdom of Cassie Bernall*, in which she described Cassie's troubled adolescent years and spiritual conversion.

Over the course of the following months, however, doubts were cast on this narrative. New eyewitness reports indicated that the conversation never happened. The brother of a survivor of the shootings claimed that another student, Valeen Schnurr, and not Cassie had confessed to believing in God. It is intriguing that appreciation of Cassie has not abated since these revelations have come to light. To be sure, the horror of these events and our sympathy for the victims do not depend on the words they said. But for many it does matter. If we are going to revere Cassie Bernall as a martyr, we need to know if she was given the opportunity to be a martyr. If choice and a demonstrable belief in God are important for a person's definition of a martyr, then our inability to know exactly what martyrs said is critically important.

1. Martyrdom of Polycarp

The *Martyrdom of Polycarp* is widely acknowledged to be the earliest martyrdom account.[16] In survey courses of the history of Christianity it is treated as the earliest story about a Christian martyr in which the term "martyr" is actually used in a technical sense. This would make it one of the most important documents from the second century and a key piece of evidence when it comes to the foundation and development of the early church and early Christians' mentality about martyrdom.[17] The account represents itself as a letter composed by the "Church in Smyrna," an important city on the coast of modern-day Turkey, to the church of Philomenium, a smaller, unremarkable town inland in Asia Minor. The church in Philomenium is instructed in the concluding chapter of the account to send the text on to other churches.

Unfortunately, many elements in the story lead us to question its reliability. The author of the text claims that he and his companions were eyewitnesses to Polycarp's martyrdom and that the letter was written sometime before the first anniversary of Polycarp's death. If we believe them, then the letter should be dated to within a year of the events themselves, which occurred between 155 and 157. There's something a little suspicious about this claim. The "letter" begins in the first person:

> We are writing to you, brothers, an account of those who were martyred, especially the blessed Polycarp, who put an end to the persecution as though he were setting his seal upon it by his martyrdom. For nearly all the preceding events happened in order that the Lord might show us once again a martyrdom which is in accord with the Gospel.[18]

This opening frames the entire account as a letter about the exemplary conduct of martyrs. The use of the first person continues throughout the opening exhortations but suddenly vanishes as the author slips into the third person as soon as the action starts. The only time the author, speaking for the supposed eyewitnesses, uses the first person again in the story is when he is describing miracles. For example, when Polycarp enters the stadium, they hear a miraculous voice addressing Polycarp:

But as Polycarp entered the stadium, there came a voice from heaven: "Be strong, Polycarp, and act like a man." And no one saw the speaker, but those of our people who were present heard the voice.[19]

The abrupt reappearance of the first person is as unexpected as the voice from heaven. The scene conjures up shades of the baptism of Jesus in the Gospels; only here the author is clear that only the inside group, the Christians, can actually hear the voice.

The same element reappears later in the story. When Polycarp is burned at the stake an extraordinary event occurs:

And as a mighty flame blazed up, we saw a miracle (we, that is, to whom it was given to see), and we have been preserved in order that we might tell the rest what happened. For the fire, taking the shape of an arch, like the sail of a ship filled by the wind, completely surrounded the body of the martyr; and it was there in the middle, not like flesh burning but like bread baking or like gold and silver being refined in a furnace. For we also perceived a very fragrant odor, as if it were the scent of incense or some other precious spice.[20]

Once again only the select few see the flames billow out and detect the aroma of precious spices. The author is employing the first person strategically, to lend credibility to the miraculous events. The first person authenticates an event that was otherwise imperceptible.

In ancient histories, as in modern histories, eyewitness statements were valued more highly than secondhand reports, or hearsay. Only those who were "given to see" the miracle actually saw it. Less special members of the audience merely saw a man burned alive. Rhetorically, it smacks of the emperor's new clothes: if you didn't hear, see, or smell the delicious miracle, it is not because the events didn't transpire, but because you were not part of the elite. Apart from these two moments and the opening and closing of the document, the remainder of the story is told in the third person. That the first person is employed only strategically is no guarantee that the text is an authentic eyewitness account; rather, it should raise our suspicions about the story as a whole.

There are other details that also might lead us to question the credibility of this story. The setting for the trial is highly unusual. Both Germanicus, the only other martyr described in the account, and Polycarp are tried in the stadium, the location in which races and other sporting events were performed. This isn't completely unprecedented, but accused criminals were usually tried in formal law courts called judicial basilicas. The setting for the trials proves a touch hazardous. When the proconsul tries to persuade Germanicus to think of his youth and recant, Germanicus "forcibly dragged a wild beast toward himself, desiring to be released as quickly as possible."[21] Looking past the spiritual steroids that enable Germanicus to forcibly drag this animal on top of himself, are we to understand from this passage that Germanicus is tried while an unrestrained "wild beast" lounges nearby? Even if the beast were chained up, it is evidently within arm's reach of him and thus close enough to cut proceedings short with a well-placed swat. Romans were sticklers for order, and it is unthinkable that any administrator would have allowed this to take place. Imagine the disappointment for everyone—both the crowd and the wild beast—if Germanicus had recanted.

A similar problem arises in the execution of Polycarp. In Polycarp's case, sentence is actually passed by the proconsul and announced to the crowd. The crowd demands that Polycarp be thrown to a lion, but the proconsul objects that the animal games have concluded. The crowd then demands that Polycarp be burned alive. Polycarp's burning, however, turns out to be a rather hands-on affair for the crowd. Apparently,

> with such swiftness, quicker than words could tell, the crowd swiftly collected wood and kindling from the workshops and

baths, the Jews being especially eager to assist in this, as is their custom.[22]

Even assuming that the stadium in Smyrna had sufficiently low walls that people could just leap over them, we have to question the probability of the sequence of the events. Does it seem plausible that the Jewish members of the audience squeezed past the other members of the crowd and jumped the barrier in order to collect firewood from nearby businesses? How did the crowd leave, gather firewood, and return so quickly? Why wouldn't the proconsul have been dismayed by the disorder and plundering of local businesses? Why would a mob riled up to the point of looting have calmly returned to their seats and allowed Polycarp to undress himself before mounting the pyre? It hardly sounds likely.

To the illegal and unlikely details from the trial we can add the host of similarities between the death of Jesus and the death of Polycarp. Polycarp retreats outside the city, prays there, enters the city on the back of a donkey, is betrayed by someone close to him, is arrested at night, and is opposed both by a figure named Herod and by blood-thirsty Jews—all of which resonates with various aspects of the Jesus story. That he is executed around Passover and stabbed in the side as he is being executed also suggests affinities with the death of Jesus. To these details other similarities can be added. The central question that arises for us is this: Is it more likely that the events just happened to transpire in a way that consistently mimics the death of Jesus, or is it more likely that these elements were exaggerated or invented in order to make Polycarp seem like Jesus?

In addressing these problems, some historians have rushed to the *Martyrdom of Polycarp*'s defense. Joseph Lightfoot, for example, argues that the parallels are "forced" or imperfect and that because they aren't perfect, they must be true.[23] The parallels between Jesus and Polycarp could be stronger, I suppose, but this does not au-tomatically mean that the story is authentic. After all, we have to assume that the author wants his story to be believable, and this means that he can invent only so many features in the text. For instance, the police chief who arrests Polycarp is called Herod. It's quite a coincidence. Lightfoot called this a faint parallel, because the status and role of the police captain are very different from those of the biblical king who interrogates Jesus. This is true. I have no doubt that the biblical Herod would be less than impressed to be played by a police captain. But would the author have been able to just invent a king of Smyrna called Herod when there was no monarchy there? It seems unlikely.

A second issue to consider is that the parallelism between Jesus and Polycarp is strategic and purposeful; it has a point. At the outset of the story the author says that the eyewitnesses are writing the story in order to provide a moral example for imitation. They write that the martyrdom is "in accord with the Gospel" and that Polycarp acted "just as the Lord did" with respect to waiting to be arrested before accepting the mantle of martyrdom.[24] The rhetorical effect of comparing Polycarp to Christ is to inculcate a set of values in the audience: if you're acting like Polycarp, then you're acting like Christ. For the author, Polycarp is a way to show what Jesus would have done in a certain setting. He is a mouthpiece for Jesus. If the parallels in the story are not as pronounced as they could be, it's because the author wants to use the basic parallelism to make a point about martyrdom.

This sort of thing happens today too. In modern society, politicians often compare themselves or find themselves compared to important political or military heroes of the past. These comparisons are *always* strategic; the intention is to get the modern politician elected and to harness the charisma of, say, John F. Kennedy or Ronald Reagan to bring that about. When these comparisons are made, they may not be precise (or even close!), but this is because they are limited by the modern politician's political program. You couldn't say that a modern politician is abolishing slavery just like Abraham Lincoln did, because slavery no longer exists. But you could compare some modern issue to slavery and use the popular goodwill toward Abraham Lincoln to your advantage.

If the parallels between Jesus and Polycarp seem faint, it is in order to preserve the realism of the account and allow the author to use Polycarp to make a larger argument. The important point, for our purposes, is that these kinds of literary flourishes make it impossible for us to imagine that the *Martyrdom of Polycarp* is a historical account of the events as they actually happened. There are too many wild coincidences, improbabilities, and illegalities for us to suppose that that was the case.

If the story is not an eyewitness account, then we have to ask: Who wrote it, when, and why? What is the larger point to which the comparisons with Jesus are directing us?

This is where things get difficult. The argument that the story is early was based on the assumption that it was also an authentic eyewitness account composed within a year of Polycarp's death. All we would need to do would be to figure out when Polycarp died, and we would know when it was written. Without the date of Polycarp's death as our anchor, we have to tread very carefully. Often when texts were forged in antiquity, their authors had axes to grind, and the texts are filled with polemic and vitriol or anachronistic theological references. We can usually use these polemical references or anachronisms to work out when the text was composed. For instance, the fraudulent account the *Passion of Procopius* purports to describe events that took place during the first edict of Diocletian and even "quotes" from the first edict. In actual fact the legal details in the trial do not fit with the first edict at all; they fit with a later period.[25] This makes it easier to pin down the date of the text. This is not the case with the *Martyrdom of Polycarp*. There is very little hostility in this story. Nonetheless, certain details in the account suggest that the story was written much later than is usually thought.

The first of these is the presence of an individual named Quintus. According to the story, Quintus had come from Phrygia to Smyrna

and had persuaded other Christians to give themselves up for martyrdom. Things did not go so well for Quintus, because when he saw
the wild beasts, he "turned coward."[26] It is apparently "for this reason,
therefore, brothers and sisters, [that] we do not praise those who hand
themselves over, since the Gospel does not so teach."[27] Quintus's anti-
Gospel martyrdom is a foil to Polycarp's martyrdom in accordance
with the Gospel. Where Quintus is rash and active, Polycarp is reti-
cent and passive. What is interesting about this story is what it tells
us about the date of the account. Quintus is engaging in a practice
that scholars have called "voluntary martyrdom," the act of offering
oneself for martyrdom.[28] The author is subtly denouncing voluntary
martyrdom by arguing that eagerness leads to cowardice and apostasy.

The *Martyrdom of Polycarp* is supposed to have been written in the
middle of the second century and to be the first text to recognize the
category of the martyr and develop a real theology of martyrdom.
This argument doesn't really make sense in light of Quintus's actions.
Why would Christians be offering themselves for martyrdom, if martyrdom as a concrete idea didn't already exist?

Some years after the death of Polycarp, around the turn of the
third century, voluntary martyrdom became an issue in the early
church. Clement of Alexandria, for instance, a Christian philosopher
and teacher in Egypt, argued that those who rushed forward to martyrdom were not really Christians at all, but merely shared the name.[29]
Clement makes it sound as if he is describing a recent phenomenon,
but in truth Christians were probably volunteering all along. It was
only in the third century, however, that Christians began to condemn
the practice. These later Christians like Clement argued that it was
only heretics who indulged in this behavior. In particular the adherents of the New Prophecy movement, or Montanists, as they were
called by their opponents, were singled out as especially enthusiastic
in their pursuit of martyrdom.

Quintus is twice described as being from Phrygia, the birthplace
of Montanism. Perhaps Quintus was a Montanist or perhaps the

author of the *Martyrdom of Polycarp* wants us to think he was. The problem is that Montanists didn't exist at the time when Polycarp was executed. Montanus, the founder of Montanism, did not begin to prophesy until 168. If Quintus actually was a Montanist or if the author wants us to think that Quintus was a Montanist, then the text must have been written after this point. If Quintus was not a Montanist and the text is just denouncing volunteerism in general, then it would make sense to suppose that the author was writing in the third century, when other Christians began to condemn this practice.

This is not the only instance in which the text presupposes a rather developed understanding of martyrdom. Not only is the author aware of people offering themselves for martyrdom; he is also concerned that some people would confuse a martyr with Christ himself. Toward the end of the account, after Polycarp has been executed, the Romans take away what is left of Polycarp's remains and burn them. The reason for this is that they are afraid that "[the Christians] may abandon the crucified one and begin to worship this man."[30] The text further notes that this was done at the insistence of the Jews. It's a peculiar concern for non-Christians to have. After all, the Romans *wanted* the Christians to stop worshipping Christ! The author goes on to state, though, that they will never be able to abandon Christ, who suffered for the salvation of the whole world, and makes a clear distinction between martyrs and Christ:

> For [Jesus], who is the Son of God, we worship, but the martyrs we love as disciples and imitators of the Lord, as they deserve, on account of their matchless devotion to their own King and Teacher.[31]

The audience for this statement is clearly the Christians. This is a piece of doctrinal instruction directed at Christians who might otherwise have thought that Polycarp was just like Jesus. This was the risk of portraying Polycarp as dying like Christ. If Jesus's death was what made him special and a savior, and martyrs died in similar ways, then some may have understood martyrs to be on a par with Christ. That the author of the *Martyrdom of Polycarp* worries about this kind of thing again presupposes that the idea of martyrdom was already well established. In the fifth century some early Christian writers like Augustine were also attempting to dampen enthusiasm for the stories about martyrs and distinguish between Christ and the martyrs, but this is after several hundred years of martyr veneration and accumulating legends. Aside from the *Martyrdom of Polycarp*, however, no other Christian authors share this concern until the fourth century.

In a similar way, the author describes religious devotional practices that didn't really take hold until the third century. At the conclusion of the piece, after Polycarp's body is burned for a second time, the Christians steal the fragments of bone and ash that remain and deposit them in an appropriate place for safekeeping. This is not just a concern for a proper burial; the author describes Polycarp's remains as "more valuable than precious stones"[32] and says that the remains were placed somewhere that Christians could gather to remember the saints and prepare themselves for their own martyrdom. The situation envisioned here is the veneration of relics.

Since the early church and even to this day, Roman Catholics, Orthodox, and some Anglican Christians view the remains of saints as reservoirs of religious power. They are believed to heal the sick and protect cities from attack, and as such they attract pilgrims. Apart from the *Martyrdom of Polycarp*, the practice of collecting and venerating the bodies of martyrs is completely unparalleled in the second century. Our next earliest references to relics are from the third century and are much less developed.[33] They may not even be firm references to relics so much as references to the distribution of mementos. In contrast, the *Martyrdom of Polycarp* does not just refer to relics; it provides an explanation for why the church in Smyrna doesn't have the whole body. That it was necessary to apologize for the absence of relics again presupposes a situation in which relic veneration was already booming. It's difficult to imagine the need to offer this explanation, if the audience wasn't expecting more, and it's difficult to imagine that the audience would have expected more before the third century.

The author has an almost precognitive ability to anticipate the sorts of practices and problems that martyrs would inspire nearly a hundred years later. The unvarnished truth is that we don't know when this story was written. There's no single piece of evidence that can help us pin down the date of the text's composition precisely, but if we have to make an educated guess, then we would say that the account was written in the third century, when voluntary martyrdom and relic collection had already emerged as religious practices.

What this means is that the earliest martyrdom account, the document that scholars believe began and fed interest in martyrdom, is a pious fraud. It pretends to be written by eyewitnesses, but in fact it was not. Although it may be based on earlier traditions, it is not an eyewitness account of the martyrdom of one of Christianity's earliest and most beloved bishops. It is a theological narrative written perhaps as late as a hundred years after the events it describes. We can tell this because it refers to practices and concerns that didn't become issues for the church until much later on. Most of the characterization of Polycarp focuses on addressing these later concerns. For example, the portrayal of Polycarp as being "like Jesus" is about contrasting Polycarp and Quintus. But as Quintus represents concerns about voluntary martyrdom, then we can't trust that he actually existed. At this point, we have to ask ourselves, what can we trust about Polycarp himself? Polycarp was almost certainly executed by the Romans, but we really don't know anything about the circumstances of his arrest, trial, and death. This makes it impossible to know the reason he was executed or the principles he died for. If all we can know is the fact of his execution, then we have to face the possibility that the martyr we admire is the invention of the author. He is a pious, appreciative, and earnest invention, but an invention nonetheless.

2. *Acts of Ptolemy and Lucius*

After Polycarp, the next document to describe the execution of individual Christians is the story about Ptolemy and Lucius in Justin's *Second Apology*. As we saw in the previous chapter, the *Acts of Ptolemy and Lucius* is something of a literary outlier when it comes to early Christian literature. It is presented as part of a Christian "apology," a kind of literature associated with ancient philosophy and with Socrates in particular, and it was composed as part of Justin's argument for why Christians should be tolerated. There's no reason to doubt that Ptolemy actually died. It's likely that a Roman citizen who found his wife enthralled with some strange new man and asking for a divorce would complain to the authorities. Justin provides so little information about Ptolemy's trial and what transpired that it is remarkable that anyone has been able to form conclusions about the death of Ptolemy. There's simply not enough to go on.

Despite its brevity, however, there's a great deal of interpretation and rhetoric in the presentation of these saints. In his description of Ptolemy, Justin is interested in depicting him as a kind of Christian philosopher. He twice notes that Ptolemy confessed to being a Christian, although the explanations for why Ptolemy did this are philosophical. Justin writes that Ptolemy confessed to being a Christian because he was a "lover of truth," a term similar to "philosopher," or "lover of wisdom," and had come to a knowledge of "the good" through the "school of divine virtue." These references to truth, instruction, virtue, and "the good" are all references to philosophical principles.

This description of Ptolemy's teachings, as discussed in the previous chapter, has as much in common with ancient philosophy as it does with earliest Christianity. As Ptolemy is executed for being a Christian, we have to assume that there was more to his syllabus than is transmitted to us by Justin. Even if Ptolemy's teachings were commonplace philosophical slogans coated in only the faintest dusting of Christianity, Justin is emphasizing the philosophical character of Christianity.

This is something that Justin believes too, but in Justin's writings there are also references to the Old Testament and the "reminiscences" of the apostles—to events from Jesus's life, to Christian liturgy, and to Christian theology. We have no way of accessing this kind of information for Ptolemy, because Justin doesn't tell us what Ptolemy actually said. We simply have to take Justin at his word. Justin himself never claims to have known Ptolemy or to have been a witness to the events he describes. Perhaps he is repeating a story he has heard from other Christians and using that story to make his larger apologetic point about the rights of Christians to exist in the Roman Empire.

If we try to reach behind Justin's version of events to the historical Ptolemy, the situation actually gets more complicated. We know from other sources that there was in fact a Christian teacher named Ptolemy who lived in Rome in the second century. We even know that this man communicated with Christian women, as we have part of a letter that he composed to a woman named Flora. As a result, some scholars have suggested that these are the people mentioned in Justin's *Second Apology*.[34]

The interesting thing is that, according to later Christians, this Ptolemy was a heretic. The Ptolemy who wrote to Flora belonged to a group of Christians known as the Valentinians. Valentinus himself was also a Christian—at one point he came close to becoming the bishop of Rome—and he and his group of friends were intellectuals who enjoyed speculating about the origins of the world and marrying Greek philosophy to early Christian scripture. To later orthodox Christians, the Valentinians were Gnostics, and they were denounced as doctrinal heretics and perverters of scripture by every generation of Christian heresy writers since. If Justin is describing the death of the very same Ptolemy, then this would mean that one of the earliest Christian martyrs was a heretic. The fact that he is valorized by Justin would only add to the irony. After all, Justin was the first Christian to claim that there were no heretical martyrs! There's a distinct possibility that, in preserving the story of Ptolemy's martyrdom, he just contradicted himself.

The issue is just as devastating for modern scholars who pro-nounce the merits of Gnosticism. Since the 1980s a succession of historians of religion have rightly pointed out that the Gnostics were unfairly maligned by their ancient critics. The "Gnostics" (if the term is even appropriate) were philosophical Christians who sincerely and intellectually asked and answered questions about the nature of the world, the identity of Christ, and the human condition. The por-trayal of the Gnostics as the archetypical heretics out to destroy the true church through the production of invidious heretical teachings is overblown, inaccurate, and the result of ancient polemic written by the orthodox, historical victors. Harvard New Testament scholar Karen King has even demonstrated that there really was no coherent group of "Gnostics" in antiquity and that our belief that this group existed is also the product of paranoid orthodox invective.[35]

At the same time, some modern scholars have valorized Gnosti-cism as a more tolerant, liberal-minded, and moderate form of ancient Christianity. Elaine Pagels has argued in a series of publications that the Gnostics were fundamentally opposed to martyrdom.[36] Her argu-ment is supported by the recent discovery and translation of the *Gospel of Judas*, which made big waves not just because the text claims to have been written by the traitorous Judas, but also because it takes a highly critical view of martyrdom. Although the precise interpretation of the *Gospel of Judas* and its approach to martyrdom can and has been de-bated, scholars like Pagels have held the *Gospel of Judas* up as a more moderate and reasonable form of ancient Christianity for post-9/11 Christians. Gnostics, she implies, are the kind of ancient Christians you want to be like. If the Ptolemy of the *Second Apology* is the Valentinian Ptolemy, then this picture of Gnosticism is also inaccurate. Both "her-etics" and "orthodox" Christians were martyred from the very begin-ning. Those who are opposed to martyrdom can't valorize the heretics as the "reasonable" ones if they died alongside "orthodox" Christians. This means that neither side has the rhetorical or moral high ground. Whether or not we think of martyrdom as a good thing, those rare instances in which it occurred were not limited to the "orthodox."

What's really remarkable for our purposes is that Justin and subsequent generations of Christians could have so wildly misunderstood Ptolemy. If Ptolemy was a Valentinian, then many people were deceived and mistaken. Certainly if later heresiologists had known this, they would not have valorized him. If Ptolemy was a Valentinian, then he's something of a cautionary tale for us modern readers. If orthodox Christians on the lookout for what they saw as heresy could fail to pick up on this, then what other kinds of mistakes have been preserved?

If it is difficult to identify and pin down Ptolemy, it is well-nigh impossible to evaluate the historicity of his fellow martyr, Lucius. Lucius is a Christian bystander at Ptolemy's trial who notices the "irrationality" of the verdict passed against Ptolemy. He protests that Ptolemy is not being convicted as "an adulterer or a fornicator or a murderer,"[37] but merely as a Christian. Urbicus, the prefect of Rome, correctly deduces that Lucius's description of adultery and fornication as crimes worthy of death was tied to the fact that he was a Christian. Lucius admits that he is and is led away saying that he is glad to have been set free from wicked rulers and that he is going to the Father and king of everything.

Again, Justin chooses to focus on the fact of Lucius's Christianity. If we assume that Urbicus followed the proper legal protocol for a court case, then a great deal of the trial has been omitted. Justin's point, however, is to emphasize that it is merely for the name "Christian" that they are convicted. This is the same point he made throughout the *First Apology*. Moreover, there's a rather suspicious detail in Lucius's conversation with Urbicus. In his complaint about the irrationality of the verdict, Lucius says, "Your judgment does not befit a pious emperor, or a philosophical Caesar—his son—or the holy Senate, O Urbicus."[38] It seems commonplace, but in fact this is clever wordplay. At the time of their execution, Antoninus Pius and Marcus Aurelius were coemperors in Rome. "Pious emperor" is a reference to Antoninus's name. "Philosophical Caesar" refers to Marcus Aurelius's reputation as a philosopher. Justin uses the same double allusion to those who "are truly pious and philosophers" at the beginning of his *First Apology*.[39]

This is not just a coincidence. That the same play on words used by Justin in the *First Apology* appears here in the *Acts of Ptolemy and Lucius* suggests that Justin is the source of both statements. Given that the remainder of Lucius's statements are also thematically similar to other parts of Justin's *First Apology*, it stands to reason that Justin invented them all. Justin has used Lucius as another opportunity to make his case. He has fraudulently but effectively harnessed the rhetorical power of the "famous last words" of a heroic martyr to further his argument. We'll never know for certain what Lucius said or even if there was a Lucius at all. All we have is a literary mouthpiece for Justin's own views.

In sum, it seems that the fact of Ptolemy's and Lucius's executions is secure. The content of their beliefs, their words at their trials, and the course of the events, however, have been heavily shaped by Justin. We don't know what Ptolemy and Lucius actually said or even what they stood for. What we know is what Justin wants us to think: that Christians were convicted merely for being Christians, but that Christianity was really just another kind of philosophy. We might sympathize with Justin's message and even his intentions, but we cannot say that this is the whole truth.

3. Acts of Justin and Companions

Shortly after the deaths of Ptolemy and Lucius, Justin found himself on trial in front of Rusticus, the Stoic tutor of the emperor Marcus Aurelius. According to Eusebius, it was the jealous Cynic philosopher Crescens who reported Justin to the authorities,[40] but the *Acts of Justin and Companions*, the account of his trial, does not provide us with an explanation, much less with any hint of scandal. Justin was arrested with six of his students, and the account of his death notes only the trial together with just a concluding note that the martyrs were led away for execution. The story is found in three distinct, progressively longer versions. Justin was an important martyr, heresy hunter, and early Christian thinker. It appears that early Christians rewrote the story twice in order to flesh out parts of the narrative that they found compelling. The earliest version is fairly brief. It is in essence just a conversation between Justin and Rusticus with a brief interrogation of each of his students. There are no miracles, descriptions of torture, or visions of heaven to liven things up.

Just as with the *Acts of Ptolemy and Lucius*, the brevity and ordinariness of the account has led many scholars to the conclusion that this is an accurate historical record of the trial as it actually happened. The fact that the trial was conducted in public and the text *could* have been composed by eyewitnesses or from the accounts of eyewitnesses has led some to assume that this is an eyewitness report, even though the text never describes itself as such.[41] We should not jump to conclusions. Just because an account is not *obviously* a forgery and fails to seize the imagination does not guarantee its authenticity. There's nothing about forgery that requires that it make interesting reading.

In the early 1980s American scholar Gary Bisbee analyzed transcripts of trials from the Roman period.[42] These were preserved mostly as part of the cache of ancient texts found at Oxyrhynchus in Egypt. Bisbee noticed that the majority of the transcripts followed a somewhat complicated formula. When Bisbee compared the *Acts of Justin and Companions* with this formula, he noticed that the *Acts of Justin* does not follow this pattern precisely. It preserves the most important structural elements of a trial, for instance, the verdict and sentence, but it meanders from the expected legal script. There are specific elements missing. This led Bisbee to argue that, although perhaps the *Acts of Justin* is derived from a court report, it has "been edited to a greater or lesser extent throughout." He goes on to say that he suspects "that entire sections of the acts have been interpolated or substantially edited."[43]

Against Bisbee, British classicist Timothy Barnes has argued that the *Acts of Justin* is authentic.[44] He makes his case on the basis of a single word. When the verdict is passed in the earliest version of the *Acts*, Rusticus says, "Let those who have refused to sacrifice to the gods be scourged and beheaded in accordance with the laws."[45] The term for "let them be beheaded" is the Greek *apachthētōsan*. According to Barnes, this is a literal Greek translation of the Latin term *ducantur*, which meant being led out for execution.[46] Barnes argues that a bilingual Roman Christian understood that Rusticus was sentencing the Christians to be beheaded and translated *ducantur* from a copy of the official court documents for his Greek-speaking audience.

This claim is not impossible, but it is important to note that the very same term is used by Justin himself in the *Acts of Ptolemy and Lucius*.[47] The *Acts of Ptolemy and Lucius* is not a copy of a court report, even if it was based on one. The presence of a single term isn't a guarantee of authenticity at all. Moreover, Justin's students were likely responsible for the preservation of both Justin's own works and the story of his death.[48] It seems highly likely that there was some intertextual editing. We know this happened with the *Acts of Justin*, which continued to be edited and expanded in light of Justin's own teachings.[49] In either case, this is just one word. What the word actually demonstrates is that the author was familiar with a court transcript, not that the text *is* a court transcript.

The evidence for the authenticity and historicity of the earliest recension of the *Acts of Justin* is much stronger than the evidence for many of the other texts we have examined. The earliest recension appears to be an edited version of a court document. The problem is very few people read the earliest version. They read what is known as the "middle recension," or recension B. This version is an expanded and edited version of the earlier text. It makes Justin appear more philosophical and Rusticus more unreasonable. This version is read because it is the version that Christian historian Eusebius preserves in his *Church History* and because the earliest version wasn't even published until the twentieth century. The irony here is that Christians continue to use the demonstrably less authentic text merely because it's traditional. What the expansion of the earliest version of the *Acts of Justin* shows is that even the most authentic texts have been edited in order to explain their meaning and significance for their audiences.

4. Martyrs of Lyons

The martyrs of Lyons and Vienne were a group of Christians arrested and executed in Gaul around 177. The story of their arrests, trials, and tortures is told in a letter apparently sent by survivors of the persecution, "the servants of Christ residing at Vienne and Lyons, in Gaul," to the churches in Asia Minor.[50] Unlike the other texts we've treated so far, the *Martyrs of Lyons* delights in the gruesome and bloody. There are detailed descriptions of torture and mutilation; the martyr Sanctus, for instance, had red-hot bronze plates pressed against "the most tender parts" of his body. The result is that he ceases to have any form, and onlookers cannot tell whether he is male or female. Blandina is so badly beaten that her *torturers* are worn out from exhaustion. The martyrs are scourged, seated in burning iron chairs, and exposed to wild animals. Even though the martyrs themselves appear to feel no pain, the authors clearly enjoy their torture.

The letter survives exclusively and only partially as part of the fourth-century historian Eusebius's *Church History*.[51] Neither the letter nor the "persecution" it describes, therefore, is attested anywhere in Christian literature until some two hundred years after the events.

Even apart from the lack of external evidence for the events in Gaul, there are excellent reasons for doubting the historicity of the account. The account begins with the circumstances of the arrests. Apparently, animosity against Christians had built up over the summer of 177, and after some time violence erupted in Gaul. The Christians were attacked by a mob and dragged to the forum, where they were questioned by the local authorities.[52] No reason is given for the arrests, but once on trial the martyrs begin to reveal more about themselves. One of the Christians, a lawyer named Vettius Epagathus, states that they had come from two churches in Vienne and Lyons. The problem is that these two towns were not just over a day's journey apart; they were in different Roman provinces. Legally, the presence of the Viennese Christians in this story is difficult to explain.

Another legal problem emerges with the evidence of some of the Christians' slaves. The slaves provide legal testimony that the Christians committed incest and cannibalism. As shocking and counterintuitive as it seems to us, under Roman law slaves had to be tortured in order for their witness to count as legal testimony. Yet the slaves are not tortured, as the law required; they simply are permitted to offer their stories. It's peculiar that the slaves are rounded up and then not tortured, that their false witness is not authenticated by torture, and that the charges of cannibalism and incest are never formally levied against the Christians. This whole enterprise is illegal and pointless.

There are some other strange details in the text. At one point the martyrs refer to the church as the "virgin mother."[53] This is a distinctive concept that does not appear anywhere else until the late third century, when another Christian writer named Methodius of Olympus introduces it in his *Symposium*.[54] There are other anachronisms too. In the conclusion to the letter the martyrs are described as reluctant to even embrace the title "martyr" before their deaths. They apparently view themselves as confessors and unworthy of any authority and respect. This formal distinction between confessors (those who are in prison awaiting execution) and martyrs (those who are dead and no longer have opinions) emerged in the mid-third century. During a period of prosecution under the emperor Decius confessors had taken to absolving other Christians of the sin of apostasy. Naturally, this infuriated the clergy, who felt that their leadership had been usurped. Christian authors who supported the church hierarchy were cautious when it came to confessors. Finally, the account opens by describing the events as "worthy of undying remembrance," an expression used by Eusebius in the *Martyrs of Palestine* and his *Church History*.[55]

Of course, it is possible that both Methodius and Eusebius had read the letter and cited from it in their own writings. And it is possible that the martyrs were filled with such humility that they unwittingly supplied a solution to the confessors' problem seventy-five years before it happened. The most likely and simplest explanation, however, is that Eusebius has edited the letter himself. The *Martyrs of Lyons*, therefore, is a theological early church letter edited by a strong-minded church historian. Eusebius is correct when he says that the letter is not *only* historical;[56] the problem is that we may not be able to discern which parts of it are *at all* historical. All we know for sure is what Eusebius or other unseen editors think about the martyrs. Although that's of interest to scholars, it's not what people imagine they're getting when they hear these stories in church.

5. Acts of the Scillitan Martyrs

In approximately 180 a group of Christians from Scillium, in North Africa, were arraigned and sentenced to die by the proconsul P. Vigellius Saturninus. Even though the text describing this event is short and scholars remain uncertain where Scillium actually was, this brief report of interrogation is critically important as the earliest evidence for Latin-speaking Christianity.[57] Not only is the text the first piece of Christian literature composed in Latin; it actually refers to "books and epistles" of the apostle Paul, which presumably were also in Latin. This makes this seemingly innocuous martyrdom account the earliest evidence for the Latin Bible and a linchpin in our evidence for the spread and development of Christianity itself.

The account is composed in the style of a transcript. The trial took place in the proconsul's *secretarium*, an office inside his residence. This was a public place, but a trial there didn't have the flashy or self-consciously public feel of a trial in law courts or an execution in the arena. Perhaps the trial took place at the end of the day when Saturninus was tired or in some haste before an official engagement, because the examination and sentencing were over in a matter of minutes. The simplicity and straightforwardness of the account led martyrdom scholar Herbert Musurillo to categorize the *Acts of the Scillitan Martyrs* as one of the most authentic of the extant martyr acts.[58] This assessment was grounded in the belief that such a prosaic text could hardly be invented. The eliding of simplicity and authenticity has meant that this text, like the *Acts of Justin and Companions*, has been treated as a historical record of events.

When read closely, however, a subtext of scriptural double entendres emerges. The reference to the books and letters of Paul in the discussion between the martyrs and the Roman judge is actually nestled in the center of an ancient literary device called a chiasmus.[59] A chiasmus is a structuring device popular in the ancient world in which thematic or verbal elements in a passage are given and then repeated in reverse order. This is most easily understood by means of an example. In the *Acts of the Scillitan Martyrs* the structure looks like this:

A. "I am a Christian." And they all agreed with him.

B. "Do you want time to deliberate?" "In a just matter like this, there is no deliberation."

C. "What are the things in your box?" "Books and epistles of Paul, a just man."

B. "Have a delay of thirty days and think it over."

A. "I am a Christian." And they all agreed with him.

Here the A statements ("I am a Christian") parallel one another, the B statements (in effect, "Do you want to think about it?") parallel one another, and sandwiched between these sets of statements is a reference to the writings of Paul. If we agree that there is a chiasmus here, then it must stem from the genius of the author. Saturninus may have been an accommodating administrator, but surely he stopped short of providing carefully structured sound bites for propagandistic Christian literature.

However, the evidence from the chiasmus alone may not be enough for everyone. Perhaps this is just a coincidence? Perhaps it is, although the reference to books at all is peculiar. It was only from the fourth century on and the persecution of Christians by the emperor Diocletian that Christians were required to hand over religious books to the authorities. In that period references to scripture became very common in martyrdom stories. It is highly unusual to find this sort of reference here in an account from the second century, before there even was such a thing as a New Testament.

More important, the reference to Paul is an interpretative key that unlocks the significance of some of the other statements made by the martyrs. In a number of places in the story, the martyrs' statements seem completely out of place. The martyrs do not answer the proconsul's questions; instead they make vague allusions to Paul in which they refer to their emperor and citizenship in heaven (cf. Phil. 3:20) and their willingness to pay taxes (cf. Rom. 13:6). For Christians hearing the story read aloud to them, the arguments of the martyrs are subtly presented as an interpretation of Paul. Although Saturninus is confused by the martyrs' vague ramblings and propensity to speak for one another, the audience understands them as acting—as Paul had told them in 1 Corinthians 12—as one body and speaking with one mind.

There is another, more technical problem with the story. There's some confusion about how many Christian martyrs were present and precisely what their names were. At the beginning of the story only six martyrs—Speratus, Nartzalus, Cittinus, Donata, Secunda, and Vestia—are mentioned. These are also the only martyrs who give individual responses during the trial. At the end of the account, when the martyrs are sentenced to die, a longer list is provided that also includes Veturius, Felix, Aquilinus, Laetantius, Januaria, and Generosa. Where did these additional martyrs come from? Were they always present as the chorus? If so, why were they not properly examined by the proconsul? Can we even be sure that they confessed to being Christians if the account does not describe this? It is possible that the first list was accidentally shortened through scribal error, but it is also possible that these martyrs were added to the second list at a slightly later date to swell the number of the saintly dead. Perhaps as the story spread and as the legend grew, additional names were added to the list of martyrs, much like a game of saintly "Telephone." Later scribes would have noticed the omission of these additional martyrs and inserted them into the story as they were copying it. In either case there is an inconsistency in the text, an inconsistency that casts doubt over the proceedings as they stand.

What this means with respect to the authenticity of the account is that the narrative is not pristine or unedited. This is only to be expected. Why wouldn't a Christian author want to shape and interpret the words of a hero or heroine? But, as a result, we cannot be completely sure that we have the actual words spoken by the martyrs. It seems likely that some Christians from Scillium died at the end of the second century. We just cannot be sure how many died, what their names were, or precisely what they said. And so—using modern standards of history—we cannot be sure that they were truly martyrs. Many Christians feel deeply personal connections to these individuals and take them as guides for how to live their lives. So it does matter to Christians how many people died at Scillium. Are we venerating saints or scribal errors?

6. Passion of Perpetua and Felicity

The *Passion of Perpetua and Felicity* is among the most famous of all early Christian texts. The reason for this is that in addition to the dramatic description of the martyrs in the arena, the glimpses of heaven in the visions of the martyrs, and the heart-wrenching youth of the protagonists, the *Passion* contains what would be both the earliest example of Christian women's writing and one of the earliest pieces of autobiography. The romantic idea that we have here a window into the heart and soul of early Christian martyrs and that we can get a sense of what they were really thinking and feeling as they approached their deaths is exhilarating. All of this assumes, of course, that Perpetua's diary was really written by her and that the editor of the text is giving us the full story.[60]

When it comes to the *Passion*, there are three potential authors—Saturus, Perpetua, and the editor—and thus three sets of questions. Is Perpetua's "diary" real? Is Saturus's vision by Saturus? And are the information and story provided by the editor accurate?

Perpetua's diary, as the most novel and thus valuable part of the *Passion*, has been subjected to a great deal of scrutiny. The "diary" was composed during the period of imprisonment prior to the execution of the martyrs and focuses on Perpetua's interactions with her family members, the weaning of her infant son, her visions, and her first experience in the arena. Some have objected that Perpetua could not be the author of this portion of the account on the grounds that it would be impossible for her to compose such a document while imprisoned.

Prisons in the ancient world were by necessity more open than they are today. They did not make provisions for inmates; thus, if prisoners were to eat, their friends and relatives had to visit them in prison. This appears to be the case in Perpetua's diary. Given this set of circumstances, it is perfectly possible that one of Perpetua's relatives smuggled her a stylus and paper. In writing from prison she was participating in a tradition of Christian prison literature. Both Paul and Ignatius of Antioch had written letters to Christian communities while imprisoned, providing evidence that some Christians did have access to writing utensils even while under guard.

Although it is believable that Perpetua wrote the diary portion herself, there are still some historical incongruities that warrant further consideration. According to the editor, Perpetua is well married, liberally educated, and from a good family. If this is the case, then we have to wonder where Perpetua's husband is. Although she describes her father, mother, and siblings, she remains silent on the identity and whereabouts of her husband. The omission might be theological. Perpetua is presented as the bride of Christ by the editor (and perhaps by Perpetua herself). The notion of being wedded to a supernatural entity in death is familiar to us from Euripides's description of

Iphigenia, but perhaps in Perpetua's case this kind of characterization demands that Perpetua's earthly legal husband take a backseat in the affairs.

On the other hand, there is a legal problem. Perpetua leaves her small child in the care of her family. Roman child custody laws favored the father, though, and if she was really respectably married, then her child would automatically have been turned over to her husband's family. There are two potential explanations for this legal problem. First, perhaps the editor is mistakenly or deliberately elevating Perpetua's social status.[61] Depending on when and for what kind of audience the editor put this text together, he might be attempting to avoid the implication that Perpetua is a concubine. We can imagine that a nicely brought-up Roman wife would have played better in front of the Sunday morning churchgoing crowd than a morally ambiguous concubine, however well educated.

Alternately, we could treat this incident as playing a role in the account's overarching theological view. One of the themes of the *Passion* is the tension between Christians and their non-Christian family members. Christians break their legal and biological ties in order to join (and die with) a new family composed exclusively of Christians. Both Perpetua and Felicity entrust their children to their fellow Christians, their family. As already mentioned, Perpetua is described and portrayed as the bride of Christ. The presence of a legal husband would undermine the metaphor. If Perpetua had a husband, the editor has taken him out in order to keep the audience firmly focused on her relationship with Christ. If this is what happened, then he has changed both how we think about her and the story itself. The reconstruction of the family in the *Passion* is a narrative reenactment of Christian understandings of the family more generally, but insofar as the events appear legally incongruous, we cannot trust their accuracy.

There is also another problem with respect to her child. When Perpetua is imprisoned, her young son stays with her, so that she can continue to breast-feed him. Shortly before her death her child is miraculously weaned, and she is able to hand him over to her family free from concerns for his well-being. In the ancient world, however, this would have seemed very peculiar. Most Roman citizens used wet nurses to care for their infants, so Perpetua's insistence on breast-feeding her own child would have struck ancient audiences as idio-syncratic. Even if Perpetua had been breast-feeding her child prior to her imprisonment, surely her family could have secured a suitable wet nurse in anticipation of her execution.

There are other incongruities as well. If Perpetua comes from such a good family, then why does Hilarianus have her father publicly beaten in court? This would be quite the affront to a man of high social status in the Roman Empire. Similarly, if Perpetua is wellborn, then why is she executed in the arena with slaves and common crimi-nals? She should have been beheaded quietly and out of sight, with-out suffering the indignity and shame of exposure in the arena. It is difficult, although not impossible, to believe that these are historical events.

In the world created by the editor we can make sense of these things. Perpetua considered herself part of this new Christian family and wanted, perhaps even requested, to be executed with her fellow Christians. Her bizarre relationship with her family members and the interesting omission of her husband can be accounted for as part of this interest in the family. In the same way, the beating of her father highlights, unrealistically, the cruelty and injustice of the Roman judges.

In addition to Perpetua's diary there is a vision of heavenly af-fairs narrated by her fellow martyr Saturus. Saturus describes how he and the other martyrs were carried by angels up to heaven, where they arrived in a heavenly garden. They were greeted excit-edly by other, more glorious angels, and they traveled to a walled structure that was full of light. Along the way they bumped into other victims of the persecution, before being ushered along to meet "the Lord." When they entered the light-filled palace, they heard the chorus, the sound of many voices chanting, "Holy, Holy,

Holy!" over and over again, and Saturus saw an old man, with white hair and a youthful face, who instructed the martyrs, almost as if they were children, to "Go and play!" The martyrs left the building filled with joy, and outside the gates they found the bishop Optatus and the presbyter Apanius. Apparently the two men were estranged from one another. The two clergymen asked the martyrs to make peace between them, but the angels intervened, telling Optatus that he must take charge of the decision making. And with some final glimpses of their fellow martyrs in heaven Saturus awoke, happier than he had been before.

When it comes to evaluating this vision, we cannot use the ordinary rules of history. Visions can't be faulted for improbability or illogicality in the same way details in a narrative can. We have no reason to think that the editor did not stumble upon this vision at the same time that he unearthed Perpetua's diary, and we have no reason to believe that one of the martyrs did not write it him- or herself.

But which martyr? The *Passion* is insistent that this vision was written by Saturus "in his own hand,"[62] but our earliest reference to this story attributes the vision to Perpetua. In his *On the Soul*, written around 207, Tertullian says:

> How is it that the most heroic martyr Perpetua on the day of her passion saw only her fellow-martyrs there, in the revelation which she received of Paradise, if it were not that the sword which guarded the entrance permitted none to go in there, except those who had died in Christ and not in Adam?[63]

There are a number of discrepancies between Tertullian's report and the *Passion*. Not only do they attribute the vision to different characters; they place it on different days. Tertullian places the vision on the day of Perpetua's martyrdom, yet in the chronology of the *Passion* the vision takes place several days beforehand. We might assume that Tertullian made a mistake, but it's not clear that Tertullian knows the version of the *Passion* that we have in our possession. The editor of the *Passion* used an earlier collection. Who is to say that Tertullian did not also utilize that collection? And, if he did, who is to say that he is not preserving the earlier tradition? There's simply no way to know.

Whatever form Perpetua's diary and visions originally took, all that we know about her and her companions is shaped for us by an anonymous and shadowy editor. In the past, some scholars have argued that Tertullian himself wrote the *Passion*, but given the disagreements over Saturus's vision, this seems unlikely. If he had, it would appear that he can't get his story straight. That Tertullian knows about the *Passion* and refers to it in 207 means that some version of the story must have circulated before then.

In addition to introducing and tweaking Perpetua's diary and Saturus's vision, the primary contribution the editor makes is to record the deaths of the martyrs. There are no historical or legal problems with the martyrdom itself, but the overall feel of the account is highly literary. In fact, the shape of the narrative and many details in the plot sound a great deal like another early Christian story, the *Acts of Paul and Thecla*.[64]

Both Perpetua and Thecla are wellborn young women who clash with powerful members of their families over their conversion to Christianity. Thecla abandons her fiancé and fights with her mother; Perpetua rejects her father's authority and demands in the courtroom. Both are portrayed as fearless women who occasionally shift genders. Thecla dresses herself in men's clothes in order to follow Paul; Perpetua turns into a man in one of her visions.

When they are in the arena, both Perpetua and Thecla participate in quasi-baptismal rituals. Thecla, who was still a catechumen when she fought with the beasts, baptizes herself by diving into a pool of man-eating seals. Perpetua's experience in the arena is also baptismal. Saturus describes himself as "well-washed" in the arena,[65] and the martyrs exchange ritualized kisses of the peace immediately before their deaths.

The most striking parallel between Thecla and Perpetua is their attitude toward those who had died without baptism. While she is imprisoned, Perpetua has a vision of her deceased brother Dinocrates, who had died before receiving baptism. He appears "dirty and pale" and in a place where he is "hot and thirsty."[66] The wound on his face that had apparently killed him is still visible to Perpetua, and Dinocrates is desperately attempting to reach the water inside an elevated basin. The basin is too high, however, and despite standing on tiptoes and straining, he is constantly frustrated. Perpetua awakens understandably distressed and resolves to pray for her brother. She prays and receives another vision in which her brother is healed and satisfied.[67] The implication is that her prayers were effective. Perpetua's intercession secures some kind of postmortem salvation for her brother. The same idea, though rare among early Christians, is found in the *Acts of Paul and Thecla*, in which Thecla prays for the deceased daughter of the kindly Queen Tryphaena.[68]

Thecla was certainly well known in North Africa in the fourth and fifth centuries, and there is evidence to suggest that the story was available much earlier, around the turn of the third century. Tertullian dismisses a text associated with the apostle Paul, which, he says, "claims the example of Thecla for allowing women to teach and to baptize."[69] The *Acts of Paul and Thecla* was written at the end of the second century. Given its positive stance on women and the similarities between Thecla and Perpetua, it is highly likely that the editor of the *Passion* knew of and was influenced by the *Acts of Paul and Thecla*.[70]

This is promising news for scholars interested in the dissemination of ancient texts, but it is a strike against the authenticity of the editor's version of events. We saw in the previous chapter that the editor of the *Passion* had taken motifs from Greek myth. Now here he uses the biography of Thecla. The editor has crafted a beautiful story, but this is more like a historical fiction than an eyewitness account. There is truth to this story, but it is hidden behind the layers of interpretation and careful editorial work. The unavailability of this truth undermines the force of these texts in the history of Christian thought and modern constructions of Christian history.

Conclusion

IT SEEMS THAT ALL of the early Christian martyr stories have been altered. From the *Martyrdom of Polycarp* to the *Acts of the Scillitan Martyrs*, these accounts have been edited and shaped by later generations of Christians. In fact, there is no early Christian account that has been preserved without emendation. Often it is the martyrs' own words that have been most clearly changed. Even in the case of the *Passion of Perpetua and Felicity*, we cannot be sure that we have the words of the actual martyrs themselves.

The conclusion is inescapable that none of the early Christian martyrdom stories is completely historically accurate. Even if portions of the accounts are possible and even probable, we can't be sure that they provide us with accurate information about the manner in which the Christians died. In the case of the six accounts we looked at in this chapter, the most historically reliable of early Christian martyrdom stories, we cannot know for certain that the details of these stories are true. Lucius is quoting Justin himself, Polycarp cannot help but act out the passion narrative, and Perpetua's familial situation casts suspicion on her famous diary. These things may seem like a light fog clouding our view of the martyrs, but the problem is that we have no way of clearing the air. We cannot know what the martyrs themselves thought and said; we can only get at what their biographers want us to think.

This matters because the reason people are interested in saints is because of what they said and did. The rationale for their veneration and canonization is grounded in who they were. If we can't know who these people were, then our connection is actually with the stories. We admire the characters and the values they embody, but we don't really know the historical martyrs. It's clear that these stories, while inspirational and heroic, are far from reservoirs of historical truth. This does not mean, however, that there were no martyrs at all or that Christians never died. It is clear that some people were cruelly tortured and brutally executed for reasons that strike us as profoundly unjust. The question is, how many? Christians have claimed that from the dawn of Christianity right up to the present day they have faced continual and relentless opposition and persecution. But is this true? Were the Christians persecuted?

CHAPTER FOUR

How Persecuted Were the Early Christians?

WHEN ASKED TO DESCRIBE THE experiences of Christians under Roman rule, many people immediately think of persecution: of thousands of Christians being herded into amphitheaters unarmed to be "thrown to the lions." Others might refer to those martyrs burned alive or beheaded or to the extreme tortures and grisly forms of execution that only the most sadistic minds could conjure up. All of this, they will say, was orchestrated by a vicious and unyielding government and took place in front of bloodthirsty crowds of Roman citizens. Christians lived surrounded by enemies and potential traitors, constantly looking over their shoulders, and always fearing the knock at the door that would bring destruction to their household. They were meek, they were kind, and they were persecuted.

This is the picture of the early church that we get from nearly two thousand years of literature, art, and—now—film. The image of Christians huddled together in catacombs or meeting in secret in one another's houses meekly observing holy days and living in fear of arrest, torture, and execution is ubiquitous. Everything from *Ben Hur* to *The Passion of the Christ* gives us the impression that Christians lived under the constant threat of brutal persecution, that they were forced to live and worship in secret, and that they could communicate with one another using only passwords and secret symbols, such as the fish.

When it comes to *why* Christians were persecuted, people are hard-pressed to supply an answer. Persecution is by its very nature about unfairly attacking a specific group because of who they are and what they believe. If an answer is supplied, it is that the Christians were new, different, and devout. Their persecutors are supposed to have been fearful and jealous. This picture—a blend of injustice and terror—comes down to us from the early church. Early Christian historians weave together a story of a church beset by great hardship and unfair persecution from its very infancy.

Christians claim that they were persecuted merely for being Christian and were treated as scapegoats whenever something went wrong. In the first half of the second century, Justin wrote an open letter to the emperor Marcus Aurelius defending Christians. He argued that Christians were arrested and condemned to die merely "for their name," not because of anything that the Christians themselves had done wrong.[1] Around 196 the Christian lawyer Tertullian complained that Roman hatred for the Christians was so great that they would use any excuse to persecute them. He wrote, "If the Tiber rises to the walls, if the Nile fails to rise and flood the fields, if the sky withholds its rain, if there is earthquake or famine or plague, straightway the cry arises: 'The Christians to the lions!'"[2]

It's easy to get carried away by this story of persecution and secrecy. It's a story that has been told and retold by successive generations of Christians to the point that it is hardwired into Christian history. We're led to believe that the Romans persecuted the Christians from the beginning and that these persecutions were fierce, bloody, and continual, but how many Christians actually died for Christ? And why were they targeted?

In this and the following chapter we examine the extent of and reasons for persecution of Christians in the early church. In this chapter we look at the evidence for violence against Christians. It's clear that Christians were never a beloved group and that during the vast majority of this period they were actively disliked. But they were not, as we will see, constantly hunted down by soldiers or regularly persecuted. In some instances the legislation that led to the execution of Christians was not even directed against them.

It's important to remember that our focus in this chapter is only on "persecution." We will not be describing the periods when Christians, although disliked, prospered and flourished or the day-to-day lives of the vast majority of Christians, who never stood before a Roman judge, paid a fine, or experienced torture. We will be assembling the evidence only for persecution. This focus only on periods of "persecution" gives the impression that Christians were targeted more than they were. When we look at the data things are clearer. Between the death of Jesus around 30 CE and the ascension of Constantine in 313, Christians died as the result of active measures by the imperial government only (1) immediately following the Great Fire of Rome in 64, (2) around 250, during the reign of Decius, (3) briefly during the reign of Valerian in 257–58, and (4) during the "Great Persecution" under the emperor Diocletian, which lasted from 303 to 305 and was renewed by Maximinus Daia between 311 and 313.[3] These dates represent the largest time span for active persecution in the period before Constantine. As we will see, not all of these episodes can reasonably be called persecution, and their implementation was often limited to specific regions and to months rather than years. Even putting these caveats aside, we are talking about fewer than ten years out of nearly three hundred during which Christians were executed as the result of imperial initiatives.

When it comes to the persecution of Christians in the Roman Empire, classicists often divide persecution into three periods: from the ministry of Jesus to the Great Fire in 64; from the Great Fire to 250; and from 250–51 (the persecutions begun under Decius) to 313 (the conversion of Constantine).[4] In contrast to Justin and Tertullian, modern historians are not at all sure that there was any persecution before 64. The historian Geoffrey de Ste. Croix puts it succinctly: "We know of no persecution by the Roman government until 64."[5]

Persecution by the Jews

AT ITS VERY CORE Christianity saw itself as a religion forged in fire. Persecution lingers in the background of every book in the New Testament. The original martyr was Jesus; the iconic founder of Christianity, its hero, leader, the Savior of the world, is portrayed by the Gospel writers as an undeserving victim. Yet according to the evangelists, it was not the Romans, but the Jews who were responsible for the death of Jesus and persecution of his followers. In the Gospel of John the Jews sought to kill Jesus because he spoke against them. The Gospel of Matthew portrays the Jews as baying for Jesus's blood and willingly accepting the guilt for his death (27:18–25). In all four of the Gospels it is Temple guards, led by the duplicitous Judas, who come to arrest Jesus in the Garden of Gethsemane.

This narrative of persecution does not end with the death of Jesus. The author of the Acts of the Apostles—for simplicity's sake let's call him Luke—describes how the Christians were systematically attacked and how one Christian named Stephen was stoned to death for blasphemy. Immediately prior to his death Stephen delivered a speech attacking the Jews for their failure to discern the work of God, their continual and repeated rejection of God's prophets, their murder of Jesus, and their failure to keep the law. For all Stephen's language of "our ancestors," this was hardly an olive branch. Then the Jews, enraged by Stephen's speech and his statement that he saw the heavens opened and the Son of Man standing at the right hand of God,

> dragged him out of the city and began to stone him; and the witnesses laid their coats at the feet of a young man named Saul. While they were stoning Stephen, he prayed, "Lord Jesus,

receive my spirit." Then he knelt down and cried out in a loud
voice, "Lord, do not hold this sin against them." When he had
said this, he died. (Acts 7:58–60)

From legal and historical perspectives, the death of Stephen sounds a
lot like a lynching or mob violence.

There are indications in the story that Luke wants us to think
of the death of Stephen as being just like that of Jesus. There are a
number of parallels between their two deaths. The attack on Stephen
is precipitated by the same accusation made against Jesus. Stephen is
accused of saying that "Jesus of Nazareth will destroy this place and
will change the customs that Moses handed on to us" (Acts 6:14). This
refers back to Jesus's prediction about the destruction of the Temple in
the Gospel of Luke (21:5–6). Also like Jesus, Stephen appears before
and is interrogated by the high priest. It is during this appearance
that both Jesus and Stephen refer to the Son of Man standing at the
right hand of God (Acts 7:55; Luke 22:69). They both cry out at the
moment of death (Acts 7:60; Luke 23:46). And, finally, at the point of
death, Stephen commends his spirit to Jesus (Acts 7:59), just as Jesus
commended his to his Father (Luke 23:46). And in the same spirit of
what will become Christian forgiveness, both Stephen and Jesus ask
God not to remember the crimes of those who were executing them
(Acts 7:60; Luke 23:34).

As already discussed, it's highly unlikely that the similarities between
the deaths of Jesus and Stephen are just coincidences. If there was any
doubt about this, it is dispelled by the evangelist Luke's fondness for
literary parallelism. He does this all the time. Throughout the Gospel
of Luke and the Acts of the Apostles the author has composed parallel
scenes that show the ways in which the church follows in the footsteps
of Jesus. A prime example of this is the descent of the Spirit on the
remaining members of the Twelve at Pentecost. Acts tells us that, after
Jesus's death, while the disciples were all together in one place, the Holy
Spirit came upon them (2:1–4). This is the moment that marks the be-

ginning of the church. It parallels Luke's description of Jesus's baptism (3:21–22). At both the baptism and Pentecost the Holy Spirit descends on the religious leader and ushers in a new era of evangelization.

In casting the death of Stephen as the death of Jesus, Luke is doing the same thing. He is saying that Christians will be persecuted just as Jesus was persecuted. It is a literary device that expresses Luke's theological perspective about the relationship of the church to Jesus and the continuity of God's activity across time. The problem is, once again, that we can't be certain that the details of the story are accurate. The historical Stephen would have had no way to know what Jesus had said at his trial or his execution, because he was at neither event and died before any of the Gospels had been written. Although it's theoretically possible that one of the Twelve told Stephen what Jesus had said on the cross, he would not have known what Jesus had said during his trial.[6]

Even though Stephen's death sounds like an isolated instance of mob violence, Luke would like us to believe that it was part of a pattern and the beginning of a dedicated persecution:

> [On the day of Stephen's death] a severe persecution began against the church in Jerusalem, and all except the apostles were scattered throughout the countryside of Judea and Samaria. . . . Meanwhile Saul, still breathing threats and murder against the disciples of the Lord, went to the high priest and asked him for letters to the synagogues at Damascus, so that if he found any who belonged to the Way, men or women, he might bring them bound to Jerusalem. (Acts 8:1; 9:1–2)

The way Acts tells the story, the church was pursued by the Jews from the very beginning. Even Saul, who would later become Paul, the apostle to the Gentiles, was involved in these affairs. There's a tension between Luke's description of the animosity of the Jews and the ineffectiveness of their actions. The situation presupposed by the story is organized persecution, and yet only a single death, that of Stephen, is reported.

The characterization of the Jews in the New Testament is a sensitive subject, and with good reason. The authors of the New Testament go out of their way to blame the Jews for the death of Jesus, and the Jews are described as being the offspring of Satan himself (John 8:44). It's difficult to overestimate the profoundly negative effects that these statements have had for the treatment of Jews, especially in Western Europe. There's no denying that the profound anti-Judaism of the New Testament contributed to the persecution of Jews by Christians from antiquity to the Holocaust.

At the same time, however, we have to consider whether intra-Jewish rivalry and concern had led some Jews or groups of Jews to target others, including the followers of Jesus. In his letter to the Galatians Paul admits that he had a hand in the routing out of Jesus followers, telling his addressees, "You have heard, no doubt, of my earlier life in Judaism. I was violently persecuting the church of God and was trying to destroy it" (1:13). That Paul himself would admit that he had participated in this practice lends credibility to the narrative of Acts, but it does not prove that Jews persecuted Christians.

The primary reason for this is that there were no Christians! Not only did the name "Christian" not yet exist, but the *idea* of Christians as a group distinct from the rest of Judaism did not exist in the lifetimes of the apostles.[7] The followers of Jesus were, like Jesus himself, Jews. There was no question of their founding a separate sect. At the time when Paul was writing he, like Peter, Andrew, James, and all of the original apostles, was a Jew. Not only were they Jews; there's no evidence that they wanted to be anything other than Jews. At the time when Jesus and the apostles lived, there were already many different branches of Judaism, which disagreed with one another on any number of things, including politics and elements of doctrine. Jews who followed Jesus were no different. They disagreed with one another, and they disagreed with other Jews. It wasn't until the end of the first century that Jesus followers began to refer to themselves as "Christians."[8] The historical period when Stephen died and Paul was writing cannot be considered a period in which Jews persecuted Christians, because Christians did not yet exist. At the very worst, and assuming that Luke is telling us the whole story, this is a situation of conflict and tension between various Jewish groups. This tension may have occasionally erupted into violence, but this does not mean that "Christians" were persecuted.

The Deaths of the Apostles

ON A MID-OCTOBER AFTERNOON in Rome in about 64 CE, the apostle Peter was attempting to steal out of the city unnoticed. He had not wanted to be a coward or a runaway, but he had been persuaded by members of his circle that he should retreat in order to fight the good missionary fight another day. Just as he was leaving the city, he spotted Jesus entering it. Seized with excitement, he approached him and asked *Quo vadis?* "Where are you going?" To this now famous statement, Jesus replied, "I am going to Rome to be crucified." A confused Peter asked, "You are going to be crucified *again?*" Jesus responded, "Yes, Peter, I am going to be crucified again." At this moment Peter came to his senses and realized that he had to face his enemies in Rome and embrace his inevitable death. He returned to his companions, informed them of his change of heart, and was arrested by four soldiers. It is not the case that Peter was reluctant. Quite the reverse, Peter returned to Rome "rejoicing and praising the Lord."

According to the apocryphal *Acts of Peter,* Peter was sentenced to die on the charge of atheism by the mad king Agrippa II. He was taken out to the place of crucifixion, where he encouraged bystanders to remember the miracles they had seen and to wait for the second coming. He then requested that he be crucified upside down. This was not because, as generations of interpreters have had it, he felt unworthy of dying in the same manner as Jesus. According to a speech Peter makes at the conclusion of the second-century *Acts of Peter*, he requested to be crucified head first in order to make a theological point. By being crucified upside down, he said, his body would stand as a symbol of humanity, which enters the world head first at birth. With a final prayer glorifying Christ as the source of his salvation, Peter died.

In the history of Christianity the martyrdom of the twelve apostles has been an important argument in favor of the truth of Christianity. After the death of Jesus his disciples graduated to the status of apostles. They started small—evangelizing Judea and the areas to the north of Galilee—but gradually they fanned out across the Roman Empire, exploring treacherous and inhospitable territories. According to various legends, all of the original apostles met untimely ends at the hands of hostile parties. Depictions of their deaths adorn the walls of churches and art museums around the world.

The willingness of the apostles to accept death for their Savior has been a key point in modern Christian apologetics. A lot is at stake in the martyrdom of the followers of Jesus. After all, the Twelve were those who knew Jesus personally, followed him around ancient Palestine, witnessed his resurrection, and spread his teachings after his death. Presumably they not only knew whether the resurrection was a sham; they would have been the ones to fabricate the idea. Why would this group of men have risked torture and death if Jesus were not really resurrected from the dead? Surely their martyrdoms are proof of the veracity of Christianity and the truth of the events described in the New Testament.

This argument is more persuasive to Christians than to non-Christians. After all, people will die for a lot of things, and in the ancient world this included country, city, virginity, religion, relatives, and—in the case of Iphigenia—good sailing weather. This does not automatically make their actions correct or their causes just. What makes this particular argument so potent for Christians, however, is that it was the apostles who were witnesses to the resurrection and ascension of Jesus. Even if we might not agree with the apostles' decision to die, we might still find ourselves conceding that they wouldn't have been willing to die if they hadn't really seen *something*.

This entire argument hinges upon the idea that the apostles were actually executed for being Christians. This means (1) that they thought of themselves as Christians, (2) that the motivation for their arrests and executions was that they were Christians rather than troublemakers, and (3) that they actually were arrested and executed. Of these three assumptions, the third is the most important. It's difficult to make the case that they died as witnesses to the truth of the resurrection if the apostles lived long, comfortable lives.

The problem here is that our sources for these events are the stuff of legend, not history. The documents that contain the stories of the deaths of the apostles, the apocryphal acts of the apostles, were written many, perhaps hundreds, of years after the events they purport to describe. Even the five earliest apocryphal acts of the apostles—the *Acts of Peter, Acts of Paul, Acts of Thomas, Acts of Andrew,* and *Acts of John*—were composed in the second century under the influence of the Greek romance novel.[9] This is to say nothing about the unreliability of the stories pertaining to the other apostles.

The fact of the matter is that we simply don't know how any of the apostles died, much less whether they were martyred. There are fifteen different versions of the deaths of the apostles Peter and Paul that were written before the end of the sixth century. While there is some overlap between the stories, they cannot possibly all be correct. What they represent are various later traditions and interpretations of the deaths of these important leaders. Even the *Acts of Peter,* the earliest version of the death of Peter, is dated by most scholars to the final decades of the second century.[10] This would mean that it was composed at least one hundred years after the date of the death of Peter given in the narrative itself. There are references to Peter's death in earlier Christian literature too. Around the turn of the second century, Clement of Rome writes that Peter was killed on account of "jealousy," not because he was a Christian.[11] Clement puts this interpretation to good work in his letter, but it goes without saying that this is just an interpretation. Not only does Clement not mention crucifixion, but he does not provide us with historical data about Peter's death or even confirm that Peter was executed upside down.

If we give any credence to the apocryphal acts and believe that the apostles attracted large crowds, then we have to concede that the apostles might have been viewed as revolutionaries. If they were arrested, then the charges levied against them may have been insurgency or inciting unrest among the people. As the death of Jesus shows, Romans had no problems executing people who caused trouble or could potentially start a rebellion. They were taking elementary precautions.

When it comes to the descriptions of the deaths of the other apostles, we have the same problem. None of the apocryphal acts can be dated any earlier than the second century. They are filled with stylized and fanciful narratives of talking animals, resurrected smoked fish, and flying magicians. Whoever wrote them never so much as met an apostle, let alone witnessed his death. Thus we cannot be sure of either the fact or the circumstances of the arrests of the apostles, much less the character or nature of their deaths. For all we know they were executed as revolutionaries or for disturbing the peace. We also do not know whether at any point they were given the opportunity to deny Christ and live. This is the key element that's missing if we're to argue that they died for Christ.

The result of this is that the fact of the apostles' deaths cannot be used as evidence for the truth of Christianity, the resurrection, or any other detail of Jesus's ministry. We know that the apostles died, but how they died, on what charges, and in what manner are far beyond our grasp. Without that information it is impossible to state that their deaths prove anything. The author of the *Acts of Peter* wants us to think that at the end Peter joyfully vindicated himself. In many ways it's an inspirational story about forgiveness. With his death he finally put to rest the guilt and shame of his denial of Jesus on the eve of the crucifixion. But all we can really say for sure, as historians, is that

Christians writing a century after the events understood the death of Peter as martyrdom and exoneration. The stories about the apostles tell us a great deal about how early Christians thought about and valued suffering and death, but they are not historical accounts and they do not demonstrate that Christians were persecuted.

From the Great Fire to the Emperor Decius

THE SUMMER OF 64 CE was a typical Roman scorcher. It was during the reign of Rome's fifth emperor, the theatrical and cruel Nero, a man notorious for marrying a eunuch slave boy and murdering his own mother. One hot summer night in July on the eve of the summer games a fire began in a small shop under the Circus Maximus. The source of the blaze is unknown; perhaps it was just a cooking fire that got out of control or perhaps it was deliberately set by enemies of the people in an effort to disrupt the following day's events. In either case the fire quickly spread to adjoining shops, fueled by the flammable goods of lamp vendors. Soon the entire Circus Maximus was aflame, and the fire spread to the dry timbers of nearby businesses and houses. The fire, called the Great Fire of Rome, burned for five days and left only four of Rome's fourteen quarters unscathed.

According to the Roman historian Tacitus, the people of Rome blamed Nero for the fire, and Nero, in turn, deflected responsibility onto the Christians. Tacitus explains that "Nero fastened guilt and inflicted the most exquisite tortures on [the Christians who] were hated for their abominations."[12] Christians were arrested and interrogated for information about others in the city. In the end "an immense multitude" was convicted and condemned to die in all kinds of extraordinary ways. Nero devised particularly cruel forms of death for the Christians. He had them dressed in animal skins and thrown to wild animals to be ripped apart; they were drenched in tar and burned alive as torches to light the night sky.

In Roman biographies of the emperors, Nero is well known for his temper and cruelty, but this does not mean that this story is completely believable. We need to exercise some caution when it comes to dealing with Tacitus. Tacitus's *Annals* dates to 115–20, at least fifty years after the events he describes. His use of the term "Christian" is somewhat anachronistic. It's highly unlikely that, at the time the Great Fire occurred, anyone recognized Jesus followers as a distinct and separate group. Jesus followers themselves do not appear to have begun using the name "Christian" until, at the earliest, the very end of the first century. If followers of Jesus weren't even identified as Christians, it's highly improbable that Christians were well known and disliked enough that Nero could single them out as scapegoats.[13] It seems more likely that Tacitus's discussion of the events in Rome around the time of the fire reflects his own situation around 115. Tacitus is evidence for growing popular animosity toward Christians in the second century, but he does not provide evidence for their persecution in the first.

In popular imagination as well as some scholarly literature the Great Fire of Rome and Nero's subsequent persecution of "Christians" begins the so-called Age of the Martyrs. Our earliest martyrdom stories date to this period, between the Great Fire and the persecution of the emperor Decius. Yet with the exception of Nero's tempestuous accusations against Christians, there's no evidence to suggest that Roman emperors themselves were that interested in the Christians during this period. For almost all of the first century, it's unclear that Roman emperors even knew that Christians existed.

Trajan and Pliny

Our first evidence for the "persecution" of Christians comes from the turn of the first century and a series of letters between the Roman emperor Trajan and Pliny, who at the time (112) was the governor of Bithynia and Pontus, in modern-day Turkey. As a conscientious governor, Pliny wrote to the emperor looking for advice on all manner of issues that arose in his administration. These letters, of which we have seventy-three from Pliny to Trajan and fifty-one from Trajan to Pliny, were largely concerned with provincial administration. Some of the letters are requests for honors for himself and his associates—a prestigious priesthood for himself and a promotion for a childhood friend, for example.[14] Others are more formal. Quite apart from the Christian question, Pliny makes inquiries about the enforcement of regulations, implementation of the imperial ban on clubs and associations, interpretation of religious customs, treatment of slaves, and use of Roman troops in the region. And, as we might expect, Pliny makes finances and building projects a primary concern. In short, Pliny writes to Trajan about everything from the celebration of the emperor's birthday to the administration of justice. There's nothing unusual about any of this; this is simply how administration worked in the Roman world, and Pliny wants to do and to be seen doing the right thing.[15]

Among these many documents is a brief exchange between Pliny and Trajan about the Christians. Pliny is saying that he has never participated in the trials of Christians prior to this point, and he is unsure about how to best proceed. The fact that Pliny has to make inquiries about this indicates that, before this point, there were no measures in place for the treatment of Christians. It's clear, then, that the Christians weren't the ancient Roman equivalent of enemies of the state. No modern governor would need to write to the Department of Homeland Security to ask what should be done about an admitted al-Qaeda operative in his or her state. Pliny would not have had to write to Trajan if Christians were high on the list of Roman concerns. His letter demonstrates a lack of familiarity with Christians and how to treat them. Pliny is uncertain about whether to sentence all Christians equally regardless of age and maturity and whether Christians should be executed as a matter of course or whether recanting their beliefs could earn them a pardon.

The cause of Pliny's sudden interest appears to be economic. In his letter he complains that many people had been attracted to Christianity and "the contagion of this superstition has spread not only to the cities, but also to the villages and farms," with the result that the temples had been already deserted and no one was purchasing animals for sacrifice. There is no special quality to Pliny's letter on this point; he writes with the same sense of urgency we see in his correspondence about the dilapidated baths in Prusa and the need for a fire company in Nicomedia.[16] But, given how much time Pliny devotes in his correspondence to the financing of building projects, it's only natural that he be concerned about the loss in revenue and the impact on the local economy. Pliny was clearly unfamiliar with the doctrines and practices of the Christians, but he had heard rumors. He had two female slaves who were also deaconesses tortured and had decided that Christianity was nothing other than a foolish "superstition." The term "superstition" was derogatory in the ancient world, as it is today, but this doesn't mean that Pliny hated Christianity. What it shows is that Pliny didn't think of Christianity as a real religion (*religio*). He didn't take Christianity seriously enough to take issue with its doctrines.

With respect to those accused of being Christian, Pliny writes that he proceeded in the following way:

> I interrogated these as to whether they were Christians; those who confessed I interrogated a second and a third time, threatening them with punishment; those who persisted I ordered executed. For I had no doubt that, whatever the nature of their creed, stubbornness and inflexible obstinacy surely deserve to be punished. There were others possessed of the same folly; but because they were Roman citizens, I signed an order for them to be transferred to Rome.[17]

Pliny's conduct was exactly what we might expect for a Roman administrator. As a governor he was able to act on his own initiative (*cognitio extra ordinem*) with respect to locals. Roman citizens could demand an audience with the emperor and had to be dispatched to Rome for trial and sentencing. Pliny devises a procedure in which he gives those accused three chances to change before sentencing them to death. Pliny is clearly annoyed by the disposition of the Christians; even though he finds nothing offensive in their doctrines, he finds their stubbornness and obstinacy to be reason enough to condemn them to death. "Stubbornness" would not have been grounds for the arrest of Christians in general, as no one would have been arrested on charges of suspected stubbornness! But once they were in front of a Roman judge, their willful stubbornness and rebellious obstinacy would have been reason enough to condemn them to death.[18]

As soon as Pliny's actions against the Christians became public knowledge, people began to take note. An anonymous document accusing members of the community of being Christian was published. The document was likely to have been the result of petty business disputes and rivalries, but Pliny felt compelled to investigate the claims, although he was adamant that the Christians were not to be sought out.

For those who denied being Christian, Pliny devised a sincerity test. He could not merely allow them to cross their fingers and repent at leisure; he had to get them to prove that they were obedient Roman subjects. Pliny had these individuals invoke the gods in words of his own choosing—there could be no room for ambiguity or slippery wordsmanship—and offer prayer, incense, and wine to the image of the emperor. Finally, he insisted that the accused curse Christ. Somehow Pliny had ascertained that real Christians would be unwilling to do these things. Among the accused were some who admitted to having been Christians in the past but insisted that this was no longer the case, worshipped the emperor, and indeed cursed Christ. Whether this was really true, and there were some for whom Christianity was a passing phase, or whether these were Christians lying out of fear of execution we will never know. One thing is certain: as long as a person sacrificed to the emperor and cursed Christ, Pliny was satisfied.

In his reply to Pliny, the emperor Trajan congratulates and commends him on his treatment of Christians. He agrees that the Christians "are not to be sought out" and that if a person "denies that he is a Christian and really proves it—that is, by worshiping our gods," then he will be pardoned.[19] Trajan recognizes the difficulty of dealing with these cases, though; he thinks that anonymous accusations set a dangerous precedent and that it is not possible to set down a general rule as a fixed standard.

These letters are something of an unexpected treasure for historians of Christianity, as they give us a glimpse into the minds of a Roman governor and an emperor. Even though Pliny and Trajan are in agreement about how Christians should be treated, they're not really that concerned with setting down a general law, much less trying to seek out Christians. Pliny and Trajan are negotiating a basic protocol for dealing with Christians in the event that one should show up in Pliny's courtroom. This is far from either formal legislation or an organized campaign. Reading between the lines of the correspondence, it seems that Pliny really just wants the Christians to go away. Once they are in his courtroom, Pliny has no option but to deal with the Christians, but he has no desire to seek them out.[20]

In his *Church History*, Eusebius writes that, with the exception of a handful of "good emperors," every one of the Roman emperors had participated in a demonically inspired program of persecution.[21] But apart from the Pliny–Trajan correspondence there is no record of imperial involvement in the handling of Christians. Even here Trajan gets involved only because Pliny asks him to, and Pliny inquires only because he has no idea what he should do. There's no doubt that Christians were occasionally arrested and executed, but this did not happen because of any organized efforts by the emperor himself.

If anonymous denunciations were off-limits and emperors were by and large uninterested in the continued existence of Christians, then we have to wonder how Christians ended up in courtrooms. There are a number of potential answers to this question. One suggestion, raised by Tertullian, is that Christians were scapegoats. Unsuccessful harvests, disease, and bad weather could have created climates in which Christians were more likely to be ill-treated. Perhaps, as Pliny implies, businessmen accused their rivals as a means of getting a leg up on the competition. Christians were vulnerable to jealous personal attacks and scurrilous rumors. In some cases the local judge or magistrate might himself have been opposed to Christians. Hilarianus, the administrator who sentenced Perpetua and her companions to die, was well known for his personal pagan piety and observance of the gods.[22] It is possible that his record with Christians was motivated by his own piety. All of this aside, there is very little evidence for the prosecution of Christians prior to 250.

We can imagine ways in which Christians found themselves in courtrooms, but this picture has to be weighed against the evidence for docile governors and friendly proconsuls. In his letter to the governor Scapula, the proconsul of Africa in 212, Tertullian notes that many governors were lenient with accused Christians, encouraging them to recant and even dismissing the charges against them. In a famous episode in Asia Minor around 185, a mob of Christians marched to the home of C. Arrius Antoninus, the governor of Asia, and demanded to be executed. The governor, no doubt irritated by the interruption, sent the Christians away, telling them that if they wanted to die, they had cliffs to leap off and ropes with which to hang themselves. If he had been following the guidelines in the Pliny–Trajan correspondence, he could have had the Christians executed, and yet this particular administrator could not be bothered to arrange trials. Not every Roman administrator was interested in Christians; many just wanted to see them go away.

The story might lead us to believe that martyrdom was widespread and many Christians were dying,[23] but this is something of an isolated example. There are no records of incidents like this in other sources—either in Asia Minor or elsewhere—until the late fourth century. Moreover, this isn't a story about Christians dying. What the story describes is thousands of Christians being *eager* to die but actually being sent home disappointed. It's easy to imagine why Christians, having heard about the death of Jesus in the Gospels and campfire stories and rumors of the deaths of the apostles, saw a death like that of Jesus as desirable. We will see later in this book just how advantageous martyrdom was for Christians. What's interesting, however, is that the Romans were not very obliging. Here we have Christians literally clamoring to die, and they were sent home alive and well. According to the story, they were not even tortured or imprisoned.

If, as the legend would have us believe, the Romans were constantly and continually persecuting Christians, then why would this particular governor have allowed the Christians to go free? Not only was he not persecuting Christians; he was actually refusing to prosecute them. The martyrdom myth maintains that Christians were constantly persecuted and died in huge numbers. Yet here, in the only example from the first three centuries after Jesus's death in which a large group of Christians could have been persecuted, we find exactly the opposite situation. Instead of Romans persecuting Christians, Christians are volunteering to die. And instead of Christians being interrogated, tortured, and executed, they are dismissed with hardly a second glance.

In this period before the reign of the emperor Decius, Christians were widely disliked. In the next chapter we explore why the Romans disliked Christians. The important thing for us to note for now is that prior to 250 there was no legislation in place that required Christians to do anything that might lead them to die. Even the correspondence between Pliny and Trajan provided guidelines only for Pliny, not for the entire empire. We have no reports of soldiers rounding up Christians, and the evidence that we do have suggests that Romans were strongly opposed to this kind of specific targeting. The climate was hostile, but there was no active persecution.

From the Emperor Decius to the Conversion of Constantine

IN JANUARY 250, THE newly acclaimed emperor, Decius, issued a decree that everyone in the empire must sacrifice to the genius (divine spirit) of the emperor.[24] It required that the sacrifice be performed in the presence of a Roman magistrate, and in return, each faithful subject would be provided with a certificate, called a *libellus* (literally, "little book"), as proof of participation. Copies of these *libelli*—forty-four in all—have survived from antiquity. They were formulaic documents signed in the presence of witnesses. One example from Egypt reads:

> (1st hand) To those in charge of the sacrifices of the village Theadelphia, from Aurelia Bellias, daughter of Peteres, and her daughter, Kapinis. We have always been constant in sacrificing to the gods, and now too, in your presence, in accordance with the regulations, I have poured libations and sacrificed and tasted the offerings, and I ask you to certify this for us below. May you continue to prosper.
> (2nd hand) We, Aurelius Serenus and Aurelius Hermas, saw you sacrificing.
> (3rd hand) I, Hermas, certify.
> (1st hand) The 1st year of the Emperor Caesar Gaius Messius Quintus Traianus Decius Pius Felix Augustus, Pauni 27.[25]

The sacrifice test was in many ways a test of loyalty. The statement that a person had always been sacrificing to the gods emphasized religious and social conformity and unity over time. Even though Decius had gained power only shortly before, the language of the certificate appeals to the idea that Decius stood in the tradition of the emperors.

In practice the decree requested no more of Decius's subjects than Pliny had demanded from Trajan's, but it struck fear into the hearts of Christians in a way that set them apart from other members of the Roman Empire. The decree itself is sadly lost, and apart from the *libelli*, we do not have any references to it outside of Christian literature.[26] From the form of the *libelli* we can deduce that the decree required that everyone participate in the cult. It was universal. No longer were Christians at risk only in the event that they were betrayed to authorities or otherwise found out. Now, for the first time, there was legislation forcing Christians to make a choice. They would be summoned before a Roman magistrate and asked to sacrifice; if they refused, they would be executed; if they sacrificed to the emperor, they would have broken their promises to God and would be facing eternal damnation.

For some Christians, the prospect of choosing between hell or death proved too daunting. Whether out of fear of torture or fear of apostasy and damnation, they elected either to try to obtain a certificate by bribery or to follow a fourth path, exile.[27] There are hints that apostasy had been a problem before the persecution of Decius. Tertullian wrote a tractate, *On Flight in Times of Persecution*, early in the third century in which he denounced flight as cowardice. But with the implementation of the Decian edict more and more Christians, especially those in areas of intense persecution, chose exile.

Among them one of the most famous was Cyprian, the bishop of Carthage. Cyprian became bishop of Carthage in the 240s, and with Decius's decree he chose to retreat to a small town in the countryside to wait things out. Exile and flight carried with them overtones of cowardice, but it was not the most serious religious crime. Many other Christians, when they found themselves in front of the magistrates, were willing to sacrifice to the emperor's genius. And if an extended vacation was difficult to explain to one's fellow Christians, emerging unscathed from a tribunal with a believable story was wellnigh impossible.

In North Africa, where the effects of the Decian decree were particularly severe, many Christians apostatized or went into exile. In many ways, Cyprian of Carthage managed to redeem himself only when he was finally martyred during the reign of Valerian in 258. After the Decian persecution was over, these apostate Christians attempted to gain reentry to the Christian churches in Carthage. In some cases exiled clergy assumed that they would be able to return to the leadership positions they had occupied before the decree. The sudden reappearance of exiled and apostate church members led to friction and tensions in the church in Carthage.

It's not difficult to empathize with those who had remained behind, who had lost family members and friends or perhaps even been tortured and imprisoned themselves and were now expected to submit to the authority of weak and morally compromised leaders. Cyprian himself had difficulties maintaining control of the *lapsi*, penitent Christians who had offered sacrifice to the emperor, and the confessors, Christians who had confessed Christ during the persecution, had been imprisoned, and were eventually released. The confessors had the moral high ground, and even Cyprian, as a former exile, had trouble managing them. The incident sowed the seeds of what would eventually become an outright schism in the church in North Africa.

There were other Christians who never made any kind of choice. This group Cyprian calls the *stantes:* Christians who were never arrested or called upon to make any kind of public statement.[28] This was risky behavior as, technically, the Christians should have all sacrificed and could be executed for not being in possession of a *libellus*. In practice, however, it would have been difficult for the local authorities to adduce who had not sacrificed, and we have no evidence to suggest that they actually tried.[29] These Christians garnered respect for having not sacrificed without even leaving their homes.

We cannot guess at the proportion of Christians who escaped persecution through flight, apostasy, and simply flying under the radar. For our purposes it's important to note both that not everyone was willing to become a martyr and that a Christian could maintain the moral high ground without ever entering a courtroom.

Christian writers describe Decius as wicked and his decree as one of the machinations of the devil. It's easy to see why they thought this. In principle the decree required that Christians apostatize or die. Just because the Christians saw the decree as a manifestation of the work of Satan in the world, however, doesn't mean that Christians were being persecuted. In fact, Decius may not even have had the Christians in mind when he passed the legislation.

Recent research into the Decian persecution has questioned whether Decius was all that interested in the Christians. Decius's original decree came as the response to a somewhat precarious political situation. He had become emperor in 249, when he entered the city of Rome in triumph. His victories over the Goths—Rome's primary external enemy—in a period of civil unrest had led to his being acclaimed emperor by his armies, but this did not mean that other Roman generals or politicians were thrilled with the idea. We tend to think of emperors and kings as all-powerful rulers who were able to crush their enemies with ease. In actual fact, the Roman emperors felt quite vulnerable. Decius himself had become emperor when he usurped the position of Philip I.

The passage of the monarchy itself was by no means assured; a dearth of successful elder sons meant that power had passed from one family to another and from general to general. Many prominent Roman senators and generals could argue that they had either the support of the army or a dynastic claim to power. Even Augustus, the successor to Julius Caesar and the most successful of the Roman emperors, had to struggle with Mark Anthony. And what well-educated Roman did not know the story of the ignominious death of Julius Caesar? According to one tradition, Decius's predecessor, Philip I, whom Decius himself defeated in a military rebellion, arranged the assassination of the child emperor Gordian III in 244.[30] Additionally, Roman emperors had become increasingly vulnerable to assassination by their own armies. Presumably even a confident and successful politician like Decius had to worry about his status.[31]

At the time Decius came to power in 249, the Roman Empire was under threat. The northern borders of the empire were being constantly raided by the increasingly aggressive Goths, and Decius had to contend with a series of comparatively minor yet nonetheless bothersome rebellions. Thus, when Decius entered Rome as military victor and emperor, he still had political rivals to handle and a divided empire to unite.[32] Decius had been a successful politician and came from an aristocratic family, but he was from the Balkans and did not have quite the reputation of an ancient Italian aristocrat. It was a delicate situation, and there was much work to be done. Decius needed to unify an empire of an almost unmanageable size and to demonstrate the legitimacy and strength of his own position.

He responded by initiating a kind of propaganda campaign that highlighted traditional Roman values and continuity with the past—the golden era of the Roman emperors. He minted special issues of coins and started a series of building projects in Rome—including the restoration of the Colosseum—in a style that recalled the early years of imperial Rome. Upon his ascension to power, Decius even added the honorary name "Trajan" to his own, thereby linking himself with the emperor Trajan, who was widely regarded as one of the most successful and well-respected emperors.[33] Decius's interest in the imperial cult was part of this program. By insisting that people participate in the cult, he was taking Rome back to its glory days and focusing attention and loyalty on himself. Decius's decree was tied to a wider renewal of traditional Roman values motivated as much by politics and personal interest as by religion or anything else.[34]

The Decian legislation had a pronounced effect on third-century Christians. Not only were Christians executed for refusing to sacrifice; the experience divided the church in Carthage. If the idea of being a persecuted group unifies people today, the reality of actually being prosecuted divided Christians in the ancient world, but the majority of Christians never allowed themselves the opportunity to become martyrs or confessors.

Since the fourth century, Christians have described Decius as a peddler of wicked decrees. But what's interesting about the Decian "persecution" is that it was short-lived and not specifically directed against Christians.[35] Nowhere in the *libelli* are the signatories required to confirm that they are not Christians or repudiate Christianity. Nor should we expect them to. The decree was about social conformity and political loyalty. That Christians experienced and interpreted Decius's actions as persecution does not mean that Decius himself intended to persecute them. If we are going to condemn the Romans for persecuting the Christians, then surely they need to have done it deliberately or at least have been *aware* they were doing it. In the words of classics scholar James Rives, it "probably did not loom nearly so large in [Decius's] mind as it has in modern scholarship" and in the imagination of later Christian authors.[36] What we have here is a short-lived piece of legislation designed to elicit social, political, and religious conformity.[37] That Christians were caught in the crosshairs of Decius's efforts to secure his empire is deeply unfortunate, but it is not evidence of anti-Christian legislation. This is prosecution, not persecution.

Valerian

For six years after the end of Decius's reign, during a period of peace and calm, Cyprian continued to struggle to maintain control in Carthage. During this time he never really earned back the respect of his congregation. Meanwhile, in the east, the new emperor Valerian was struggling to regain Antioch from the Persians. The Persians had captured and sacked the city shortly before Valerian's ascent to power in late 253, and Valerian traveled east in 254 to combat the threat, staying there until his capture in 260. During this time Valerian composed two letters to the Senate about Christians. The first was issued in 257 and demanded that the church leaders participate in pagan rituals and that Christians stop meeting en masse in cemeteries. After the first edict failed to make any sizable impact, he issued a second, stronger statement about Christians in 258, in which he directed that bishops, priests, and deacons were to be put to death at once.[38] Additionally, Christian senators and high-ranking officials were to lose their status and property and, if they did not apostatize, be executed as well. Christian women of senatorial rank were to lose their property, as were members of the imperial household who, additionally, were to be bundled off to the imperial estates, where their views would make them less of a liability.

It is interesting that, given that the Decian "persecution" occurred less than a decade earlier, there were already Christians in such high-status positions. The fact that there were Christians in positions of authority so quickly after Decius's supposed "persecution" suggests that the effects of the decree were not widely felt. Participation in government and politics was a very public affair that necessitated involvement in religious rites and oath taking and brought great scrutiny. It's difficult to imagine that all of these high-ranking Christians had both excelled in public office and concealed their Christian identity from a supposedly antagonistic and inquisitional government. Furthermore, it's surprising that Christians could and did achieve power and status in the government, if—as tradition has us believe—they were being systematically persecuted by that same government. That both Valerian and, as we will see, Diocletian ejected Christians from public office demonstrates that Christians not only lived peacefully among the Romans, they flourished and rose to positions of prominence and power.

Valerian's second letter was the first piece of legislation that was specifically directed against Christians. It is important to note that he was concerned only with leaders of the church and high-status Roman citizens. He had little interest in routing out all the Christians, young and old. Valerian, like a great number of Romans, viewed Christians as potentially subversive and antiestablishment. In the next chapter we examine why this was; the important point for now is that Valerian did not want this anti-institutional mind-set to work its way into the leadership of the empire. Although he was ambivalent about rank-and-file Christians, he did not want to see Roman values corrupted by Christianity.

This was certainly restrictive, but the same principle existed until extremely recently in Great Britain. Until October 2011 the king or queen of England was prohibited from marrying a Roman Catholic. He or she could marry a member of any other Christian denomination or religion, but not a Catholic.[39] Autumn Phillips, the wife of Elizabeth II's grandson Peter, actually converted from Roman Catholicism before her marriage in 2008. Similarly, in the United States, provisions in the state constitutions of Arkansas, Maryland, Mississippi, North Carolina, South Carolina, Tennessee, and Texas make it impossible for atheists to hold public office.[40] This legislation is discriminatory and outdated, but it expresses the same concern about the suitability of political leaders. In the same way, Valerian's suppression of Christianity was not about persecuting Christians in general; it was about preserving the integrity of the Roman government and limiting the influence of what was seen as a potentially destructive group. The exercise of power may have been sharp and the principles discriminatory, but it is important to recognize that this was not an attack on Christians in general.

Only a handful of Christians seem to have died as a result of Valerian's second letter in 258. Although there are some highly literary martyrdom accounts describing the deaths of individual bishops and church leaders from the period 257–59, the content of many of these stories, some of which imitate the style and form of earlier martyrdom accounts, is of dubious origin.

As for Cyprian, our Carthaginian bishop, the persecution under Valerian provided an opportunity for vindication. Cyprian was arrested and tried quite publicly by Galerius Maximus, the proconsul of Carthage, on September 14, 258. The trial was extremely brief. Maximus confirmed Cyprian's identity, invited him to sacrifice, and provided him with the opportunity to think things over. Cyprian rejected Maximus's offer, was sentenced to die, and was led directly to the place of execution, where he was beheaded.[41]

In 260, after several years defending the eastern parts of the empire from the Goths and the Persians, Valerian met with King Shapur I of Persia to arrange a truce. Shapur betrayed Valerian and seized him as a prisoner. According to Lactantius, a later Christian writer, Valerian lived out his final years in degrading captivity.[42] For Christians, the period following Valerian's capture was one of prosperity. After Valerian's death his son Gallienus revoked his legislation, and Christians enjoyed more than forty years of undisrupted peace. They may have been disliked, but they were again able to climb the social ladder, accumulate wealth, build churches, and assemble in full view of everyone. As before, Christians weren't hiding in catacombs; they were out in the open.

The Great Persecution

Up until this point we have seen Christians caught up in general legislation designed for everyone, the expulsion of Christians from positions of power, the execution of powerful Christians, and sets of procedures designed to deal with Christians in the courtroom. We have not seen widespread general persecution of the sort described in modern-day sermons. But with the accession of the emperor Diocletian, we find something quite different. His legislation inaugurates the first and only period of persecution that fits with popularly held notions about persecution in the early church.

Like Decius, Diocletian was aware of the precariousness of his own position. His reign followed closely on the heels of fifty years of political turbulence in the empire.[43] Between 268 and the accession of Diocletian in 284, no fewer than eight emperors had been assassinated, most often by their own troops, and the empire was plagued by civil war and barbarian invasions. At the same time inflation and the debasement of the coinage threatened the economic stability of the empire.[44] This instability and the vastness of the Roman Empire prompted Diocletian, in 286, to divide the empire into two—a Western empire, ruled by Maximian as coemperor (a junior emperor), and an Eastern empire, which he himself controlled. In 293 he further appointed two more coemperors—Galerius and Constantius Chlorus—and promoted Maximian to full emperor. This system of government, known as the tetrarchy (rule of four), lasted under successive emperors until 313 and was designed to promote military stability and success.

Because of the division of power, Roman emperors were able to personally address military threats in different parts of the empire simultaneously without abandoning Rome to potentially treacherous politicians and generals. The tetrarchy made a sprawling empire bordered by enemies and potential enemies both more manageable and more stable. At the same time, the existence of four emperors made it difficult to convey the notion of a united empire. The public profile of the tetrarchy had to be carefully managed in order to convey a sense of unity and cohesion. Even portraits of the emperors displayed in sculpture and on imperial coins depicted the four emperors with identical facial features.

Like those of Decius, Diocletian's edicts were concerned with furthering this sense of unity. Diocletian also had genuine religious concerns and a particular interest in sacrifice. Coins minted during his reign often depict him sacrificing. Toward the end of the third century he had taken action against the Manichaeans, whose religion he saw as deriving from Rome's enemies, the Persians.[45] In addition to issues of piety, politics, and stability, there were philosophical differences and personality clashes at the court of Diocletian that had made Christians unpopular there.[46] Unlike Decius's, his regulations took the form of several increasingly severe pieces of legislation. These edicts gradually rescinded the legal rights of Christians in the Roman Empire. Diocletian was attempting to undo the amiable position of his predecessor Gallienus, who had tolerated the presence of Christians in the empire.

The persecution itself came in waves. It began on February 23, 303, with the destruction of the newly constructed church in Nicomedia. The publication of the first edict the following day made the holding of Christian meetings illegal and ordered the destruction of Christian places of worship and the confiscation of Christian scriptures. Christians were denied the right to either petition the courts or respond to legal actions brought against them, making them especially vulnerable in judicial contexts. Christians with distinguished social status lost their rank, and imperial freedmen were enslaved. Everyone, including Christians, was now expected to sacrifice before engaging in any legal or official business.

When it came to the terms of the edict, there was more room for maneuvering than we might think. Most Christians rarely attended churches and did not own copies of Christian writings.[47] Provided they did neither of these things, the only limitations for this kind of Christian were in the legal process. A letter from a Christian named Copres to his sister Sarapias tells us that Christians found a way around the legal prohibitions. Copres tells Sarapias that, since he had discovered that those "who present themselves in court are being made to sacrifice," he has "made power of attorney in favor of his brother." Presumably Sarapias's brother was not Christian and was happy to help. He and his brother had also consulted an advocate about how best to preserve their land holdings.[48] There were, therefore, ways around the edict, and some non-Christians were willing to help.

Despite the fact that the persecution is named for the emperor Diocletian, it is sometimes thought that it was his coemperor, Galerius, who was the more brutal. Galerius wanted to have those who refused to sacrifice burned alive, but Diocletian's goal was apparently to have the edict enforced "without bloodshed."[49] If this is true, then Diocletian may have been a little naive on this point. In any case, local governors and proconsuls exercised their discretionary powers and executed Christians who did not comply with the order. And in the East some Christians were burned alive, as Galerius had originally requested. Prior to the publication of the edict Christians were enjoying a period of relative quiet. The church in Nicomedia that was pulled down at the beginning of the persecution faced the imperial palace, almost as a direct confrontation or challenge to imperial power. Certainly, before the edict was published, Christians were not hiding. They had, from the Roman perspective, the audacity to build in the emperor's own front yard.

The ferocity and extent of the persecution were very different in the Latin West than in the Greek East. In the West only a portion of the legislation was enforced and even then somewhat sporadically. Although in northern Africa executions began in Cirta, modern-day Algeria, in May 303 and were severe, the persecutions in Britain and Gaul, the area of the empire controlled by Constantius, were relatively mild. Lactantius tells us that things progressed no further than the destruction of church buildings, and Eusebius protests that no buildings were destroyed there at all.[50] Persecution appears to have died out in the West during the year 304 and was officially ended by the emperor Constantius in July 306. Constantius went further, though: he not only granted Christians in Britain, Gaul, and Spain freedom; he even restored their confiscated property to them.[51]

In the East, the region controlled by Galerius and Diocletian, the persecutions continued and progressed. In the first fifteen days after the publication of the first edict, the imperial palace in Nicomedia caught fire twice. Whatever the actual cause of the fire—Lactantius tells us Galerius was trying to frame the Christians, while the future emperor Constantine credits a bolt of lightning from heaven—suspicion fell on the Christians.[52] A second edict was published in the summer of 303, ordering the arrest of Christian clergy.[53] According to Eusebius, the impetus for the second edict was a series of political uprisings in Melitene and Syria in which Christians were believed to have been implicated.[54] Eusebius writes that so many priests were arrested, it put a strain on the entire prison system. Apparently, common criminals had to be released in order to deal with the overcrowding. This may seem like a huge number, but it's important to remember that Roman jails were a short-term measure for holding accused criminals before their trials. The idea of detaining and feeding prisoners for years at the expense of taxpayers would have seemed laughable.[55] Prisons were holding cells, and the fact that they were overcrowded should not lead us to believe that tens of thousands of people were arrested.

In November 303, in preparation for the celebration of the twentieth anniversary of his reign the following year, Diocletian issued a third edict.[56] This edict provided an amnesty for the imprisoned clergy providing that they sacrificed.[57] Many clergy balked at the notion of sacrificing, but it does appear that some were nominally compliant. In an interesting passage in the *Martyrs of Palestine* the church historian Eusebius writes that one Christian was brought to an altar with hands bound and maneuvered through the sacrifice like a marionette doll before being set free.[58] It's not clear how widespread this sort of thing was or whether this was a sheepish apostate's explanation for his freedom. If it is true, it appears that the local authorities just wanted to process the accused Christians as quickly and efficiently as possible. They weren't interested in conscience or conversion.

The fourth and final edict, issued in the spring of 304, was the most severe.[59] It required that everyone—men, women, and children—gather in a public space to offer sacrifice. If they refused, they were to be executed. For such a firm piece of persecution, the fourth edict is curiously undiscussed. It is never referred to by Christians in the West, by Lactantius in his *On the Deaths of the Persecutors*, or by Eusebius in his *Church History*. Eusebius mentions this edict only in his *Martyrs of Palestine*. It is difficult to deduce from Eusebius exactly how far-reaching the persecution was. Of the ninety-nine Christians executed in the *Martyrs of Palestine*, only sixteen can be said to have been actively sought out by the authorities.[60] Either the circumstances of the arrest of the other Christians are unknown, or it appears that the Christians presented themselves to the authorities. This doesn't mean that the persecution was trivial, but it does force us to reappraise the picture of Romans hunting down Christians in the middle of the night.

How bad was the Diocletian persecution? One problem is that martyrdom accounts set during this period are of little help to us. They are increasingly stylized and show, in the words of classicist de Ste. Croix, "an increasing contempt for historicity."[61]

Some Christians doubtless bribed their way out of punishment. Eusebius tells us that many others offered sacrifice and apostatized. Christians may have been persecuted, but that does not mean that they died. Governors in Palestine appear to have been enthusiastic persecutors, but others apparently boasted of having perfect blood-free track records.[62] We do not know how bad the persecution was, but we know that the edicts were not uniformly enforced and that even in the East, where Christians tell us the persecutions were the worst, Christians were rarely sought out.

It seems likely that, in its original form, the Great Persecution lasted until Diocletian's retirement in 305 and was briefly renewed by

Maximinus Daia from 311 to 313. Even if we assume that the persecution did not abate with Diocletian's retirement in 305 and continued until 313, we are talking about a period that could not have lasted more than a decade and that in many regions of the empire lasted no more than a couple of years.

Persecution or Prosecution?

THAT IN THE FIRST three centuries of the Christian era Christians were prosecuted at imperial request for no more than twelve years hardly constitutes sustained and continual persecution. There is scant evidence for Christians actually being *targeted* or actively sought out by the authorities. The shrill complaints of early Christians who say that the Romans were constantly out to get them were overblown. What do we make of this? What was the reality?

Scholarly treatments of this issue, especially by classicists, have sided with the Romans. The continual refrain is that persecution was "sporadic and local," meaning that, apart from the Decian decree and the persecutions of Valerian and Diocletian, Christians were not prosecuted by the imperial government. When Christians were marginalized, denied legal rights, ostracized from society, or otherwise threatened, this situation is categorized as "prejudice" or "social marginalization." When Christians claim, for instance, that they are aliens and exiles in society (1 Pet. 1:1; 2:11), this is not persecution. There is clearly a difference between the situation in Asia Minor that led the author of Revelation to write his apocalypse and the circumstances of Christians during the reign of Diocletian. Some scholars have attempted to articulate the difference by suggesting that first-century Christians "perceived" that they were persecuted even though they didn't suffer from "real persecution."

Implicit in this argument is a particular definition of "real persecution." The implication is that "real persecution" is imperially organized, is active, and involves execution. The problem with this implied definition of persecution is that it fits better with the way persecution works in the modern world than it did in the ancient world. There were some instances of imperial persecution, which we have examined here. At the same time government was organized very differently in the ancient world. In addition to the emperor, who could issue mandates for the whole empire, there were provincial governors, who had (as we have seen) a great deal of power in their individual provinces. If a governor chose to persecute Christians in his province, the persecution might be local in the sense that it was only in that region, but this doesn't mean that it was not serious for the people concerned.

An additional problem is caused by the scale of the persecutions. Modern technologies of violence make it possible for us to exterminate thousands of people with the push of a button. The horrifying violence of the twentieth century means that the deaths of four or five people, while tragic, hardly register on our collective scale of violence. And nonviolent persecution doesn't count in scholarly appraisals of persecution in the early church. We are desensitized to violence.

Conclusion

THERE'S NO DOUBT THAT Christians thought they were persecuted; they ruminate on it, theologize about it, bewail, lament, protest, and complain. Nor should we underestimate the reality of their experiences. There is no doubt that Christians did die, that they were horrifically tortured and executed in ways that would appall people today, however uninterested they are in human rights. We can imagine that for a small community the death of even a single member would have had a devastating effect on the group and left a lasting imprint on the ways in which they thought about themselves. We do not need to conclude that the authors of Revelation and 1 Peter are hysterical when they complain about being persecuted, but their experiences do not line up with either the mythology of Christian persecution or modern definitions of persecution in which persecution is centralized and state-led.

At the same time, the statements of apologists like Justin Martyr, Tertullian, and Eusebius do not fit with the evidence. We need to be wary of the claims of Christians that they were everywhere and always persecuted, when, in fact, they were not. Even if we do not agree that persecution must necessarily be imperially initiated, there needs to be greater subtlety in the way we describe the experiences of early Christians. There is something different about the experiences of a Christian after the implementation of Diocletian's fourth edict, a Christian who dies as the result of mob violence or impudence, and a Christian unable to hold public office. It is important to use language that reflects these different circumstances, because the failure to do so has contributed to the misconception that Christians were always and everywhere under attack. As clouded and difficult as this question is, one thing is clear: Christians were not the victims of sustained and continual persecution by the Romans on either an imperial or provincial level. They were very rarely the victims of imperial persecution, and we cannot always be sure that this persecution was directed against Christians. The Roman emperors and even some governors seem largely uninterested in Christians. Although they found Christians irritating, it appears that many, if not most, administrators were willing to turn a blind eye to their existence.

Even in those few cases when legislation demanded that Christians sacrifice publicly to the gods, it's difficult to tell what kind of structures were in place for tracking down those who were noncompliant. During the Decian "persecution," Christians *could* have been called to account for failing to produce a certificate of participation in the imperial cult. It's just not clear how often that happened. In the case of the fourth edict of the Diocletian persecution, roll calls of citizens were apparently taken in order to check who had and had not sacrificed. But this happened only in select regions and for a very short period of time. It was really only after Diocletian's fourth edict in 304, only in select regions in the empire, and presumably only until his retirement in 305 that we find the kind of situation assumed by the myth of Christian persecution.

The so-called Decian persecution raises something of an issue for us. There is little evidence to suggest that Decius had Christians in particular in mind when he issued his decree. The decree may have affected Christians more than others, but this doesn't speak to Decius's intent. If persecution is to be defined as hostility toward a group because of its religious beliefs, then surely it is important that the Romans intended to target Christians. Otherwise this is prosecution, not persecution. The death of a Christian or group of Christians might be unjust, but it is not persecution as it has traditionally been defined. This leads us to the prosecutors. Why did the Romans execute any Christians at all?

CHAPTER FIVE

Why Did the Romans Dislike Christians?

ALTHOUGH PERSECUTION WAS RARE, DISLIKE of Christians was fairly widespread, and some Christians were in fact put to death by Romans merely for being Christians. Before we judge the Romans too harshly, we should approach the issue from their perspective. Romans are not known for their cruelty; in contrast to the ancient Assyrians, who gained a reputation for brutality and sadism, they were known for being comparatively beneficent rulers.[1] This is partly the result of the Romans' own propaganda and partly the conclusion of modern scholars. In assessments of Roman treatment of Christians, this supposed kindness has been used in two diametrically opposed ways: on the one hand, it is used to highlight the extraordinary quality of their prosecution of Christians and to amplify the sense of injustice. The Romans were usually so kind, the argument goes, that their treatment of Christians was out of character and cruel. On the other, it is used as evidence of Roman innocence; the Romans were so kind that we must conclude that the Christians deserved it.

It is worth examining what it was about Christians that was so objectionable to the Romans.[2] When we talk about persecution, we often assume that it has no basis in logic, that it is sustained by rumor, fear, prejudice, and irrationality. Romans saw themselves not as persecutors, but prosecutors. We have to ask what the Romans thought they were accomplishing when they executed Christians and whether the prosecution of Christians can technically be called persecution.

Just because Christians were prosecuted or executed, *even unjustly*, does not necessarily mean that they were persecuted. *Persecution* implies that a certain group is being unfairly targeted for attack and condemnation, usually because of blind hatred. We have to know, then, why Christians were being arrested and executed and whether the reasons were a part of general legal practice or whether the Christians were being singled out. As we look at episodes of "persecution," we need to constantly ask ourselves: Is this religious persecution or is this ancient justice?

Before we turn to the question of Christians in particular, we first have to look at persecution and violence in the ancient world in general. We live in a world in which peace, toleration, and variety are valued and prized. We assume in the West that people have the right to practice their beliefs freely, and we attempt to make punishment painless or as painless as possible. Because of this it is shocking—even to supporters of the death penalty—to think that people were executed for crimes other than high treason or murder and that some forms of execution were designed to be as painful, prolonged, and humiliating as possible. Punishment in the Roman world was quite different.

Violence in Perspective

The reality of the ancient world was that the dominant political power called the shots. Many different groups of people had heroic figures who qualify as martyrs. One reason for this is that conquered groups were subject as a matter of course to certain kinds of political pressure: taxes, political oversight, forced participation in foreign religious festivals and practices, and so on. If a political power was tolerant, it was because it viewed tolerance as expedient, not because it was bound by international humanitarian laws or regulations.

Perhaps the first thing we have to note, though, is that the bar for capital punishment was a great deal lower in the ancient world than the modern one. Under Roman law a person could be executed not just for treason or murder, but also for less severe crimes such as accepting bribes while serving as a judge or for defrauding a client. We know from an ancient Roman legal document called the *Twelve Tables*, written around 450 BCE, that a person could be executed in all manner of brutal ways for comparatively petty crimes, including burning crops planted by a farmer or making disturbances at night. For slandering someone in a song, for instance, the penalty was to be clubbed to death. Those convicted of false witness would be thrown off the Tarpeian Rock, a steep cliff overlooking the Forum in the heart of Rome.

In 18 BCE, the emperor Augustus introduced new legislation governing marriage called the *lex Iulia de adulteriis* ("Julian law on adultery"). Under this new law a married woman who was caught in the act in her father's house could be put to death with her lover by her father. The situation was even more dangerous for slaves. In addition to being executed for any of the usual crimes, they were liable to be crucified for attempting to run away or for theft.

Capital punishment was a regular occurrence in the ancient world, and the methods of execution were similarly brutal. The *Twelve Tables* describes being beheaded, crucified, buried alive, drowned at sea, beaten to death, hanged, and impaled. In a show of characteristic fairness, the method of execution was tailored to fit the crime. Arsonists, for example, were often burned alive.

What this means for us and our study of persecution is that the execution of Christians is more exceptional to us as modern readers than it was at the time. If it actually happened, Nero's brutal execution of Christians for arson should shock us only insofar as the Christians were unfairly accused. The fact that Nero would have had Christians burned alive, however, was perfectly in keeping not just with Nero's own penchant for cruelty, but also with the general principles of Roman punishment. Torture and public execution were common for a whole host of crimes, and it is within this context that we should judge the treatment of Christians.

The Romans as Persecutors

IN A LOT OF ways it is peculiar that the Romans could be accused of persecuting anyone at all. In comparison with the Seleucids— who, according to the Maccabean literature, had Jews carved up and sautéed—the Romans were very tolerant and accepting rulers. In fact, the model for Roman interaction with foreign deities and religion was one of tolerance and adaptation. The most familiar example of this, still taught in high-school mythology classes today, is the way that Greek deities were romanized, so that Athena became Minerva, Aphrodite became Venus, Zeus became Jupiter, and so on. When the Romans assumed control of a new city or region, they incorporated elements of the local religions into the Pantheon in Rome and allowed the conquered group to continue to worship their own deities largely undisturbed. This meant that in the first century the Pantheon in Rome was a religious curiosity, housing not just the Roman and Greek deities, but also statues and representations from other religions.

The view, propagated by the Romans themselves, that the Romans were tolerant and largely benevolent rulers should not be too concretely identified with modern understandings of religious toleration. The historian Peter Garnsey has suggested that "Roman-style polytheism was disposed to expand and absorb or at least neutralize other gods, not to tolerate them."[3] Religious freedom and the idea that people have the right to maintain and practice their religious traditions undisturbed is very much a modern idea. For the Romans, as for all premoderns, religious freedom did not exist as such. The Roman form of toleration was about subsuming foreign deities and traditions into the Roman system, not about allowing people an inalienable human right.

At the same time, as classicist Clifford Ando has shown, when Romans did allow the perpetuation of foreign systems of law and religious traditions, they did so both as a means of displaying their magnanimity and largesse and because they conceived of religious institutions as local.[4] In theory, therefore, toleration depended on the goodwill of the emperor and local administrators and a friendly arrangement between small local religious groups and governing bodies. What this means is that interference in the administration of non-Roman religious practices and institutions, or, as it is frequently labeled, "persecution," was always an option permitted under the Roman law. Religious freedom was a privilege, not a right.

Persecution of Non-Christian Groups

PRIOR TO CHRISTIANITY THERE were only two clear-cut instances of Romans targeting specific groups because of their religious orientation. The first was the extermination of the Druids, a subset of the Celts who lived in Gaul and Britannia, modern-day France and Britain. Although some writers speak approvingly of the Druids' science and philosophy, most authors speak of their brutality. According to Julius Caesar and the geographer Strabo, the Druids practiced human sacrifice.[5] The late-first-century author Pliny the Elder says that human sacrifice survived in Gaul even to his own time, and Tacitus writes that the Druids practiced human sacrifice and consulted human entrails in prophecy.[6] There were political reasons for eradicating the Druids as well. They wielded considerable influence over local kings and, as the local intellectual elite, galvanized intertribal resistance to Roman encroachments into Britain. Whatever the political benefits, however, it was the reputation for human sacrifice that formed the justification for the Roman suppression of Druidism. A succession of emperors attempted to suppress the Druids in the first century CE: Augustus initiated these attempts, Tiberius continued them, and Claudius abolished their order. Outright elimination was difficult, however. It was only when large groups were assembled in one place, as was the case in 60 in Anglesey, an island off the coast of Wales, that the Romans were able to take the moral high ground with a tidy massacre.[7]

The second example is the laws prohibiting worship of the god Bacchus in 186–181 BCE. Bacchus, or Dionysus, is commonly known as the fun-loving god of wine, but the truth of his character is darker and more sinister. In Greek plays, Bacchus is described as an effeminate, dangerous deity who brought Asian magical practices into Greece. He is depicted as a source of moral corruption and chaos. To the morally conscientious Romans, who saw the household and familial virtues as the building blocks of society, the cult of Bacchus was potentially threatening. Adherents of Bacchus, or Bacchants, were known for throwing wild parties, for incest, and for their general lack of sexual self-control and social respectability.

The treatment of the Bacchants and the legislation against them are interesting. We might ask why the Romans were so threatened by the Bacchants. Surely every society has its social outcasts, its counter-cultural misfits, and its libertine nonconformists?

Apparently, there were rumors that the crimes of the Bacchants were more serious than the ancient equivalent of "Pagans Gone Wild." According to the Roman historian Livy, sex and alcohol were just the gateway drugs, for the Bacchants had brought to Rome a whole host of more serious crimes:

> When wine, lascivious discourse, night, and the intercourse of the sexes had extinguished every sentiment of modesty, then debaucheries of every kind began to be practiced, as every person found at hand that sort of enjoyment to which he was disposed by the passion predominant in his nature. Nor were they confined to one species of vice—the promiscuous intercourse of free-born men and women; but from this store-house of villainy proceeded false witnesses, counterfeit seals, false evidences, and pretended discoveries. From the same place, too, proceeded poison and secret murders, so that in some cases,

not even the bodies could be found for burial. Many of their audacious deeds were brought about by treachery, but most of them by force; it served to conceal the violence, that, on account of the loud shouting, and the noise of drums and cymbals, none of the cries uttered by the persons suffering violence or murder could be heard abroad.[8]

When we read between the lines, the accusations against the Bacchants seem like sensationalized gossip. These are rather convenient reasons for why no one knows about the murders. Livy goes on to tell us a story at the end of which a former Bacchant describes the secret mysteries of Bacchus to the consul of Rome. Apparently men who would not submit to sexual congress with other men were sacrificed to the gods, and the cult initiated people only under the age of twenty in order to win converts who were still young and impressionable.

The result of the revelation was a period of persecution during which many adherents were killed or imprisoned, places of worship were destroyed, and a decree was leveled against the cult of Bacchus. This decree, passed in 186 and known as the *senatus consultum de Bacchanalibus*, restricted gatherings to a mere handful of attendees who could meet only with a special license. In cracking down on the Bacchants, the Romans were protecting their society from decay, corruption, and immorality. They were especially suspicious of the Bacchants because they were a foreign cult that had been imported to Rome. That they had the potential to spread among the youth in the capital only made the situation worse. Many of the concerns about the Bacchants also applied to ancient Christians. Pliny's description of Christianity as a "superstition" carried connotations of ideological contagion. The concern that a foreign and rapidly spreading religious cult with a bad reputation could poison the well of Roman values was as applicable to the Christians as it was to the Bacchants.

The extent of and motivations for the persecution are hotly debated. Whatever the truth of the matter, justification for the mistreatment of these groups was grounded in serious crimes: murder and human sacrifice. There were other motivations, of course: these groups were politically dangerous and socially subversive. In the case of Gaul, the Druids were a key part of local resistance to Roman conquest; in the case of the mysteries of Bacchus, the Bacchants had brought superstitious subversion to the doorstep of the empire. The justification for their suppression was crimes against humanity, but the motivation for and benefit from their elimination were both social and political. The same complicated set of religious, political, and social concerns surrounded Roman attitudes toward Christians.

What the Roman suppression of the Druids and the Bacchants demonstrates is that there was a precedent for Roman attitudes toward and treatment of the Christians. It is not the case that the Romans were uniformly "tolerant" and made a huge exception for the Christians. There was both a rationale for allowing the continuation of indigenous religious practices and an established method for dealing with indigenous practices that threatened Roman values and stability.

Why Were the Christians Prosecuted?

TERTULLIAN STATES THAT CHRISTIANS are used as scapegoats in times of social unrest and anxiety, and Justin complains that Christians are persecuted merely for their name and in spite of the virtuous lives they lead. There is some corroborating evidence for this explanation in the writings of other early Christians and in the letters of Pliny, who, as we saw, would try anyone accused of being a Christian. Even given the violent nature of the ancient world and the ease with which criminals were sentenced to death, we still have to ask ourselves: Why was it that the Romans disliked Christians? And why did they prosecute them on occasion or at all?

Pax Deorum *and the Roman Imperial Cult*

When we look at the rare instances in which Christians were prosecuted, the motivation for this can often be tied to political and environmental stability. Decius, as we saw, was attempting to bring about unity and conformity in the empire. This conformity, he hoped, would bring stability and peace to an otherwise divided empire. This underlying logic was also at work in other episodes of imperial prosecution. Valerian's condemnation of Christians came at a time when the Roman Empire was under threat; the Persians had successfully captured Antioch, an important city on the coast of Turkey. Diocletian, who was much more cognizant of the role of the Christians than Decius had been, also lived in a time of political uncertainty. By eliminating dissenting groups, he hoped to unify an empire at risk of falling apart.

But there was a more amorphous notion of stability at work here too. Tertullian complains that in times of natural disaster or failing crops the Christians were blamed.[9] Christians were held accountable for the weather, floods, and disease. This may seem to us illogical and a sign that Christians were being unfairly victimized, but it is important to try to understand this from the perspective of the ancient Romans.

Roman society, like most ancient societies, presumed that there was an intimate connection between the gods, the success of the Roman Empire, and social order. It was not just the case, as in the Old Testament, that gods punish those who disobey them and reward those who are obedient and respectful; the whole of the empire was sustained and nourished by a system of delicate social structures and religious practices. The success of the Roman Empire hinged on the favor of the gods, a favor cultivated by piety and order. It was a delicate balancing act, and with the empire threatened both internally, by ambitious politicians vying for power, and externally, by hungry barbarians testing the limits of Roman power, the empire was always in a precarious situation.

The Romans did not connect their military success with the idea that their gods were simply more powerful than the deities of conquered cities and peoples. They maintained that they had identified and cultivated the proper methods for addressing the gods and that they had managed to persuade the gods to support their actions more frequently than the actions of their opponents.[10] As a means of sustaining social and divine order across the expanse of the empire, Roman emperors used the imperial cult as a kind of empire-wide religious structure. As an institution, the imperial cult was rather unimposing, but it served to unify all members of the empire behind its figurehead leader. It reminded people of the history of the empire, its power, and their individual duties. It worked, in some ways, as an ideological tax or a test of allegiance. The imperial cult was as much about political allegiance and stability as it was religious affiliation. It united all quarters of the empire and was instrumental in the sustenance and stability of it.

A key question, when it comes to our evaluation of Roman treatment of Christians, is the extent to which the Romans were targeting the Christians for their *beliefs*. Was the adherence to the Roman imperial cult a religious issue or a political one? If it was a political issue, then we can understand why the Romans would insist that the Christians participate in it. If it was a religious issue, then we might be more inclined to sympathize with the Christians.

In the ancient world religion was, in some senses, everywhere. All aspects of one's social, legal, professional, and moral life were governed by religious principles. If ancient Romans wanted to keep money in a bank, they would deposit it in a temple for safekeeping; if two businessmen wanted to conduct a transaction, they would swear a religious oath; recruits for military service took an oath of allegiance; and candidates for government and politics first had to become pontiffs (or priests) in particular religious organizations. It is difficult, therefore, to talk about practices that were *not* religious.

In the past it has been argued that the Roman imperial cult was just a political organization. It is certainly true that the imperial cult

served political and social functions. But merely because the imperial cult was interwoven with political stability and social conformity
doesn't mean that it and traditional Greek and Roman religious practices had no religious content or significance. In the past scholars
have described traditional religions (or "paganism") as just ritual.
Pagans, it was thought, just went through the motions; they didn't
really believe in the gods to whom they sacrificed. Christians, by contrast, really believed in the ideas that they professed.

This picture of belief and ritual in the ancient world isn't really
about the ancient world at all. It developed in the wake of the Reformation in controversies between Protestants and Catholics. During
this period Protestants emphasized belief as the core of what it means
to be Christian. This concept is encapsulated in Luther's slogan *sola
fide*, "by faith alone." When early Protestant thinkers looked back on
the early church and their relationship with it, they identified with the
first followers of Jesus. They compared their own relationship with
the Roman Catholic Church to the relationship of the early church
and paganism. In this comparison Catholics were the Romans, and just
as Protestants thought that Catholicism was encumbered by empty
rituals and idolatry and devoid of faith, so too moderns thought that
the Greeks and Romans were just going through the motions. They
were just ancient Catholics: mindless automatons looking to make a
quick buck off of meaningless rituals.

More recently, scholars have realized that the stereotype of
Roman religion as perfunctory—the religious equivalent of brushing
one's teeth—is incorrect. We clearly don't know what was going on in
people's heads, but there's no reason to assume that Romans weren't
deeply and truly committed to their religious traditions. Additionally,
we shouldn't be put off by the fact that religion has political, economic, and social elements. It's easy to characterize as mercenary ancient religious practices that involved paying for animals to sacrifice,
greasing the palm of a local priest or priestess for access to prophecy,
or asking a deity for success in business, politics, or war. But the in-
termingling of religion with all aspects of life was very common in the

ancient world. Everyone—Jew, pagan, and Christian alike—thought that religion permeated every part of a person's life. This state of affairs doesn't mean that religion is insincere, any more than praying to God to heal a sick relative is a form of divine exploitation.

It is simply anachronistic to divide ancient motivations into the religious and the political. They were tangled up together. For us, the state is—in theory—exclusively political and should not interfere in questions of personal belief, religion, faith, or God. In reality religion and politics are thoroughly entangled with one another, but we idealize the separation of church and state and the freedom of individuals to practice their religious traditions. For ancient Romans the state was both political and religious, and more important, Christianity sounded highly politicized. What this difference between modern and ancient views of politics and religion means is that we tend to misread what was happening in the ancient world.

It is claimed that Christians were persecuted for their religious beliefs, as if the treatment of Christians was a clean-cut case of religious persecution. But if we make the (arguably anachronistic) move of divorcing religion and politics, then the prosecution of early Christians is better understood as politically motivated. If the Roman emperors had a problem with Christians and Christianity, it was because they threatened the stability of the empire and appeared to make divisive political claims. Roman emperors did not take issue with nonthreatening things like baptism or hymns; they had problems with those aspects of Christianity that sounded like treason or revolution.

One reason the Romans took exception to Christians' refusal to participate in the imperial cult was that the vast majority of people in the ancient world thought nothing of participating in it. When the imperial cult was criticized in the ancient world, it was usually for the vainglorious celebration of individuals and personalities. Diehard republicans and aristocrats may have felt that it was occasionally gaudy and self-congratulatory, but as a *religious* practice it didn't raise any eyebrows. In the marketplace of ancient religions, pledging one's allegiance to the emperor and, by extension the Roman Empire, was easily done. It did not require the abandonment of a civic, household, or personal god. It was but one facet of ancient religious life.

Christians had inherited their strong sense of monotheism and condemnation of idols from Judaism. In the martyrdom stories Christians often cite or allude to the biblical book of Daniel, in which Daniel states that he will not sacrifice to idols (e.g., 3:18).[11] During the first fifty years after the death of Jesus, followers of Jesus had benefitted from this system. They were a small, relatively anonymous organization, and they were regarded by the administration as Jews. Jewish authorities and synagogue leaders had found a way to negotiate a role for themselves in the imperial cult that neither offended their religious sensibilities nor caused trouble with the Romans, but the Christians did not.[12] As Christians became more visible and identifiable as a group distinct from the Jews, this became more problematic. In the eyes of the state, they were transitioning from an ancient religion with specific traditions that shaped their participation in the imperial cult to a new, rapidly spreading superstition.

For the Romans, participation in the imperial cult was something that bound the empire together. Much like the pledge of allegiance, it was a communal ritual that solidified social ties between individuals on a local level and disparate regions and groups on an imperial level. In times of political or social instability, the imperial cult became particularly important as a form of steadying the ebb and flow of potential unrest.

The Christians, as is by now clear, would not participate in the imperial cult, and to the Romans, this state of affairs was dangerous. From an ancient perspective, the presence of a religiously noncompliant group in any community was a threat to that community. Human flourishing was a delicate affair, and religion was one way in which health, political success, independence, good harvest, fine weather, and all aspects of everyday life were managed. The Christians threatened all of this. They threatened to disrupt the *pax deorum* ("peace of the gods") and, in doing so, invited destruction on everyone. For the Romans, Christians' nonparticipation in the imperial cult was threatening. Their stubbornness was not just disrespectful and iconoclastic; it could potentially bring down the empire.

Subversion

In addition to the general threat that Christians posed to stability and success, their actions seemed inexplicable. Roman judges weren't entirely sure *why* Christians wouldn't participate in the imperial cult. Even though religion was everywhere, there was an understanding that what we would now call religious sensibilities should not interfere with political duties or social order. Christians rejected not only the imperial cult, but often military service. The idea that a person would refuse to serve in the military for religious reasons, for example, was almost unheard of before Christians. Today, we may defend the rights of an individual to refuse military service on religious or ideological grounds, but this is because we recognize and respect the concept of pacifism. But to ancient Romans pacifism didn't exist *as a concept*. Although some philosophers and playwrights occasionally criticized military society, such objections were rare. The refusal of military service, therefore, was confusing and strange. It was part of a pattern of Christian behavior that resisted—seemingly for no good reason—everyday ideals and social structures. Christians were socially subversive, and the limits of this subversion were unclear. If a Christian man wouldn't participate in the military or the imperial cult, a Roman judge might wonder whether he was a good father, citizen, taxpayer, or worker. Christian subversiveness was, in the eyes of the Romans, far-reaching and dangerous.

The situation grew only murkier when it came to Christian arguments about *why* they wouldn't participate in society. In the *Acts of Justin and Companions*, during the trial of the philosopher Justin Martyr, the Stoic philosopher and judge Rusticus grows increasingly frustrated. The Christians don't play by the rules; their responses to questions are incomprehensible. When Rusticus asks Justin to obey the commands of the emperor, Justin responds by saying that he obeys the laws of God. And when Rusticus asks one of Justin's students, a young man named Liberian, why he won't sacrifice to the emperor and "be pious," Liberian responds that he *is* pious and he worships God alone. Perhaps Justin's and Liberian's answers seem reasonable to us—we can understand why a Christian would refuse to worship the emperor and would instead worship God alone—but we have to look at the conversation from Rusticus's point of view.

The Greek word for "piety" that both Rusticus and Liberian use in the trial is *eusebeia*. Although this word is used to refer to religious piety toward the gods, it had a much broader use in antiquity. It referred to the respect that a child should show for a parent, a wife for her husband, a slave for a master, a human being for deities, and a citizen for the emperor. In other words *eusebeia* meant something much more like the modern English word "respect." Everyone respects those above them in the social hierarchy. Naturally, this meant that a person might be respectful to lots of parties: a Roman wife owed respect to her husband, to politicians, to the gods, to her father, and to the emperor. For Rusticus, Liberian's claim that he could not be respectful to the emperor, that he could be respectful only to Christ, would have come as a shock. Refusing to show *eusebeia* to anyone but Christ was rude, politically and socially subversive, and—to a Roman—completely illogical.

It is like modern defendants who say that they will not recognize the authority of the court or of the government, but recognize only the authority of God. For modern Americans, as for ancient Romans, this sounds either sinister or vaguely insane. Even modern societies work on the basis of a social contract by which individual beliefs are subsumed under the state. When militia groups defend their illegal actions on the basis that they don't recognize some aspect of American law, they are still thrown in jail. This is essentially the state of affairs for the Romans. It's merely that their political and social norms were intrinsically wrapped up in religion, as was everything in the ancient world. We cannot really blame Rusticus for being taken aback. We react much the same today.

In the same way, when Justin responds to Rusticus's question about obeying the laws by saying that he keeps the laws of God, Justin is undermining the authority of the courtroom and the emperor. The idea that a person could not obey both God and emperor was utterly alien and strikingly dangerous. To a Roman judge it sounded like sedition and political—not religious—subversion.

This phenomenon is not limited to the *Acts of Justin*. Once they were arrested, early Christians could hardly be accused of trying to secure their release. They were by and large uncooperative and stubborn. In the martyrdom accounts themselves Christians fail to answer the questions that are put to them. Even simple questions such as "What is your name?" or "Where are you from?" are met with vague, evasive, and nonsensical answers. According to the second-century *Martyrs of Lyons*, a martyr named Sanctus refused to give the judge any information about his name, citizenship, nationality, or background and instead answered all questions by saying, "I am a Christian." In early Christian stories about martyrs, this kind of impudence is found in abundance. Although we might be able to empathize with Christian refusals to worship the emperor, this sort of behavior was for some the kind of unnecessary stubbornness that invited trouble. To an ancient Roman observer this practice seemed perverse. Is it really necessary to refuse to give one's *name* in a trial? Even in modern American trials in which defendants regularly "take the fifth" in order to avoid answering questions, they're not usually evasive about their own names. To the Romans, and in anyone's estimation, the Christians were difficult in the courtroom.

It is possible that their stubbornness and difficult conduct in the courtroom were themselves a crime. The historian A. N. Sherwin-White suggests that by refusing to obey the orders of the Roman magistrates, Christians were guilty of *contumacia* ("contempt").[13] Pliny complains about this in his letter to the emperor Trajan when he writes that, regardless of the content of their confession, "their pertinacity and inflexible obstinacy ought to be punished."[14] It is certainly true that Christians were inflexible to such a degree that Roman judges found them intolerable and obstinate. This does not mean, however, that this formed the basis for their arrest and sentencing. If it had, we would expect to find the technical term *contumacia* used in either Pliny's letters or the early Christian martyrdom stories.[15] All the same, even if it were not the legal grounds for the prosecution of Christians, it probably contributed to their bad reputation and secured harsher sentencing in the event of their arrest.

The problem, when it comes to Christians, is that Christians changed the definition and language of what it means to be religious. They used political and legal terminology in new ways and refused to engage in ordinary, everyday practices on the grounds that they were against their "beliefs." To a Roman judge, Christians' appeals to Christ their "king" sounded like political subversion, especially when they insisted on portraying their king as superior to the emperor. Add to this the Christian refusal to engage in the imperial cult, and they could be accused of undermining the system that made the Romans successful. From the perspective of the Romans, the inexplicable stubbornness of Christians literally threatened the fate and future of the Roman Empire.

Superstition

Christians were stubborn, petulant, difficult, and, at times, completely incomprehensible, but their situation might have been different if they had been able to persuade the Romans that Christianity was a bona fide religion. An important point, when it comes to the question of religious persecution, is whether the Romans thought that Christianity was a religion at all. In his *Letter to Trajan* Pliny describes Christianity as a *superstitio*, a "superstition." What should we make of this?

In the ancient world, as today, superstition and religion were conceptually distinct categories. We tend to think of superstition as nonrational, unproven, unscientific, and traditional, whereas religion is institutionalized and systematized. The distinction has less to do with the content of religion and superstition than the way that people are evaluating that content. In the same way, Pliny engages in some conceptual roughhousing. By refusing to allow that Christianity was a *religio*, or "religion," Pliny is denigrating the Christians' position.

At the same time, perhaps he really means it. Historically, the definition of a religion has been constantly changing. Even today in America, in a society that prizes religious freedom, it's not possible to claim that just anything is a religious belief. I may be a huge Red Sox fan and describe baseball as "my religion," but I'm going to have a hard time convincing my employer that every home game during baseball season is a "religious holiday" and that I should get to miss work in order to attend the games. In the event that I lost my job to attend baseball games, it's highly unlikely that I could curry much sympathy for my predicament, that anyone would believe that I was being discriminated against or persecuted for my religious beliefs. This is because we have a generally accepted definition of what counts as religion and what kinds of behavior are protected by the First Amendment.

From the perspective of an ancient Roman, Christians were an irritating novelty. They had emerged quickly, seemingly out of nowhere, and made frustrating and incomprehensible claims about what was and was not religious. More problematic, they were contagious. When Pliny and other ancient Romans describe Christianity as a *superstitio*, they do so in the context of describing its rapid spread.[16] That Christians denied the existence of non-Christian deities seemed akin to atheism. That they insisted on talking about "faith" in God rather than their knowledge of the gods was bizarre.[17] That they removed themselves from certain aspects of society and held such eccentric beliefs seemed like superstition. Being designated as a *superstitio* meant that Christianity was akin to a disease. It wasn't a true religion or philosophy; it was foreign and inherently anti-Roman.

Cannibalism and Incest

Like many other religious groups with membership requirements, Christians met privately. This wasn't because they were persecuted but because they didn't own dedicated public spaces and were meeting in people's homes. Many other groups also met privately. After all, what's the point of being a highly selective group with initiation rituals if just anyone can show up? The air of secrecy that surrounded these initiation rituals could be a boon to mystery religions. Wealthy young aristocratic Roman men were drawn to exotic religious mystery cults imported from the east and dedicated to foreign deities like Isis and Mithras. Secrecy adds to the mystique. Who doesn't want to know what happens inside Yale's famous Skull and Bones society? At the same time, secrecy can breed suspicion and rumor, and early Christians seem to have fallen prey to this.

In particular, two rumors about Christians, which quickly became accusations, circulated from the second century on. These were that Christians practiced incest or other kinds of sexual perversion and that they practiced cannibalism. Our sources for these rumors come to us mostly from Christian writers themselves, who responded to them with frustration and outrage. There's a vague allusion to "crimes" that Christians are purported to have committed, possibly during ritual meals, in Pliny's letter to the emperor Trajan, but he doesn't go into detail and, in any case, finds the accusations to be baseless.[18] The notions of incest and cannibalism first appear explicitly in Justin Martyr. Justin's version of the rumor describes how in the aftermath of a feast someone would conveniently "knock over" a lamp, leaving the room in darkness, so that the participants would be able to drink human blood and have sex with one another without repercussion. The third-century writer Tertullian repeats the same story, adding more detail about the logistics. He supplements Justin's version by saying that Christian men had to be careful to note where their mothers and sisters were positioned before the lights were extinguished.[19] This was not, as we might assume, so that a young Christian man

could *avoid* sexual relations with his biological relatives, but rather so
that he could indulge in them.

Athenagoras, another Christian writing around 177, brings a little
up-market mythological sophistication to the accusation when he
writes that Christians were accused of "Thyestian feasts [and] Oedi-
pal couplings" (cannibalism and incest).[20] The third-century Christian apologist Minucius Felix records one version, which he claims
was spread by the well-known Roman grammarian and orator Marcus
Cornelius Fronto. He writes:

> Now the story about the initiation of novices is as disgusting
> as it is well known. An infant covered with flour, in order to
> deceive the unwary, is placed before the one who is to be initi-
> ated into their rites. The novice, encouraged by the surface of
> flour to strike without harm, kills the infant with unseen and
> hidden wounds. I can hardly mention this, but they thirstily
> lap up the infant's blood, eagerly tear his body apart, make a
> covenant over their sacrificial victim, and by complicity in the
> crime they bind themselves to mutual silence. These rites are
> more foul than any form of sacrilege.[21]

Given the improbability of confusing a flour-dusted infant with
the kinds of flat, circular inanimate bread so popular in the Roman
Empire at the time, we have to wonder where these rumors came
from. Why on earth would people think that Christians ate children?

There are two theories about the origins of this myth. The first
has to do with the language that Christians used to describe their
rituals. For example, in the Gospel of John, Jesus tells his disciples:

> Very truly, I tell you, unless you eat the flesh of the Son of Man
> and drink his blood, you have no life in you. Those who eat my
> flesh and drink my blood have eternal life, and I will raise them
> up on the last day; for my flesh is true food and my blood is
> true drink. Those who eat my flesh and drink my blood abide

in me, and I in them. Just as the living Father sent me, and I live because of the Father, so whoever eats me will live because of me. (John 6:53–57)

To modern ears, this may not sound so shocking. Since the early modern period Protestants and Roman Catholics have disagreed about the significance of this language. Is it symbolic or literal? If literal, how do we account for the distinctly waferlike appearance of the body of Christ? Does Jesus mean that his followers are actually *eating* him? The debate is whether the bread is *really* the body of Jesus. The knowledge that we're dealing with consecrated bread and trying to explain its relationship to the body of Jesus makes the accusation of cannibalism unthinkable.

But imagine you'd never attended any kind of communal celebration and this was all you knew about the communal meals held by Christians. Even if communal meals were a feature of your own religious practices—as they were for many in the ancient world—we can imagine that the subtleties of this passage were lost on those who merely heard it read aloud. To outsiders eavesdropping on a conversation about the Gospels as they browsed the offerings at their local tannery or butcher's shop, references to consuming the "blood" and "flesh" of human beings sound like cannibalism. It's easy to imagine how a mistake could have been made. This is the position that Justin Martyr takes in the *First Apology* when he writes that the "body of Christ" was confused with human flesh.[22] Perhaps, then, it was the taking of the Gospels out of context that led to this misunderstanding, and the scandalous rumor of people eating human flesh was beefed up with details of infants and initiation rituals.

This same explanation can account for the accusations of incest. The language of brotherly or sisterly love (*philos*) used by Paul in the New Testament to describe the ways that Christians related to one another was banal enough, even in the ancient world. But put this together with Christian insistence on referring to one another as "brother" and "sister" and references to the opaquely named "love feasts," or *agape* meals, in other Christian sources, and there's some room for interpretation.[23]

An alternative theory is that the accusation of cannibalism was a common form of ancient slander. In antiquity, as today, certain practices were taboo and regarded as morally repugnant perversions. Just like today, cannibalism was one such taboo in the ancient world. If you wanted to launch an attack on a particular individual or group, you might make your invective juicier with lurid details of their sexual perversions or predilection for human flesh. Accusations of cannibalism were particularly associated with foreigners and people who lived in faraway places. The historian Herodotus describes a range of cannibalistic practices among ancient peoples—the Indian Issedones and Callatiae practiced cannibalism in preference to burial or cremation, the Massagetae and Padaei pragmatically killed and ate their elderly while they were still fresh, and Scythian warriors drank the blood of those they killed in battle. These characterizations became stereotypes; by the common era "everyone knew" that the Scythians were cannibals. When Christians were called cannibals, they were being aligned with these far-flung barbaric groups.

Ironically, a prime example of this phenomenon is found among Christians themselves. Epiphanius of Salamis, a fourth-century Egyptian bishop with something of a lurid imagination, accuses the Gnostics or Borborites of something very similar. Amid descriptions of sex on altars and consuming semen as an offering to God, Epiphanius writes in his *Medicine Chest* that when a woman becomes pregnant, the heretics abort the fetus, dismember it, and eat it, declaring the meal "the Perfect Passover." It's unlikely that the Gnostics, or any other kinds of Christians for that matter, ever participated in these kinds of rituals, but that's not the point. Invoking this taboo was so effective that it would be difficult for anyone to mount a defense of a person or group accused of cannibalism.

Charges of incest worked the same way. Incest was a serious crime. It was, according to ancient myth, enough to drive a person to gouge out his own eyes. And it made for salacious gossip. For example, Suetonius, the lively biographer of the *Twelve Caesars*, made incest one of the many sexual perversions in which the emperor Caligula indulged.[24] Charges of incest seem to have been common in Roman politics as a means of undermining an opponent. The frequency of the accusation demonstrates the taboo nature of the act. For slander to be effective it has to have some teeth—there's no point accusing someone of going over the speed limit, for instance. Accusations of grave immorality or impiety tarnished the intellectual, political, or religious credibility of others, but they were especially effective when it came to small misunderstood groups like the Christians.

There's no evidence that Christians were tried or arrested for being cannibals. But the rumors swirled around them, and, just as in 1950s America it was impossible to shrug off the accusation of being a Communist sympathizer, there's no doubt that these rumors contributed to the generally negative perception of Christians among their contemporaries. In the *Martyrs of Lyons*, the author writes that the terrified slaves of the Christians (yes, the Christians owned slaves) accused their owners of incest and cannibalism out of fear that they would be tortured.[25] The scene is familiar to readers of Arthur Miller's *The Crucible*. Even though slaves were tortured as a part of due process under Roman law, here the slaves were hurling accusations and gushing rumors even before they were through the metaphorical door or strapped to the literal rack. Whether the story has any truth to it, it probably gives us a good sense of the ways in which these rumors affected early Christians. The Christians in the narrative were not tried for incest or cannibalism; they were tried for being Christians, but the rumors that surrounded early Christians didn't help their cause. It predisposed people to dislike them. That the same accusations crop up in France, North Africa, and Rome suggests that these labels were commonly attached to the Christians. Whether the root of the accusation was mistaken identity or sharp polemic doesn't matter in the end. Bad publicity was damaging regardless of whether or not it was accurate.

Conclusion

THE SUNDAY SCHOOL NARRATIVE of a church of martyrs, of Christians huddled in catacombs out of fear, meeting in secret to avoid arrest, and mercilessly thrown to lions merely for their religious beliefs is a macabre fairy tale. When Christians appeared in Roman courtrooms, they were not tried as heretics, blasphemers, or even fools. Christians had a reputation for being socially reclusive, refusing to join the military, and refusing to swear oaths. Once in the courtroom Christians said things that sounded like sedition. They were rude, subversive, and disrespectful. Most important, they were threatening. Even if the actions of the Romans still seem unjust, we must admit that they had reasons for treating Christians the way they did. The fact that religion and politics were so intimately blended with one another means that it is difficult to parse the motivations of Roman administrators as either religious or political. But from the Roman perspective and from the perspective of members of most ancient religious groups and political organizations, the Romans had the moral high ground. They were protecting the empire from the wrath of the gods and its effects. That Christians were executed should not surprise us; this is a world in which people paid the "ultimate price" for seemingly small offenses.

As we have seen in the past two chapters, a close look at the evidence shows that Christians were never the victims of sustained, targeted persecution. Even the so-called great persecutions under the emperors Decius and Diocletian have been vastly exaggerated in our Christian sources. In general, when Christians were executed, it was for activities that were authentically politically and socially subversive. In the case of the emperor Decius, it seems that the so-called persecution of Christians wasn't aimed at Christians at all. It was a way of bringing about social and political unity in the empire, something much more like a pledge of allegiance than religious persecution.

When we put this together with the actual evidence for the persecution of Christians we saw in the previous chapter, we can see that things were much less serious than the shrill rhetoric of early Christians suggests. The Romans rarely persecuted Christians, and when they did, they had logical reasons that made sense to any ancient Roman. This was not blind hatred or mindless persecution. Christians posed a threat to the security of the empire. In a world in which treason and sedition were capital offenses, it makes sense that the Romans executed Christians. This does not mean that—to us—the actions of the Romans are defensible, ethical, or just, but it does make them intelligible. It also means that, with the exception of the climax of the Great Persecution (303–5), there is nothing about the Roman treatment of early Christians that fits with the commonly held myth of Christian martyrdom.

CHAPTER SIX

Myths About Martyrs

IMAGINE AN ARID DESERT ROAD. It is a major highway for merchants transporting goods and for merchants traveling from one urban center to another. The route is plagued by bands of terrorists who prey upon wealthy merchants and foreigners. The vigilantes attack the convoys, destroying private property and gruesomely executing those who transport it. The terrorists are the very same group responsible for suicidal attacks on established churches in neighboring cities and numerous other acts of violence and brutality. Although their numbers are small and their means limited, the sickening violence of their actions makes them notorious throughout the civilized world, in which they are vilified and feared. Their ultimate aim is a martyr's death, a death that they believe will bring them honor, glory, and heavenly rewards.

The people in question are not modern-day terrorists, but a group of ancient Christians known as the Circumcellions. The name Circumcellion is believed to come from the fact that they lived in areas around (*circum*) martyr shrines (*cellas*). They were the vigilante wing of the Donatist church in North Africa in the fourth and fifth centuries.[1] The Donatists were locked in a conflict with the Catholic Church championed by more moderate European-style Christians, like Augustine. Even though Augustine's Christians called themselves

Catholic and orthodox and championed unity, it was probably the Donatists who had the better claim to represent North African Christianity. The split between the two groups began early in the fourth century after the first Diocletian edict when bishops and priests had handed over religious writings to the authorities in order to avoid persecution. Those who had remained in the urban cities—most notably in Carthage, the largest city in North Africa and one of the largest and most prosperous cities in the Roman Empire—appointed their own priests and bishops, an act that eventually led to a split between the new and old clergy.

If we look at the history of the struggle between these two groups, it's easy to feel sympathy for the Donatists. From the Donatists' perspective, they were the church of the people, the group that stood courageously against the Romans, while their wealthier leaders fled to safety or, worse, collaborated with the prosecutors. They fought back using the only thing they had—their lives. At the same time, however, it's difficult to feel anything but disgust at the actions of the Circumcellions. They terrorized the countryside and killed innocent Christians who had played no part in their oppression and marginalization.

The church fathers describe the Circumcellions as mad and suicidal. Apparently it was because of "their mad desire for martyrdom . . . [that they] kill themselves by means of the sword or by fire, so that, by dying violent deaths, they might acquire the name of martyrs."[2] It is possible that the Circumcellions have suffered from some extremely bad publicity and that they were neither as violent nor as suicidal as church historians would have us believe.[3] What they bring to light, though, is one of the most common misconceptions about early Christian martyrs: the idea that they were humble pacifists who meekly accepted torture because of their love of Jesus. This description of Christian martyrs is often compared—whether explicitly or implicitly—with that of martyrs from other religions. In recent years the focus of this discussion has been on Muslim martyrs, but in the past Christian martyrs have been contrasted with representatives from other major religions and even from various individual Christian denominations. The point of these comparisons is that Christian martyrs are good; they are true martyrs. But when we look at the evidence, we see that even if we would call them good, Christian martyrs are a lot more complicated—for good and for bad—than their reputation would lead us to believe.

Suicide and Voluntary Martyrdom

AROUND 180, A CROWD gathered to watch the execution of a Christian bishop named Carpus and his deacon, Papylus. It was a moving sight. The two men were tied to the stake and set aflame, yet rather than crying out, they bore their sufferings with self-control and courage. In the crowd, a woman named Agathonike watched the spectacle with great interest. She apparently saw the "glory of the Lord" and interpreted this as a sign that she should join the martyrs in death. Throwing off her cloak, she declared, "Here is the meal that has been prepared for me! I must share and eat this glorious repast!" The bystanders cried out to Agathonike to have pity on her son, but she responded that God would care for him and threw herself joyfully onto the stake. She was then raised up on the stake, and as soon as the flames touched her, she cited Psalms and cried out for God to assist her. She died, and her remains were collected together with those of the other saints.

This is all we know about Agathonike. Was she a slave? Was she respectably married? How old was her son? Was she even a Christian before she witnessed the execution of Carpus and Papylus? Did she come to the execution with the intention of killing herself? We simply don't know. Narratively, the author's claim that Agathonike has a vision of the glory of the Lord is completely unsubstantiated. She does not say what she saw or even that she saw a vision; she merely states that this is a meal that has been prepared for her. The only clue to her identity comes in the reference to her clothing. The fact that she is described as wearing a cloak may suggest that she is dressed as a philosopher. Ancient Greeks and Romans thought of the gymnosophists of India—an ascetic group who immolated themselves on funeral pyres—as philosophers, so perhaps we're supposed to think of Agathonike as something like a gymnosophist. But who Agathonike really was and why she decided to throw herself alive onto a bonfire remain complete mysteries.

There's no way around it: by any modern person's estimation, Agathonike's death is a suicide. In the earliest version of the story she is just a bystander. She has not even been arrested, much less been sentenced to death. Yet to the author of the account there doesn't appear to be anything surprising about Agathonike's behavior. In fact, the author describes her as just another one of the martyrs. Like the other martyrs she speaks words from Psalms as she "gives up" her life to God, and, like those of the other martyrs, her remains are gathered as holy relics for veneration. A later Latin author edited out these details, but at the time this story was written down in Greek there was no problem with the idea of bringing about one's own death. This is suicide, and even today Agathonike is a saint.

This is not the only case of suicidal behavior in early Christianity.[4] As we saw earlier, Tertullian claims that in Asia Minor in the second century thousands of Christians banged on the door of the Roman proconsul's house and demanded to be executed as Christians. The Roman official sent them away, but this seems to have come as something of a disappointment to the fired-up Christians who had to return home empty-handed and corporally intact.

There are more subtle examples too. Justin Martyr describes two voluntary martyrs in the *Acts of Ptolemy and Lucius*—Lucius and an unnamed man. The interesting thing is that Justin Martyr, one of the pioneers of Christian orthodoxy, doesn't treat Lucius's death as different from Ptolemy's. He doesn't even remark upon the unnamed man except to tell us that he came forward of his own accord. Although Justin doesn't apply the term "martyr" to either individual, he seems to think that their deaths are virtuous and good. There is no hint of condemnation here, and, in the case of the anonymous Christian, if Justin had felt in the slightest bit embarrassed by his conduct, he could easily have not mentioned him at all. After all, the *only* thing we know about this man is that he volunteered for martyrdom.

It might seem shocking to us that esteemed saints and church writers like Justin accepted volunteering for death. After all, Christians are particularly outspoken when it comes to condemning suicide in the modern world. In the Roman Catholic Church, for instance, suicide is seen as a crime against God. Although the current position is more compassionate, it used to be the case that those who had committed suicide were not even permitted burial on holy ground or funerals in Catholic churches.[5] The truth of the matter is that this viewpoint took many centuries to emerge, and most people in the ancient world accepted suicide, and even saw it as noble and courageous.[6] In instances of failed wars or political coups the best way for a general or conspirator to save face and protect his family was to commit suicide. Socrates committed suicide. Even though he was condemned to die, he still willingly drank poison to end his own life. And this, technically speaking, is suicide. None of the descriptions of noble death intimate that those who take their own lives are cowardly or desperate. On the contrary, suicide was generally seen as the ultimate act of self-control and an honorable end to a person's life.

Among ancient Jews too, suicide was in certain circumstances viewed as a badge of honor. One of the heroes of the Maccabean revolt is Razis, an elder of the people in Jerusalem, who was loved by everyone, well regarded, and called a "father of the Jews" (2 Macc. 14:37). When Razis learned that the soldiers were approaching his house to kill him, he fell upon his own sword in an effort to end his life. His aim was a little off, though, and he did "not hit exactly" the right spot. So he ran from his house through the crowd to a steep rock. He turned to face the crowd, hurled his entrails at them, and, calling on God to give them back to him in the afterlife, threw himself off the rock.

In collections of martyrdom stories, the narrative of Razis's death is often excluded, but in 2 Maccabees he is quite clearly a hero. His death forms part of a pattern in which the deaths of heroes precede periods of renewed military success for the Jews. A historical theologian might say that this is because the deaths of the martyrs serve as sacrifices to atone for communal sin and that, with the sins cleared away, the Jews are able to be successful. A sociologist might argue that these dramatic acts of resistance serve to mobilize the people who remain. In either case there is a pattern: remarkable deaths lead to magnificent victories. The fact that there's no difference between the death of the suicidal Razis and the deaths of the other Maccabean martyrs demonstrates that at the time Razis's death wasn't viewed as unusual or different. It was considered morally identical to all the other martyrdoms in the book.

It's within this context that we have to view Christian treatments of martyrdom. That second-century writers appear not to have been bothered by examples of martyrdom that we see as suicidal should not surprise us. Many people in the ancient world were unfazed by and even admired this kind of behavior. Although later Christians would condemn volunteering oneself for martyrdom precisely because it was a kind of suicide, at the time many Christians, including bishops and priests, actually sought out suffering and death.

The circumstances under which Christians came to see voluntary martyrdom as a bad thing are equally interesting. Chronologically speaking our earliest objector is Clement of Alexandria, a Christian philosopher who fled Alexandria out of fear of arrest around 202. Clement denounces voluntary martyrdom as something done by heretics:

> We . . . say that those who have rushed on death (for there are some, not belonging to us, but sharing the name merely, who are in haste to give themselves up, the poor wretches dying through hatred to the Creator)—these, we say, banish themselves without being martyrs, even though they are punished publicly.[7]

Most scholars believe that Clement is talking about the adherents of the New Prophecy, or the Montanists, whom Clement and subsequent generations of Christians denounced as especially eager for martyrdom. In the history of the church and its scholarship, people have been easily seduced by Clement's claims about Montanism. Some scholars have even argued that voluntary martyrdom was so essential to the New Prophecy that it was the single feature that distinguished adherents of the New Prophecy from other Christians.[8] The trouble is that there is simply no evidence to defend this claim. Other than the writings of the orthodox Christians who are attempting to condemn voluntary martyrdom, there is no evidence to suggest that Montanists were more enthusiastic supporters of voluntary martyrdom than the so-called orthodox Christians.[9] Clement alters this picture, however, in a very self-serving way. As someone who himself had fled martyrdom, he was at risk of being labeled a coward. It was in his best interests to supply doctrinal reasons for his conduct, and one way to do that was to condemn eagerness for martyrdom as heresy.

That some orthodox Christians had begun the process of denouncing voluntary martyrdom as "something the heretics do" began to sway people's opinions about suicide and voluntary martyrdom. The decisive shift, however, came with Augustine. In his *City of God* Augustine denounced voluntary martyrdom as suicidal and argued that the Bible prohibited it.[10] Augustine's strong and sharp condemnation of suicide was not only the result of abstract moral reasoning or a philosophical debate that he had with himself; it was also a matter of practicality and urgency. Augustine was responding to the sack of Rome, during which many women were raped and subsequently killed themselves. Additionally, he lived in North Africa in the era of the Circumcellions. We shouldn't doubt that Augustine was genuinely appalled by the actions of the Circumcellions, but this wasn't only a question of morality. Donatists—and Circumcellions—were competitors for the souls of the faithful. Augustine's denouncement of suicide was in part a practical measure. We cannot assume that he would have thought about the question, were it not for the Donatists and events in Rome.

What all of this goes to show is that when Christians died, it was not always as the result of persecution or even prosecution. The Donatist controversy really began only after the accession of Constantine and can best be characterized as a struggle between two brands of Christianity in North Africa. Interestingly, some early Christian martyrs were, by modern standards, suicidal. Although these Christians may not have been in the majority, we cannot pretend that they didn't exist. Christians were eager to die. The rejection of voluntary martyrdom and suicide has historical origins as well as ethical grounds. The history of suicide and voluntary martyrdom in Christianity might have been very different, were it not for Augustine's experiences and the Donatists in the fifth century.

Violence: Real and Rhetorical

WHEN IT COMES TO the Circumcellions, the most troubling aspect of their conduct is not that they killed themselves, but rather that they killed others. They went into orthodox churches and attacked congregants while they worshipped. They bludgeoned their fellow Christians to death. They tried to persuade people they encountered to kill them, threatening them with violence if they did not comply. Their aim was to become martyrs and ascend directly to heaven. Christian martyrs are supposed to be pacifists who meekly accept their fate without resistance or violence. This characterization of Christian martyrdom has become even more important since 9/11, as Christian passivity is cited as one of the fundamental differences between Christian and Muslim martyrs. One way of dealing with the Circumcellions is to dismiss them as outliers or aberrations. They're not even orthodox, the argument goes, so how can they be read as examples of *Christian* martyrdom?

There are other examples of violence, however. A Coptic martyrdom account called the *Martyrdom of Shenoufe and Companions* describes something similar.[11] In this story a young Christian soldier named Eusebius grabs a sword in the courtroom. Naturally, the Roman soldiers kill Eusebius in self-defense. Eusebius's actions would, in modern terms, be classified as insanity, and maybe even terrorism, but the author of this story portrays him as a martyr.

Examples of outright physical violence are rare in Christian martyrdom stories, but they are there. Much more common is the use of violent language and imagery to describe the actions of the saints. The Christians are at war with the devil and his minions, who are actively out to get them. In one of the visions recorded in her prison memoir, for instance, Perpetua describes herself as being changed into a man and fighting an Egyptian—who is meant to be the devil—in the arena. It is, we might say, just a dream. But it is a dream of violence and battle.

The same imagery of military conquest and satanic involvement is found in other martyrdom accounts. The fourth-century *Acts of the Abitinian Martyrs* concludes, "Here one battle in the great war is brought to an end; here the devil is overcome and conquered; here the martyrs of Christ rejoice"; it further notes that "the adversary of the Lord was conquered by the most glorious striving of so many martyrs and was overcome by so many and so great a crowd."[12]

Nowhere is this conflict more apparent than in the *Martyrs of Lyons*. In this story the devil is an actor in the events that transpire in Gaul. He orchestrates the torture and executions. But Satan is no impartial observer; he is involved in the individual struggles of the martyrs, attempting to seize control of their bodies. For example, in the case of Sanctus, the first martyr to conquer Satan, Sanctus's actual body becomes the location for a battle between good and evil, Christ and Satan. After Sanctus's body is tortured to the point that he is no longer recognizable, the narrator notes:

> But his body bore witness to his sufferings, being all one bruise and one wound, stretched and distorted out of any recogniz-

ably human shape; but Christ suffering in him achieved great glory, overwhelming the Adversary, and showing as an example to all the others that nothing is to be feared where the Father's love is, nothing painful where we find Christ's glory.[13]

The same phenomenon is found a few sentences later, in the description of the tortures of Biblis. Biblis has not endured torture as well as Sanctus. During the tortures she has recanted her beliefs and cursed Christ. This, apparently, is when the devil overplays his hand. He mistakenly thinks that Biblis is a coward and that by torturing her more he will get her to multiply her sins, curse Christ again, or otherwise compound her betrayal. Instead, the additional tortures rouse Biblis as if from sleep; she renews her confession and denies the slanders levied against Christians. She is saved and the devil is frustrated.

The battle with the devil culminates in the description of Blandina in the arena. She is hung on a stake in a cruciform pose that arouses the admiration of her fellow martyrs, who look at Blandina and see their Savior in her. The efficacy of Blandina's actions is summed up using the language of victory and triumph:

Thus for her victory in further contests she would make irreversible the condemnation of the crooked serpent, and tiny, weak, and insignificant as she was she would give inspiration to her brothers, for she had put on Christ, that mighty and invincible athlete, and had overcome the Adversary in many contests and through her conflict had won the crown of immortality.[14]

Blandina's triumph is both personal and cosmic. As a lowly slave girl, "tiny, weak, and insignificant," she became the leader of the martyrs. Even though the group was composed of Roman citizens, slave owners, highly educated orators, and soldiers, it was Blandina who led them. She is the perfect embodiment of a Christian ethic that rejects gaudy wealth and status and appreciates the poor and downtrodden. At the same time her accomplishment is about much more than herself. The reference to the "crooked serpent" is an allusion to Genesis. The devil is here equated with the serpent in the garden of Eden, and Blandina crushes him.[15] She is an actor in a cosmic drama that spans the course of human history. The hidden message is that Christians take their place in this battle alongside Christ. If the Romans thought this was a run-of-the-mill execution, they were wrong. Blandina's actions and death matter. She conquers the Adversary.

On the one hand, the portrayal of martyrs as engaged in a battle to the death with Satan is easily understood. The stakes are high here, and the martyrs really are going to die. This is not, in many ways, an exaggeration. On the other hand, there are aspects of the portrayal of this battle with the devil that should worry us. People, real people, are aligned with and identified with Satan. They are possessed by the devil in the same way that Christians are filled with the spirit of Christ. It's easy to miss, but in referring to "the devil's" or "Satan's" efforts to overwhelm the Christians, we forget that there are human actors in these events. Judges, torturers, and "the crowd" are dehumanized. Just as the martyrs are filled with Christ, their opponents are filled with Satan. In some instances we don't even notice that there are other people. It is the devil who attempts to overwhelm Biblis. The fact that there were people involved is lost.

It's easy to understand why Christians who were being tortured and killed would feel this way. This is a theological explanation that makes sense of a terrible and horrifying injustice. It reassured and strengthened Christians both in the narrative and in the audience. The same kinds of explanations are found in Christian apocalyptic literature, like the book of Revelation. One way for Christians to deal with their precarious situation in the world was to imagine themselves as participating in a cosmic battle between God and Satan. This understanding of the world gave purpose and meaning to their experiences and suffering. We can hardly blame them. Given the horrors that are described in the *Martyrs of Lyons*, why shouldn't the authors feel that the people treating them this way are literally agents of the devil?

The problem is what happens when this vision of the world is translated into settings in which Christians are not the underdogs. In situations where Christians have the military, political, and financial power to take steps against their "demonically inspired" enemies, this worldview can legitimize all kinds of violence. Once a group, idea, or person is labeled evil, then any measures can be used in opposition, even if these measures themselves involve torture, imprisonment, and execution. The fact that these stories envision actual physical possession by the devil only makes the problem worse. In a world in which one's enemies are no longer people but agents of evil, those people are completely dehumanized. They are no longer deserving of compassion, forgiveness, understanding, or empathy. No one clamors for basic human rights for demons. Early Christian martyrdom stories set a precedent for later generations of Christians to see the world in this way. Once a group claims to be persecuted, they invoke (whether explicitly or implicitly) the idea that their opponents are acting for the devil.

Nowhere was this danger more acutely realized than during the Crusades. In 1095 Pope Urban II called upon all Christians to join in a war against the Turks, promising a remission of sins for those who participated. This began a series of religious wars, nine in total, that lasted into the thirteenth century. The motivations for the Crusades were complicated. At the time when the First Crusade began, Jerusalem had been under the control of Muslims for centuries. Many have questioned whether those involved were as concerned with the Holy City as they were with the financial and political rewards that the venture could bring.[16] We should, of course, try to understand the motivations of the Crusaders on their own terms and consider the validity of their view that they were under attack.[17] But even if we do, and irrespective of their motivations and their feelings of vulnerability, it is undeniable that the Crusaders committed unspeakable acts of violence. Historian Jeremy Cohen's work, for example, explores descriptions in contemporary accounts by Jews of Crusader bands, in 1096, forcing Jews to convert. If they refused baptism, they were murdered or driven to suicide.[18] Such events are nothing short of horrifying.

It comes as some surprise, therefore, to find that Europeans thought of the Crusades as an opportunity for martyrdom.[19] Pope Urban II had stated in his speech at Clermont in 1095 that the new war "contains the glorious reward of martyrdom."[20] Not only those who died in battle, but also those Christians who were captured during the fighting and refused to apostatize were described as martyrs. This might seem more reasonable to us, but it is important to remember that these soldiers were captured as part of a preemptive strike launched by European forces. Moreover, Crusaders offered exactly the same choice—convert or die—to Jews. What is interesting is that at the time they saw themselves as the defensive party, and however we might interpret the campaigns in the Levant, the treatment of Jews in the Rhineland cannot be justified as "defensive." That Christians could see their actions, which ranged from warfare to pogroms, as holy war and martyrdom illustrates just how dangerous this worldview can be. It's a lesson that we should heed today. There is always the possibility that we have no sense of our own position in a conflict. Even though we cast ourselves as martyrs, we might be Crusaders.

Passivity

It's easy to see why the violence of the martyrs is problematic. Paradoxically, a chief complaint of modern liberal theologians like Gustavo Gutiérrez is that some theologies of suffering accept violence and oppression too readily. The martyrs should fight more! Take, for example, the *Martyrs of Lyons*. In the story of Biblis, it is the application of additional torture that brings Biblis "to her senses." It is, in some ways, a good thing because, according to the author of the story, it brings her salvation. There's a subtle implication, though, that torture and suffering lead to salvation. The theological justification for suffering as a good thing is often tied to the idea of imitating the passion of Jesus. The suffering of Christ was a good thing, so suffering *like* Christ is also a good thing. As the author of the *Martyrdom of Polycarp* would say, "We love the martyrs as disciples and imitators of the Lord."[21]

This idea of accepting suffering and martyrdom willingly as an imitation of the death of Jesus is found throughout Christian martyrdom literature. In theological terms it is called the "moral exemplar" model of salvation and refers to the idea that the death of Jesus saves us by offering a model of self-sacrificial love that we ourselves can imitate.[22] Self-sacrificial love is still highly regarded in modern society. Many people expect parents, mothers especially, to be willing to risk their own lives in order to save those of their children.[23] We think of those who put themselves in harm's way for others—police officers and firefighters, for instance—as heroes, but we also think of certain kinds of self-sacrifice as expected.

As much as we admire those who are willing to sacrifice themselves for others, there are also circumstances in which this is inappropriate. Modern theologians have criticized the idea that imitating the suffering of Christ means obedience and submission in circumstances of oppression. The idea that suffering is personally redemptive—an idea that lies at the heart of Christian ideas about martyrdom—has had and can have a damaging impact in the lives of many. If the idea of suffering unjustly is praised, then people might be encouraged to stay in dangerous or personally harmful situations because it's what Jesus and the martyrs would have done. Black womanist theologian Delores Williams, for instance, points out how the valorization of redemptive suffering has led to the subjugation of African American women.[24] In a similar way studies have demonstrated that the doctrine of redemptive suffering "has encouraged compliant and passive responses by women suffering in abusive relationships."[25] As the Archbishops' Council, a leadership body within the Church of England, recently stated in the set of guidelines *Responding to Domestic Abuse*, "There are major objections to comparing the suffering resulting from domestic abuse with the suffering of Jesus and Christian disciples or martyrs."[26]

This is not merely ancient violence; these are serious pressing issues that continue to have relevance today. It's easy to see how martyrs perpetuate that Christly model of accepting unjust suffering as good. Some of the martyrdom accounts actually encourage their audiences to seek out martyrdom. The Donatist *Acts of the Abitinian Martyrs* describes its purpose as twofold: as a means of preparation for martyrdom and as a form of memorialization. The Donatist author of the *Martyrdom of Maximian and Isaac* goes further:

> Now brothers and sisters, all these conditions which led them to the heavenly kingdom come round to you. These exemplars compel you. This situation drove them on first to these glories for your sake. The multitude of your own confessions made you teachers through your oft repeated professions of faith. Now they advise you concerning martyrdom. Their pattern which encourages others likewise now encourages you. Now they are holding out their arms to you from heaven, waiting for the time when they will run to meet you.[27]

The image of martyrs stretching out their arms from heaven beckoning members of the congregation to join them is as powerful as it is disturbing. The message is not just, "Be like the martyrs," but much more specifically, "The martyrs want you to join them by suffering."

At the same time, these criticisms are part of the misguided impression that early Christian martyrs *are* passive and accepting of violence against them. The martyrs, however, are not portrayed as meek or helpless. Their acceptance of death should not be confused with an acceptance of oppression. In the *Martyrdom of Marian and James*, the martyr's statement that he is a Christian is a proclamation that arouses a frenzy of activity:

> And by this prophecy not only did the martyr's faith triumph over the pagans; it sounded a trumpet-call, as it were, to arouse his brethren to emulate his courage, so that in the midst of these temporal plagues the saints of God might grasp at the opportunity for a death that was precious and holy.[28]

The martyrs are not powerless or even disarmed in the face of such persecution. In some circumstances their confessions are acts of violence: the confession is a "spiritual sword" against the demonic proconsuls.[29] In the end, the tyrant is "torn asunder" by the battle line of the Lord's unconquered martyrs, and the devil lies defeated and ruined. The violence of the martyr's confession is problematic, but it is a powerful antidote to the idea that the downtrodden should be content with or even embrace their lot.[30]

Justice and Revenge

WHEN PEOPLE THINK OF saints, they imagine that they are kind, sweet, humble, and charitable. They are the embodiment of self-sacrificial Christian virtues: individuals who love God so much that they are willing to lay down their lives for him. For the most part, they are. Early martyrs, however, tend to have an edge to them. Accompanying their defiance, endurance, and resilience is a quiet confidence. They are confident not only in their future vindication, but in the destruction of their accusers and attackers.

When people think of Perpetua and her companions in the arena in Carthage, they tend to think of innocence and youth. Perpetua and Felicity were exposed and vulnerable. Milk still dripped from new mother Felicity's breasts. They were weak, alone, unable to defend themselves, and unwilling to fight. They sang songs and prayed. But there was a steely resolve to the martyrs, a defiant streak—not only confidence that they were going to a better place when they died, but certainty that they would see the destruction of their enemies in the future. The night before the games, as the condemned celebrated their final meal, a crowd gathered at the prison. Presumably the people had come to take a good look at the prisoners who were to be executed the next day. The martyrs were not happy to be treated as curiosities. They "boldly flung their words at the crowd, threatening them with the judgment of God." Saturus goes a step further and says, "Take a good look at our faces, so that you will be able to recognize us on that day."[31] Whatever the crowd might think, Saturus does not refer to the contest in the arena, but rather to *that* day: the Day of Judgment. On that day, Saturus implies, the martyrs will be there, watching. Saturus wants the crowd to remember their faces, so that when they face God and are punished for their crimes, they will recognize that, in the grand scheme of things, the martyrs won.

Many martyrs imply that their judges and executioners will face judgment after they die. Others go further, implying that they themselves will participate in eschatological judgment. In the North African *Martyrdom of Marian and James*, an embellished, almost fraudulent account based on the *Passion of Perpetua and Felicity*, the martyr Marian has a vision of heaven. In his vision he arrives at a heavenly courtroom, in the center of which is a towering tribunal. Instead of an ordinary Roman prefect, a judge of handsome countenance is sitting there, and the platform is so high that instead of one step, there are many. The judge is ordering that people be executed, but when Marian arrives he hears a voice saying that they should "bring up Marian." Marian looks and sees Cyprian, the former bishop of Carthage who was recently executed, at the judge's right hand. Cyprian reaches out and helps Marian up the scaffold, and Cyprian and Marian sit and watch as the others are tried.

That Marian does not receive judgment and is set apart is expected. As we've already discussed, martyrs assumed that by dying for Christ, they would not face judgment in the afterlife. This scene goes further than that. Both Cyprian and Marian are sitting with the "judge" on the side of judgment. Although the scene does not explicitly describe Marian judging the dead, and we cannot be certain that the scene refers to eschatological judgment, the fact that he is elevated over the masses and sits alongside God suggests that he is participating in the administration of heavenly justice. As with Saturus, there's an expectation that on the Day of Judgment the martyrs will get to voyeuristically enjoy the judgment of the dead.

It's easy to empathize with the martyrs. Why wouldn't they look forward to the downfall of their enemies? Why wouldn't they want to be there to see it? Who hasn't entertained the occasional revenge fantasy about someone responsible for a wrong? And the idea has biblical roots. It goes back to the book of Daniel, to the horrible punishment visited on the families of Daniel's accusers and to the expectation that the wicked will be resurrected to shame and ignominy. It becomes explicit in the emergence and development of early Christian ideas about hell, in which persecutors and sinners suffer exquisite eternal torments. In the parable of the rich man and Lazarus in the Gospel of Luke (16:19–31), the rich man, condemned to hell for no other reason than being wealthy, is able, as he is tormented in the afterlife, to see the vindicated beggar Lazarus. The same sentiment is more explicitly laid out by Tertullian in his description of the afterlife. Tertullian imagines himself rejoicing in heaven and laughing at the fate of the damned:

> What ample breadth of sights there will be then [when we are in heaven]! At which shall one gaze in wonder? At which shall I laugh? At which rejoice? At which exult, when I see so many kings who were proclaimed to have been taken up into heaven, groaning in the deepest darkness. And when I see those governors, persecutors of the Lord's name, melting in the flames more savage than those with which they insolently raged against Christians! . . . I believe that they [these spectacles] are more pleasing than the circus or both of the enclosures, or than any racetrack.[32]

The existentialist philosopher Nietzsche argued that this perspective, this revenge fantasy, was connected to the Christian rejection of traditional notions of flourishing. He argued that Christians had inherited from the Jews an "unfathomable hatred" that led them to argue that "only those who suffer are good; only the poor, the powerless, the lowly are good; the suffering, the deprived, the sick, the ugly, are the only pious people."[33]

Nietzsche's statements about the emergence of this kind of re-venge fantasy in Christianity are overly simplistic and anti-Semitic, but his assessment of Christian understandings of the afterlife as vengeful has some truth to it. This interest in sanitized revenge is not limited to those interested in martyrdom. It's a larger phenom-enon that comes up frequently in Jewish and Christian apocalyptic literature. It may not fit with our understanding of the selflessness and kindness of the saints, but in their literary portrayal the martyrs, like other Christians, eagerly looked forward to the Day of Judg-ment, so that they could have their revenge on those who mocked and doubted them.

The Sunday school myth of martyrdom does not emphasize, or even acknowledge, the vengeful side of early Christian theologies of martyrdom and justice. Martyrs are portrayed as sweet and forgiving. Those aspects of early Christian martyrdom that seem unpalatable or morally repugnant and that might complicate our picture of Christian martyrdom are whitewashed and sanitized. If we are going to appeal to martyrdom in modern discourse, however, we cannot misrepresent our heritage. We cannot perpetuate the myth that Christian martyrs are always forgiving.

Rewards in Heaven

ONE OF THE THINGS I often hear from my students is that Chris-tian martyrs are different from and better than other martyrs, because they die without having any ulterior motive. They die for Christ and for Christianity, not because they want to "get something" in return. This is in contrast, I'm told, to martyrs in Islam, who are promised seventy virgins in heaven. If we put aside the risk of exhaustion that might accompany tending to a heavenly harem of this size, there's no doubting the appeal of an idyllic eternal life surrounded by dedicated and compliant young women. My students are wrong, though, if they think that martyrdom in Christianity doesn't confer any rewards on its practitioners. To really get a sense of what's better about being a martyr, we have to compare what people thought about the fate of the martyrs with that of ordinary Christians.

As a culture we don't like to think about death. In fact, when polled about how they would like to die, an alarmingly significant proportion of people say that they want to live forever (as if this is a viable option). Christians are no exception. When someone dies, we comfort their relatives by telling them that their loved one is now in heaven, with Jesus, or at peace. We have good intentions, but this isn't technically what most of the Bible says about the afterlife, and this isn't what most branches of Christianity—ancient or modern—actually teach. Roman Catholics maintain that people go to purgatory; Protestants tend to think—with Paul—that the dead will be resurrected at the end of the world; and almost all Christians think that the final decision on our postmortem fate will be made on Judgment Day. Until then we will sleep in the ground, tread water in purgatory, or wait in heavenly holding pens.

In the ancient world there was a considerable diversity of opinion about the fate of the dead. In Christianity ideas about immortality and resurrection appear to have developed on something of an ad hoc basis. There was a basic principle of judgment at the end of time, but it was skeletal in comparison with Dante's circles of hell. The earliest followers of Jesus did not initially think about the fate of the dead. They thought that Jesus would return, bringing about the end of the world, within their own lifetimes. They had good reason for thinking this. In one conversation with the disciples, Jesus had told them, "There are some standing here who will not taste death until they see that the kingdom of God has come with power" (Mark 9:1; Matt. 16:28; Luke 9:27).[34] The understanding that the end of the world would arrive within their own lifetimes meant that the first generation didn't have to give too much thought to the question of what would happen to the faithful between death and Judgment Day.

As time went on Christians realized that the end of the world was not just around the corner. In the beginning this realization seems to have caused unrest and confusion. In 1 Thessalonians, Paul has to reassure the Thessalonians that those who have "fallen asleep" would in fact be resurrected at the end of the world. Paul's argument for the resurrection of the dead, as intimated in 1 Corinthians 15, may have won the day in the end, but it was not at all clear to ancient Christians precisely what would happen after death. There was great disagreement. Some early Christians appear to have subscribed to ideas of astral immortality, others to the idea of eschatological resurrection of the body, others to the immortality of the soul. As to the timing of these events, that was also unclear.

This was not the case for martyrs. At the moment of their deaths they proceeded immediately to the heavenly realm, where they would receive the rewards of martyrdom. Death becomes the moment of departure to God. The immediacy of the martyr's transition to heaven is emphasized in a number of stories. In the *Acts of the Scillitan Martyrs*, Nartzalus declares, "Today we are martyrs in heaven!"[35] In the same way Polycarp's last prayer asks God, "May I be received this day among [the martyrs] before your face."[36] Other martyrs actually hurry to their deaths: the third-century martyr Pionius purportedly says that he is hurrying so that he might "awake all the more quickly, manifesting the resurrection of the dead."[37] Of course we do not know whether martyrs actually said these things, but at a minimum the early Christians who wrote these accounts and heard them read out believed them to be true. Whatever the eventual fate of Christians in general, all martyrs went directly to heaven.

As a reward, bypassing the interim period between death and the Day of Judgment is significant. The martyrs do not have to sleep in the ground or wait in purgatory or some other shadowy realm for the second coming. They are already comfortably ensconced in the heavenly court.

Their rewards are greater, though, for they avoid eschatological judgment. Their fate has already been positively decided. If there were pervasive or widely held beliefs about the afterlife among ancient Christians, one of them was the judgment of the dead. All good things must come to an end, and this end is most properly marked with eschatological judgment. Judgment was not, for the majority of people, optional. Paul himself writes, "All of us must appear before the judgment seat of Christ, so that each may receive recompense for what has been done in the body, whether good or evil" (2 Cor. 5:10). If there was one crime that guaranteed punishment, it was denying Christ. In Mark, Jesus states, "Those who are ashamed of me and of my words in this adulterous and sinful generation, of them the Son of Man will also be ashamed when he comes in the glory of his Father with the holy angels" (8:38). If Christians in general were confident that they would fare well at the heavenly tribunal, martyrs were sure of it. For the martyrs, the ordinary rules of judgment did not apply. Not only did they go directly to heaven at their deaths; they escaped judgment altogether. To paraphrase the words of Polycarp, that's not bad for an hour's work.

Once in heaven, the martyrs participated in the heavenly banquet, feasting and rejoicing with Christ until the end of time. A commonplace throughout the martyrdom stories is that the martyrs receive crowns in heaven. The origin of these crowns was probably in the crowns given to the victors in athletic contests, but in heaven they are symbols of the elevated status and special rank of the martyrs. Revelation goes further, promising those who conquer like the Lamb (i.e., die) a seat on the throne of God (3:21). A seat on the throne of God implies not just exalted status, but also, potentially, that the martyr co-rules with God in heaven.[38] This is indeed a lofty reward for a mere human being.

Not only do martyrs get to go to heaven more quickly than other Christians and enjoy a better kind of afterlife; the quality of that afterlife is predicated on how much they suffer. In the *Martyrdom of Marian and James* the martyr Aemilian reveals a vision in which he converses with his pagan brother. Aemilian's brother asks him, "Will all of you [martyrs] receive equally the reward of heavenly gifts without distinction?" Aemilian compares the martyrs to the stars of heaven and says that some will be greater than others. His brother pushes further and

asks, "Is there some distinction? Which of you are higher in merit-
ing the goodwill of the Lord?" Aemilian answers, "There are two
[of us] who are superior to the rest . . . those whose victory is slower
and with greatest difficulty, these receive the more glorious crown."[39]
Even though this is a vision, the message is very clear. Those martyrs
who suffer the most have "more glorious crowns" in heaven. If there
is, in this formulation of the afterlife at least, a ranking of the martyrs
predicated on suffering, then we can infer from this that the rewards
of those who are not martyred are even smaller.

Not all martyrs are fixated on their heavenly rewards. Others are
more pragmatic and principled. The Roman martyr Apollonius, who
probably died at the end of the second century but whose story comes
from centuries later, is willing to allow for some doubt. In a lengthy
speech the martyr is purported to have said that even if, as the Romans
think, it is a mistake to say that the soul is immortal, that there is
judgment after death, and that the good soul will be rewarded at the
resurrection when God will judge everyone, then "we would gladly
endure this deception, for by it we have learned to live the good life,
looking forward to the hope to come, even while suffering."[40] Apollonius is willing to concede both that there may not be rewards after
death and that it would be worth dying for Christ anyway, because he
has taught Christians how to live a good life. The character of Apollonius more closely resembles what modern Christians think of when
they think of martyrs. He appears as a kind of narrative forerunner
to modern martyrs like Oscar Romero, but he represents a minority
opinion in the early church. Most stories about martyrs emphasize
the centrality of heavenly rewards.

Of course, we don't know what the martyrs actually said. These
statements tell us what early Christians *thought* about martyrdom.
Martyrdom had some distinct advantages over dying as a faithful
Christian at the end of one's natural life. Although there are no nubile
young virgins to greet Christian martyrs, the martyrs go directly to
heaven and not only avoid judgment, but can actually participate in
the judgment of their enemies. Once in heaven the martyrs receive

crowns of immortality, victor's palms, and potentially thrones. In contrast, other Christians had to wait until the end of time, hope that their conduct had secured them reward, and then join the ranks of the heavenly choir. There are no references to crowns or thrones for the average dearly departed Christian. There was, according to some early Christians, hierarchy in the distribution of heavenly rewards: the greater the suffering, the greater the reward.

What this means, of course, is that there are demonstrable advantages to being a martyr. The fate of martyrs is secure, and their rewards are immediate and guaranteed. In a world in which Christians are convinced of the reality of the afterlife, martyrdom is an easy choice. If the decision is between an hour suffering now followed by an eternity of rewards versus a few years scratching together a life now followed by an eternity of torment, then there really is no choice. This is just good investing.

Some martyrs even looked forward to watching their tormentors be judged and suffer at the end of time. They taunted their executioners that they would see them at the Last Judgment and threatened them with eternal damnation. These stories show that there was an element of self-interest in Christian martyrdom and that those who died did so in anticipation of heavenly rewards, rewards that often outstripped those of other deceased Christians.

Conclusion

CHRISTIAN MARTYRS ARE COMMONLY portrayed as having a blend of humility, courage, determination, love, and selflessness. We are led to believe that they do not instigate their own arrests, offer themselves for death, commit acts of violence, or behave in ways at odds with modern teachings about suicide. One of the things that is thought to make Christian martyrs better than other martyrs is that their actions are motivated by goodness and love. They do not have any interest in or expectation of reward in the hereafter. They die as meek lambs out of love for Jesus.

This picture, as we have seen, is overly simplistic. Even if this is generally true, it is not *universally* true. Many martyrs died deaths that were, by modern standards, suicidal. It was not, as heresiologists want us to believe, only heretics who "rushed" toward death. There was little difference between the behavior of orthodox Christians and the behavior of heretical ones. Although only a few martyrs were physically violent, the imagery and language of martyrdom are aggressive and replete with fantasies of vengeful justice. Christians saw themselves at odds with the world and eagerly anticipated the suffering and destruction of those who oppressed them. These are not the meek and forgiving saints of Sunday school. They are, quite literally, soldiers for Christ.

So far we have seen that many cherished and widely held beliefs about martyrs are far from the mark, that persecution was not as severe as Christian authors and two thousand years of tradition would lead us to believe, and that we have very little evidence for what the martyrs themselves actually said. Given that the myth is so far from reality, we have to wonder how we ended up with this picture. Where does this myth of persecution and martyrdom come from?

CHAPTER SEVEN

The Invention of the Persecuted Church

IN HIS 1867 INTRODUCTION TO John Foxe's *Book of the Martyrs*, William Bramley-Moore notes, "The history of Christian martyrdom is, in fact, the history of Christianity itself."[1] Given everything that we now know about the overblown nature of the idea that Christians were continually persecuted, we have to wonder where this idea originates. How did the history of Christianity become so inextricably linked to the history of persecution?

There are seeds of this idea in the writings of the New Testament, of course. Followers of Jesus expected to be persecuted. In the Gospels Jesus tells his disciples that they should expect to find themselves arrested and brought before judges in tribunals. He counsels them that they should not be concerned about this, because the Holy Spirit will tell them what to say (Matt. 10:17–20; Luke 12:11–12). Similarly, in the speech immediately before his death, Stephen weaves a history of the Jewish people in which God's chosen ones have always been rejected and maligned by the Jews (Acts 7). Read alongside one another, these and other scriptural passages lay the foundations for the notion that Christians were always persecuted in the past and should expect to be persecuted in the future. They do not, however, speak to the reality of the situation at the time or in the years to follow. Even taken together with the shrill rhetoric of early church writers like Irenaeus,

Justin Martyr, and Tertullian, where did this history of a church of martyrs come from?

Antecedents can be found in the New Testament and writings of the early church fathers, but the idea of the persecuted church truly developed in the fourth century and later, with the dawn of Christian historiography. The credit seems to lie with historians like Eusebius of Caesarea, Christianity's first great church historian, and with anonymous hagiographers who preserved, edited, and invented the overwhelming majority of the martyrdom stories we have today.

It's probably clear how dependent we are on Eusebius just from how many times I have had to refer to him up until this point. Eusebius is our sole source for the names and narratives of a large number of the martyrs in the first three centuries of the common era. Drawing upon the work of earlier authors, Eusebius composed an account of the rise of Christianity that forms the outline for modern histories of the church. If we take Eusebius out of the equation, then our knowledge of the second and third centuries becomes very clouded.

It was Eusebius who made martyrdom a nearly continuous presence in the life of the church. Christians had described themselves as suffering for Christ long before Eusebius, but the process of redefining the *church* as a persecuted church was really initiated in his *Church History*. Eusebius was willing to grant that there were good emperors who had not persecuted the Christians and even massaged the facts when it came to the reputations of good emperors, but these can fade into the background when compared with the frequent descriptions of execution.[2] This is not just documenting the past, though. As we see in this chapter, Eusebius, like all historians, had an agenda and purpose in writing. His portrayal of Christianity as a church of martyrs was strategic. It allowed him to use martyrs to further other claims he wanted to make.

In this chapter we look at how and for what purposes Eusebius furthered this myth of Christian martyrdom. In the nineteenth century, Eusebius was branded a liar for his unfair representation of the early church.[3] This may be a vast exaggeration, but it is true that Eusebius tells only the parts of Christian history that he deems worthwhile. He suppresses the voices of those who disagree with him and ignores information that does not fit with his argument. Moreover the *way* that he chooses to tell history shapes the way we have understood it.

In some ways it is odd that Eusebius writes about persecution at all. He lived the first forty years of his life in a period of peace and completed the *Church History* during the reign of a promising pro-Christian emperor, Constantine. He acknowledged that before the Great Persecution there was a period of peace during which Christians were promoted to positions of authority.[4] Given that Eusebius knows about these things, we have to ask why he writes the history of the church in the way that he does—what is the myth of Christian martyrdom doing for Eusebius?

What we see in the course of this chapter is that the development of a history of martyrdom was a deliberate and strategic attempt to improve the image of Christians, to bolster the position of the church hierarchy, and to provide security for orthodoxy. Eusebius uses the history of the martyrs as a means of drawing battle lines for the established church orthodoxy against heresy. What we think is the truth about persecuted martyrs from the early church is in fact the retrojection of issues about orthodoxy from the fourth century when the church was more powerful and more centralized. And the church in the centuries that followed bought this retrojection hook, line, and sinker.

Eusebius's History of Persecution

EUSEBIUS WAS BORN IN Caesarea in Palestine and studied under the Christian teacher Pamphilus during the Great Persecution before he became bishop in 314/5.[5] He composed three documents that relate to Christian martyrdom.[6] The first is *On the Martyrs of Palestine*, a collection of accounts of martyrdoms that took place in Palestine during the reign of the emperor Diocletian. Some of the martyrs of the Great Persecution were apparently known to Eusebius personally, and he dwells on their suffering and deaths far longer than those of the others. He also composed a now lost compendium of Christian martyrs.[7] The third text is Eusebius's *Church History*, an account of the origins of the church from Jesus Christ up to Eusebius's own time.

The *Church History* was produced in multiple editions. The seven books of the original version were begun and completed during the period of peace that preceded the Diocletian persecution. At the time Christians imagined that this détente was permanent; they had no expectation of future violence. It was during this period too that Eusebius had begun to jot down the stories of the martyrs in his now lost collection. During the Great Persecution, Eusebius traveled outside of Palestine, to Phoenicia, to Egypt, and possibly even as far as Arabia.[8] He was apparently arrested and imprisoned, although one of his fellow prisoners would later accuse him of being a coward and traitor.[9] It was only in 311, after the emperor Galerius had decreed toleration, that Eusebius decided to write the *Martyrs of Palestine* and appended a short version of it to the *Church History* with a concluding statement about persecution under the emperor Maximinus Daia. Soon enough, however, Eusebius began to feel that this was inadequate and started work on the second edition of the *Church History*, which would come to number ten books. All of Eusebius's writings about persecution were composed during periods when Eusebius himself and Christians more broadly were no longer experiencing persecution. They were written in periods of peace.

Just because Eusebius knew and was interested in martyrdom does not, of course, mean that he was interested in preserving the facts any more than the other editors of martyrdom stories we have examined. The fact that there is some literary and thematic overlap between the martyrdom stories preserved independently from Eusebius, comments made by Eusebius in the *Church History*, and his description of the martyrs of Palestine suggests that Eusebius was either altering or borrowing from his sources. One brief example should suffice here. In Eusebius's version of the *Martyrdom of Polycarp*, the body of

Polycarp is taken and burned by the Romans just in case the Christians might switch to worshipping Polycarp instead of Christ.[10] The same concern and justification for withholding of the body appear in other writings by Eusebius. Late in the *Church History* Eusebius says that the bodies of martyrs are dug up and cast into the sea "lest any, as they thought, regarding them as gods, might worship them lying in their sepulchers."[11] It's curious that the only two references to Romans taking an interest in the bodies of martyrs for this reason are both connected with Eusebius. Would Roman authorities have been especially interested in Christians worshipping martyrs in their tombs—particularly when, during the Diocletian period, the Roman solution to that problem would have been to destroy the sepulchers themselves?

The concern about martyrs' bodies fits with Eusebius's agenda. He likes martyrs, but he wouldn't want anyone to get the wrong idea and start worshipping them. We cannot be completely certain in which direction the lines of influence go. Was Eusebius so charmed by the *Martyrdom of Polycarp*'s turn of phrase that he transferred its argument to other portions of the *Church History*? Either Eusebius borrowed from his sources or interpolated into them. In either case, though, what this example shows us is that Eusebius's interests were not strictly in recording historical information, but also in providing an interpretation of the past that fits with his vision for the church.

When it comes to the *Church History*, scholars have puzzled over what kind of book this is. Is this part of the historical tradition of the ancient Greeks? Is this, as Eusebius insists on referring to the Christians as a "race," a national history? Is it literary or philosophical history? Or is it, by virtue of the fact that it describes events pertaining to Christians, a new kind of writing that dropped out of heaven? One thing is for sure: Eusebius calls his work *historia* and wants us to think of it as such. In an exhausting 167-word opening sentence, he follows the conventions of Greek historical writing and lays out the objectives of his work. He intends to describe "the succession of the holy apostles" from the time of Jesus to his own day; the important transactions reported in the history of the church by those who governed it, those who were ambassadors for the Word; those who "fell into utmost error" (the heretics), who ravaged "the flock of Christ unsparingly like grievous wolves"; the disasters that befell the Jews as a result of their plot against Jesus; the "wars waged by the heathens" against the Christians; and the character of those who "underwent the contest of blood and torture."[12]

It is interesting that when Eusebius describes his own work, he invites comparisons between different aspects of this history, especially between the history of persecution and the history of heresy. For example, there is a great deal of military terminology in the preface to the story of the *Martyrs of Lyons*:

> Other writers of history record the victories of war and trophies won from enemies, the skill of generals, and the manly bravery of soldiers, defiled with blood and with innumerable slaughters for the sake of children and country. . . . But our narrative of the government of God will record in ineffaceable letters the most peaceful wars waged in behalf of the peace of the soul, and will tell of men doing brave deeds for truth rather than country, and for piety rather than dearest friends. It will hand down to imperishable remembrance the discipline and the much-tried fortitude of the athletes of religion, the trophies won from demons, the victories over invisible enemies, and the crowns placed upon all their heads.[13]

Here Eusebius contrasts his work with other historical narratives, narratives that deal with "victories of war and trophies won from enemies, the skill of generals, and . . . slaughters for the sake of children and country" with his own record of "*peaceful* wars waged in behalf of the peace of the soul, . . . men doing brave deeds for the sake of truth" and between "athletes for religion" and "demons . . . [and] invisible enemies."

In the past, he tells us, the historians described the battles of those who fought for the sake of petty things like offspring and country, but the Christians, he says, are focused on a kind of "warfare" that is better than that of their predecessors, because it is not interested in this world. He is recording the battle between warriors for truth and piety and the heretics. The enemy forces are the heretics who attack the Christians "like grievous wolves" and the unseen forces that provoked the martyrdom of the righteous. The fact that Eusebius describes the heretics as being like ravenous wild animals takes the comparison further. They are not just grouped with the persecutors by virtue of the fact that they are opposing the Christians; they are like the wild animals that the Christians fought in the arena. The effect of this is to blur the line between the wolflike heretics who attack the truth of the church and the unseen forces who attack the martyrs.

It's subtle, but linking a group you dislike to a group that *everyone* dislikes is a powerful rhetorical trick. The same thing happens today when a political group is accused of "terrorizing" others. After 9/11 the term conjures up images of violence and external forces conspiring against Americans. So even if those in the group in question are actually American, they are instantly aligned with malevolent external forces. They're not even Americans anymore. In this situation subtler language is actually *more* effective. If someone came out and called me a terrorist, I'd defend myself. But if they used language applied to terrorism to describe me, I'd have a more difficult time pinning down the errors in what they were saying.

The same thing is happening here in Eusebius. Readers come away with the impression that the heretics and the demons are in league with one another. The orthodox Christians, the church, are just like the martyrs. The heretics that Eusebius is denouncing are just like the demons that attack the Christians.[14] Even from the beginning, then, Eusebius starts weaving the themes of his history together, so that he can group different sets of opponents into a single class. In this situation martyrs now stand for the church. They become a kind of litmus test for orthodoxy and truth. If a martyr endorsed a bishop, then we know that bishop to be good. If a martyr condemned a heretic, then we should steer well clear. Eusebius uses this strategy throughout the *Church History* in order to support ideas and individuals in which he believes and denounce those with whom he disagrees.

Martyrs and Heresy

When martyrdom stories are printed in modern collections, they are excerpted from other texts, from either medieval manuscripts or larger histories, such as Eusebius's *Church History*. This provides us with useful resources for the study of martyrdom but sometimes conceals what the authors of these sources were trying to do. In the *Church History* Eusebius interlaces his stories about the deaths of martyrs with anecdotes about things the martyrs said and did during their lives. These anecdotes almost always relate some kind of official church teaching or describe the martyrs condemning their heretical contemporaries. The result is that Eusebius is able to make the martyrs into the champions of orthodoxy and the natural opponents of heresy. For readers, who see martyrs as the champions of the church, the martyrs model how to interact with heretics. The rhetorical effect is a lot like endorsements today: if a former president whom I admire endorses a particular candidate today, I might be inclined to support that candidate purely because I admire the former president. In the same way, when important and well-respected martyrs were used to support Eusebius's orthodoxy, then admirers of the martyrs were also more likely to support Eusebius's orthodoxy.

For example, in a discussion of the goings-on in the church in Rome in the mid-second century, Eusebius uses the martyred bishop Polycarp to condemn the heterodox Marcionites. The Marcionites were a group of Christians active in Rome in the second century who used as their canon only the Gospel of Luke and the writings of Paul. They were denounced, among other reasons, for rejecting the

Old Testament. In Eusebius's version, Polycarp is explicitly associated with the condemnation of the heretic Marcion. Eusebius relays a story, derived from the second-century heresiologist Irenaeus but not present in other independent copies of the martyrdom account, that Polycarp once encountered Marcion on the street in Rome and denounced him:

> And Polycarp himself, when Marcion once met him and said, "Do you know us?" replied, "I know the firstborn of Satan." Such caution did the apostles and their disciples exercise that they might not even converse with any of those who perverted the truth; as Paul also said, "A man who is a heretic, after the first and second admonition, reject; knowing he who is such is subverted, and sins, being condemned of himself."[15]

The behavior modeled by Polycarp is the act of withdrawing oneself from the company of schismatics and the public denouncement of those deemed heretics. The model for orthodox Christian interaction with heretics that Eusebius is holding up for his audience is one in which the good Christian will completely avoid the company of the heretic.

The story is very similar to another anecdote about saintly avoidance of heresy. Eusebius writes:

> On the authority of Polycarp, that the apostle John once entered a bath to bathe; but, learning that Cerinthus was within, he sprang from the place and rushed out of the door, for he could not bear to remain under the same roof with him. And he advised those who were with him to do the same, saying, "Let us flee, lest the bath fall; for Cerinthus, the enemy of the truth, is within."[16]

It is interesting to note how the pattern of saintly self-segregation reproduces the lines of apostolic tradition in Asia Minor.

According to Eusebius, Polycarp had learned Christianity at the feet of the evangelist John as a catechumen.[17] The evangelist, of course, had learned Christianity from Jesus himself. The quaint, almost romantic picture of Polycarp as a child allows Eusebius to use Irenaeus's stories about Polycarp to construct a pedigree for his bishops that stretched back to Jesus. The connection between John and Polycarp is then restated in terms of their attitude toward heresy. Not only had Polycarp learned the teachings of Jesus from the apostle John; he had learned how best to behave when one runs across a heretic. The weaving of histories of apostolic succession and martyrdom into his ecclesiastical history allows Eusebius to amplify the rhetorical effect of his refutation of schismatics. He takes the authority of the martyr and marries it to apostolic orthodoxy in order to further his own agenda. This is about using an important hero in the ancient church to silence dissenters in his own time. It would be akin to a modern politician "discovering" a letter from George Washington that makes a definitive statement on gay marriage or some other controversial issue. It would have a devastating impact on the modern political debate. This is exactly what Eusebius is doing. He is using traditions about apostles and the martyrs (the ancient version of the founding fathers) to propagate his own views.

A subtler instance of Polycarp rejecting heresy emerges out of the martyrdom account itself. The Phrygian Quintus, whom we encountered in the *Martyrdom of Polycarp*, presents himself to the authorities and asks to be martyred, only to recant at the last moment. As we discussed earlier, the description of Quintus as a Phrygian has been interpreted by some as a veiled allusion to the New Prophecy (or Montanism), an ecstatic religious practice popular in Asia Minor and Carthage in the third century. The New Prophecy emerged in Phrygia, and its adherents have traditionally been portrayed as eager and enthusiastic believers in martyrdom whose reckless, provocative conduct led to their executions.[18]

There are two versions of the story: the version preserved in Eusebius and a version attributed to Pionius, who later died as a martyr himself. It is unclear whether, in the Pionian version, we are meant to understand that Quintus actually is a Montanist. In the early third century, when the New Prophecy was in its infancy, the name "Phrygian" might not have connoted Montanist.[19] By the time of Eusebius, however, the use of the term "Phrygian heresy" as a cipher for followers of Montanus was well established, especially in the writings of Eusebius himself, as was the orthodox caricature that the Montanists were especially enthusiastic martyrs.[20]

But Eusebius is not content to leave the denouncement of the Phrygian heresy at that. He goes further and edits the *Martyrdom of Polycarp* to make the disjuncture of orthodoxy and heresy even more apparent to readers. In the Pionian version, the contrast between Quintus and Polycarp rests on the fact that Quintus offers himself for martyrdom, whereas Polycarp is patient, "in accordance with the Gospel." Eusebius removes the reference to Gospel-style martyrdom and focuses on Quintus's cowardice. He describes Quintus as belonging to the "race of Phrygians," an emendation that draws out the contrast with the God-fearing "race of Christians."[21] The identification of the Christians as a race is found in both the Pionian and Eusebian versions of the account, but only Eusebius uses the category of race to describe Quintus. In doing so Eusebius widens the gap between the orthodox Christians and the heretics. The contrast between Polycarp and Quintus is not just one of adherence to or deviation from the Gospel; it becomes, in Eusebius's version, a question of race and ethnicity. One is now either a follower of the martyrs and member of the race of Christians, or one is not. The drawing together of two components of human identity works to widen the chasm between us and them: if you are not with us doctrinally, you are not even of the same race.

The same phenomenon is at work in Eusebius's presentation of the *Martyrs of Lyons*. Having described the sufferings, trials, and glorious deaths of the martyrs in the opening of book 5, Eusebius turns to things that the martyrs had purportedly said and done while they were imprisoned. There's a sudden shift in the tone and style of this section of the letter. Whereas the bulk of the letter (5.1.1–57) is preserved as a continuous narrative, this section (5.2) and the heresiological letters produced by the martyrs of Lyons and referenced by Eusebius (5.3) are disjointed and quite different in content from the narrative of their trials and execution. They deal with the status of the martyrs, their relationship to Christ, and their views of contemporary heretical groups such as the Montanists. It is possible, therefore, that these antiheretical excerpts have been appended by Eusebius to the account of the martyrs' deaths as part of his larger compositional plan.

According to an additional letter, to which Eusebius only refers, the martyrs of Lyons composed letters railing against the adherents of the New Prophecy, the Montanists:

> The followers of Montanus, Alcibiades and Theodotus in Phrygia were now first giving wide circulation to their assumption in regard to prophecy—for the many other miracles that, through the gift of God, were still wrought in the different churches caused their prophesying to be readily credited by many—and as dissension arose concerning them, the brethren in Gaul set forth their own prudent and most orthodox judgment in the matter, and published also several epistles from the witnesses that had been put to death among them. These they sent, while they were still in prison, to the brethren throughout Asia and Phrygia, and also to Eleutherus, who was then bishop of Rome, negotiating for the peace of the churches.[22]

It's difficult to know if this additional correspondence between Gaul and the other churches existed. It's curious that a group of martyrs from a church that had no institutional pedigree would take it upon themselves to write this kind of letter. The frequency with which Eusebius refers to martyrs as defenders of orthodoxy makes it more likely that this comes from Eusebius himself. Regardless, Eusebius describes the martyrs as "prudent and . . . orthodox" and as supporting the work of the bishop Eleutherus. There's a unity in Eusebius's axis of orthodoxy: martyrs and bishops working together to condemn the heretics.

This is Eusebius's brilliant insight: by equating bishops with martyrs and persecutors with heretics, he can detach the rhetoric of persecution from the reality of persecution and use it to condemn those he opposes.[23] Eusebius knew that there were bad bishops and that there had been heretical martyrs, but in those moments where he makes heretics the new persecutors he lays the groundwork for a dangerous idea: that those who disagree with us are the same as those who persecute us and that even in periods of peace the church is always under attack. It is an idea that remains with us today.

Martyrs and Bishops

When conspiracy theories about early Christianity circulate, they often depict an organized cohort of Catholic priests and bishops, meeting in secret at night in hooded cloaks in order to fabricate evidence, mislead or control the populace, and generally work mischief for their own ends. For those who enjoy a good iconoclastic conspiracy, it's an appealing image. Yet when it comes to the early church, it's an idea unlikely to hold much water. The reason for this is not that people in the early church were more honest and less power hungry than at any other point in history, but rather that the early church was much less organized than Christian history has led us to believe.

According to the Roman Catholic and Anglican Churches, bishops can trace their line in an unending succession all the way back to the earliest days of the Jesus movement. The most famous example of this is the pope in Roman Catholicism, who is believed to be a direct spiritual descendant of the apostle Peter. Yet recent archaeological and historical studies of the church before the conversion of Constantine have shown that bishops were not very powerful and that the church was thoroughly disorganized.[24]

Part of the problem was that Christians didn't really go to church. In *The Second Church*, Yale historian Ramsay MacMullen demonstrates that churches were capable of accommodating only 5 percent of the Christian population in any given region. This means, of course, that 95 percent of Christians weren't learning about Jesus or what it meant to be a Christian from priests or bishops as part of ordinary weekly meetings. Additionally, when Christians were able to gather together, it was largely thanks to the benevolence of the wealthier members of the congregation. In the early days Christians met in the houses of these more prosperous Christians. This gave the householders a great deal of unofficial power and influence. As the hosts, they were the ones who actually controlled access to religious meals, scripture, and community. Just as today one wouldn't want to offend one's host at a dinner party, so too in the ancient world the host had a great deal of social capital. The situation did not change that much once Christianity moved out of individuals' homes and into churches. Someone had to finance the construction of these buildings, and unless bishops were exceptionally wealthy, they could find themselves socially indebted to the aristocrats who funded Christian churches and basilicas.

In reality, therefore, bishops were much more dependent on the laity for their survival and authority than has traditionally been thought. Christian bishops had to fight, argue, and persuade others to acknowledge their authority and to follow their instructions. They sometimes had to deal with the reality of competing clerics in the same location. Apostolic succession worked much better in theory than in practice.

By the time Eusebius became bishop of Caesarea around 315, a new vision of the church began to develop. The fantasy of a well-ordered, centralized, and monolithic church had always been around, but Eusebius wanted to make it a reality. In periods of peace, Christians were able to imagine themselves as a church of the present. It was no longer necessary to look to the future for redemption and vindication; they could create the Kingdom of God in the here and now. This possibility and the exciting vision for the church required a new version of the church's history. Eusebius provided it. Drawing upon the work of Irenaeus and other early church writers, Eusebius set about telling the history of the "apostles" from the time of Christ to his own day.[25]

When it came to establishing the idea of authoritative bishops as the standard for the church, Eusebius was wise to use the rhetorical power of the martyrs. He used martyrs both to establish the succession of bishops in particular regions and to bolster the authority of individual bishops. Nowhere is this more apparent than in his interweaving of martyrdom, persecution, and bishops in his history of Gaul—in particular in his establishment of Irenaeus as the bishop of Lyons.

In the late second century, when Irenaeus lived and wrote, the churches in Gaul were comparatively small and inconsequential. It's difficult to deduce how Christianity spread to France or how widespread it was there. In fact, Eusebius's rendition of the *Martyrs of Lyons* is one of our only Christian writings from France during this period. Apart from what we can glean from Irenaeus, the *Martyrs of Lyons* is all we have.

In the *Martyrs of Lyons* one of the first individuals to be sentenced is Pothinus. The account of martyrdom leads into a discussion of letters written by the martyrs during their imprisonment. At first glance these seem like housekeeping issues or notes on other topics referred to by the authors. Then Eusebius reaches their final letter:

> The same martyrs also recommended Irenaeus, who was already at that time a presbyter of the parish of Lyons, to the above-mentioned bishop of Rome, saying many favorable things in regard to him, as the following extract shows: "We pray, Father Eleutherus, that you may rejoice in God in all things and always. We have requested our brother and comrade Irenaeus to carry this letter to you, and we ask you to hold him in esteem, as zealous for the covenant of Christ. For if we thought that office could confer righteousness upon any one, we should commend him among the first as a presbyter of the church, which is his position."[26]

The death of Pothinus, the presbyter-bishop of Lyons, in 177 had created a vacancy. Apparently before their executions the remaining imprisoned Christians commended Irenaeus to the bishop of Rome as first among them. Letters of recommendation were an important part of social interaction in antiquity, so it is reasonable that Irenaeus would have carried these kinds of letters of introduction. It is, however, slightly strange that ordinary correspondence should make it into Eusebius's grand *Church History*. Perhaps something more significant is happening here. If we read between the lines of this statement, it seems that the martyrs are asking the bishop of Rome to appoint Irenaeus as the succeeding bishop. A little farther on in the *Church History*, this seems to be precisely what happened:

> Pothinus having died with the other martyrs in Gaul at ninety years of age, Irenaeus succeeded him in the episcopate of the church at Lyons. We have learned that, in his youth, he was a hearer of Polycarp. In the third book of his work *Against Heresies* he has inserted a list of the bishops of Rome, bringing it down as far as Eleutherus (whose times we are now considering), under whom he composed his work.[27]

Here Irenaeus is tied to not one, but two martyred bishops: first Pothinus, whom he succeeded, and then Polycarp, whom he apparently heard as a child. Eusebius is shoring up Irenaeus's martyrological connections. All of this introduces and validates Irenaeus's list of Roman bishops.

The picture we get from Eusebius is that Irenaeus, a keen fighter of heretics and chronographer of episcopal traditions, was a friend of the martyrs and was recommended for the rank of bishop by the martyrs themselves. By the time this letter reached Rome, its authors would have been dead already and moved from the category of confessors to that of martyrs. It is interesting that these Christians were writing to the bishop of Rome, because this assumes that the bishop of Rome had influence and perhaps even authority over ancient

France in a manner similar to the pope's influence and authority over the church today. This is a charming picture of order and harmony in which martyrs defer to and support the bishops. Eusebius is able to establish, quite concretely, the lineage of the episcopacy in Gaul and to justify its origins.

This romantic picture of harmony and hierarchy is anachronistic. In the late second century the bishop of Rome had nothing like the power that the pope has today. The famous passage from Matthew in which Jesus promises Peter, "You are Peter, and on this rock I will build my church" (16:18), which is today used to legitimize the papacy, was never quoted in full in any Christian literature until the third-century writer Tertullian.[28] Even then Tertullian does not cite the passage in order to demonstrate the authority of the bishop of Rome over the entire church. If the imprisoned confessors in Gaul wrote to the bishop of Rome, it was because they had strong ties to Rome, Rome was a center of finance and commerce, and the bishop of Rome was an important figure there. It was not because they were asking the head of the church for guidance. For many centuries bishops struggled to find their footing as authority figures in the church. They found themselves at odds with confessors, monks, and those who controlled the shrines of saints in their regions.[29] The picture that Eusebius gives us is incorrect, but it does valuable work in supporting church hierarchy and unity.

Why does Eusebius use the martyrs to help him with this project? The history of the church in France is at best murky. There were no early stories or legends about apostles founding the church in Gaul, and so it was difficult for Eusebius to fit Gaul into his vision of a church founded and shepherded by apostles. This doesn't mean that Eusebius invented the history of bishops in Gaul, but he has shaped it for us in a very particular way. Whatever resources were available to Eusebius, he has chosen to tell the history of bishops in Gaul using martyrs. The death of Pothinus as a martyr clears the stage for the ascendancy of Irenaeus, and the martyrs themselves act as Irenaeus's character references.

We don't know whether this letter of recommendation from the martyrs to the bishop of Rome actually existed, and Eusebius never quotes from it, but it serves a valuable purpose. At the time when Eusebius was writing, there did not yet exist a legend about how Christianity was brought to Gaul by this or that apostle. In the absence of a founding story involving one of the original Twelve, martyrs are the next best thing. Eusebius uses them to give authority to the bishopric of Lyons. In selecting the next bishop, the martyrs do the kind of work that an apostle or a bishop would have done. In this way, the shaky origins of the church in Gaul are here supported using the words and wishes of Christian heroes. Irenaeus's reputation and credentials are enhanced by virtue of the fact that he was supported by the martyrs.

This pattern is not limited to the church in Gaul; it continues throughout the *Church History*. In book 6 Eusebius discusses the flaws of Novatus, a schismatic, someone who had caused a break in the church by separating himself and founding a rival group. He had apparently set himself up as bishop in Rome as a rival to Eusebius's orthodox leader. Eusebius cites at length from a letter detailing the arguments and evidence against Novatus. One of his concluding points mentions Moses, an otherwise unknown "blessed martyr, who lately suffered among us a glorious and admirable martyrdom." Apparently while Moses was still alive, he refused to "commune with [Novatus] and with the five presbyters who with him had separated themselves from the church" on the grounds that they were schismatics.[30] This story is essentially identical to the stories about Polycarp and the apostle John avoiding heretics.

Here though, the problem is not a heretic, but a schismatic. Novatus was a rival to the bishop of Rome and a threat to Eusebius's history of the church in which there was a single unbroken thread of bishops that stretched back to Jesus. Eusebius uses every weapon in his arsenal to attack Novatus, claiming that he was possessed by Satan when he was younger, calling him arrogant, referring to the bishops who denounced him, and so on. The story about Moses is the final argument in an already damning case. The story may or may not be true and may or may not have been present in Eusebius's source. It is clear, however, that Eusebius uses it to show that, once again, the martyrs dismissed any challenge to the singular, unified, unchanging orthodox church.

The consequence of Eusebius's history of the persecuted church is that he divides the church into two groups: orthodox, as represented by orthodox bishops and martyrs, and their opponents—the heretics, schismatics, and persecutors. Eusebius's targets are the dissenting voices within the church: those with whom he disagrees, those who threaten the idea of a single line of authoritative bishops, and those who question the tenets of orthodoxy. By polarizing Christianity in this way, Eusebius forces those groups outside of the church. At the same time, those within the church who might be inclined to disagree are reminded that they are either on the side of the martyrs or on the side of the heretics and persecutors. Eusebius creates and uses this idea of a persecuted church filled with martyrs in order to advance his agenda. Eusebius helps to create the "persecuted us against the aggressive them" mentality that is used as a powerful rhetorical device to this very day. Before the rise of the emperor Constantine, this polarized view of the world had existed among Christians who saw themselves as outsiders battling Satan at the end of time; with Eusebius this idea becomes institutionalized. The persecuted "us" is now the establishment.

Christians had complained about persecution before Eusebius, but, as the first church historian, Eusebius encodes the understanding of the church as persecuted into the history of Christianity itself. In the early modern period thousands of Christians would look to this history and feel obligated to give up their own lives, because they thought that this is what it meant to be Christian.[31] What they didn't know was that this history of Christianity was a fourth-century invention.

The Growth of the Martyrdom Tradition

IT USED TO BE thought that people wrote martyrdom stories because they were persecuted. The truth of the matter is that the explosion of martyrdom stories, and hagiographical literature in general, occurred only once comparative peace had settled across the empire. It was during this period that martyrdom stories flourished and grew, were edited, and sometimes crafted out of thin air. It was, as Bollandist hagiographer Hippolyte Delehaye remarks, during the fourth century that Christians became more interested in telling romantic fictions than preserving historical facts. As early as the fourth century, he notes, Christians were plagiarizing foreign legends about saints and adapting them to fit their own local heroes.[32] The fifth-century *Passion of St. Lawrence* (St. Lawrence is the patron saint of Rome), for example, is influenced by the stories of the martyrs of Phrygia described by the historians Sozomen and Socrates.[33] The *Life of St. Agnes*, about one of Christianity's most famous female saints and one whose name is read daily as part of the Catholic Mass, exists in two versions: the version provided by Ambrose, bishop of Milan and Doctor of the Church (ca. 339–97) and the version attributed to Pope Damasus I (366–84). The problem is, they disagree about the manner of Agnes's death—the great Doctor of the Church and the pope disagree with one another. Perhaps more troubling, for us, is the fact that the version attributed to Pope Damasus sounds a great deal like the legend of the death of St. Eulalia.[34] In a similar vein, the slightly lazy author of the fifth- or sixth-century *Passion of Philip of Heraclea* "borrows" passages from the work of the third-century writer Clement of Alexandria and places them in the mouth of his hero.[35] The fourth century becomes the turning point for martyrdom literature. We are no longer dealing with stories that are authentic. We are teetering precariously on the cusp of crude plagiarism and fanciful invention.

The reasons for the explosion in martyrdom literature were largely connected to the emergence of the cult of the saints in late antiquity. The tourist industry surrounding martyrs was in its infancy, but by the end of the fourth century the presence of a saint's remains in a town was enough to entice wealthy pilgrims to it. The reason it was so easy to forge or invent martyrdom stories in this period is that, unlike the New Testament but like the overwhelming majority of early Christian literature, stories about martyrs weren't canonized. This meant that when they were copied, the scribes responsible had considerable freedom to alter, expand, edit, or invent traditions as they saw fit. Sometimes authors were just adding to an earlier tradition. They set down in writing campfire stories or gossipy oral traditions, the origins of which are completely unknown. Other times they edited a text to make it more orthodox, placing creeds, statements of faith, or denouncements of heretics on the lips of the saints. On still other occasions, we find texts that seem to have been composed out of whole cloth or out of scraps of information as a means of bringing local saints up-to-date or filling in the gaps.

The Growth of the Cult of the Saints

ONE OF THE PRIMARY reasons that hagiographers felt compelled to invent, supplement, and expand martyrdom stories was in order to support what is commonly known as the cult of the saints, the religious buildings and rituals involving the veneration of the saints. People gathered at the site of a saint's grave to celebrate the saint's birthday, they made dangerous pilgrimages across vast distances to visit their heroes, and, often, they sought something else—forgiveness, healing, and communication with something beyond and greater than themselves. People believed that, even though the saints were in heaven in the palm of God, the saints were also fully present at their shrines.[36] As a result, martyr shrines and churches were a place where the boundary between heaven and earth collapsed, and pilgrims had what seemed to be immediate access to help and hope for the future. The power of the saints was such that people clamored and even paid to be buried near the saints (*ad sanctos*) in order to secure themselves a front-row seat at the resurrection. The same impulse persists even today, not only in the vast crowds that flock to the Vatican to see the tombs of the popes, but also in the thousands who line up to see Kate Middleton's wedding dress on display in Buckingham Palace. People long to have direct contact with their heroes.

Because the martyrs had suffered so much in life, it was believed that their remains had special healing properties. Because the healing miracles that people hoped for were rooted in the martyr's own experience of pain, the stories played a key role in the saint's mystique. The reading of a saint's martyrdom was reported to have magical qualities itself: sweet scents filled the church, those who had offended the saint began to quake with fear, and the infirm and disabled felt miraculous power fill their bodies.[37]

At the same time and for all these reasons, the cult of the saints and the preservation of a saint's remains and memory were big business. Martyrs could draw a crowd. The possession of a martyr's remains, especially a famous martyr's remains, brought a town not only protection and fame, but also visitors. Pilgrims to a martyr's shrine needed places to stay, things to eat, and a commemorative lamp or comb to take home with them.[38] Every town wanted to have the remains of a famous martyr.

Of course, not every town actually had a martyr. It might, however, have had a local hero who was rumored to have died under this or that emperor. But more information was needed. In order to solicit justification for the construction of expensive churches and attract visitors from neighboring towns and provinces, a town needed more than just a rumor; it needed a legend.

One example of this phenomenon is the *Martyrdom of Theodotus of Ancyra*. According to this story, Theodotus was a Christian shopkeeper from Ancyra in Turkey who was apparently executed around 313. When not harboring Christians in his shop, Theodotus took to recovering and burying the remains of Christian martyrs. At one point in the story Theodotus leaves Ancyra and goes to the small town of Malos to collect and bury the remains of a martyr whose corpse had been thrown into the river there. While in Malos, he meets with a group of Christians, including a priest named Fronto, and picnics in a pleasant spot that Theodotus declares would be a wonderful site for a chapel dedicated to a martyr. Meanwhile, in Ancyra seven virgins were drowned after refusing to participate in a pagan ritual. Theodotus is informed of this development in a vision and returns to Ancyra to retrieve the bodies and bury them, with the result that he himself is arrested. Despite the pagan governor Theoctenus's offers of power, money, and a prestigious pagan priesthood, Theodotus cannot be persuaded to recant. And so he is tortured and killed. Just before the guards burn Theodotus's body, Fronto arrives from Malos bearing kegs of Malos's famous wine. The guards can't resist the delicious beverage and quickly become drunk, allowing Fronto to load the donkey up with the body of the martyr. Unguided, the donkey wends its way back to Malos to the very spot that Theodotus had identified as a location for a martyr chapel. And there Theodotus's remains are duly buried.

In the nineteenth century Hippolyte Delehaye declared that the text was a forgery and suggested that Theodotus never existed.[39] The more recent discovery of a chapel dedicated to St. Theodotus in Malos and a review of the detailed knowledge of the local geography found in the tale have prompted some to take a less skeptical view, but even these scholars recognize that the story would have been composed much later than the events.[40] For our purposes, the interesting thing is the author's focus on the relocation of Theodotus and the promotion of Malos. Malos was a small town, and the author's detailed knowledge of its geography tells us that the author knew the town itself. Many of the story's plot details are about explaining how and why the remains of a saint who came from and died in a more important city ended up buried in such an inconsequential place. The answer here, as in so many stories about saints, is divine intervention.

This interest in explaining the construction of churches and the physical location of saints is common in stories from the late fourth century and later. They were written to justify and support the existence of a particular religious site. In the case of the *Martyrdom of Theodotus of Ancyra*, the story also serves as advertising for the town's most well-known export—its wine. To this day Kalecik (ancient Malos) still produces the most famous wine in the region. Just as fans of C. S. Lewis's fantasy *The Lion, the Witch, and the Wardrobe* try Turkish delight when they visit England, no ancient pilgrims are going to leave Malos without sampling the wine and purchasing some for their relatives. It's a way to step into the story and identify with its hero. And, for the locals, it's a way to promote local commerce.

Theodotus was, according to the story, a relic collector. He gathered the remains of martyrs and had them properly interred. As a man and a mere shopkeeper, this makes him something of an anomaly, for many such figures in Christian history were wealthy aristocratic women. Neither arranging for formal and elaborate burials nor building churches was cheap in late antiquity. As a result, public buildings were often financed by wealthy individuals, groups, or families, and the collection of martyrs' remains was undertaken by people of means.[41]

One example of this is a woman named Lucina, who appears in the late-fifth- or early-sixth-century *Passion of Saint Sebastian*. Sebastian is one of Rome's most famous martyrs. In Michelangelo's *Last Judgment* in the Sistine Chapel, he is depicted in heaven with arrows still lodged in his chest. He was a soldier of the praetorian guard in Rome who was shot through with arrows—an experience that he survived—before being bludgeoned to death with clubs. After his death Sebastian was unceremoniously dumped in the sewer. He appeared to Lucina in a vision and urged her to retrieve his body and bury him next to the bodies of the apostles Peter and Paul in the catacombs, which she did.[42] The year was apparently 290. This is where the problems emerge. According to separate accounts, in 253 Lucina herself had moved the bones of St. Paul to her private estate on the Via Ostiensis, in Rome, but there is no mention of this in the *Passion of Saint Sebastian*. Did she forget where Paul was?

Things get even stranger in another late text entitled the *Passion of Processus and Martinianus.* This is the story of the deaths of Peter and Paul's jailors, who had apparently converted to Christianity and ended up as martyrs themselves. Apparently Lucina was also present to collect their bones, even though they had died at the end of the first century. Once all of the evidence is assembled, Lucina appears in no fewer than eleven separate martyrdom stories, the narrative settings of which span well over *two hundred years.* Good diet and exercise notwithstanding, life spans like this have not been seen since the patriarchs of the Old Testament.

Perhaps Lucina existed at some point and was responsible for moving the bones of a martyr; perhaps she represents real women who were responsible for collecting the remains of their deceased Christian siblings; or perhaps she never existed at all and is the stuff of legend.[43] Lucina's appearance only in fifth- and sixth-century hagiography suggests that she is a later invention, but why would later editors insert Lucina, and other women like her, into these stories at all? By the turn of the sixth century there were competing stories about the final resting places of important saints like Peter and Paul. In her work, ancient history scholar Kate Cooper suggests that these stories involving Lucina were intended to adjudicate between the claims in these various burial traditions.[44] It was the editor's way of explaining the presence of a saint's remains in various different locations at different points in time. It avoided offending whichever wealthy patron had paid for the erection of the latest mausoleum. The end result was a convoluted and confused biography for the fictional bone gatherer Lucina.

This phenomenon is found throughout the stories of martyrs. What's happening here is that martyrdom stories are being changed, altered, and edited in order to support a particular cult's claims about relics. When the provenance of a saint's bones was unknown, a story would emerge in which a local religious figure had a vision in which the saint led them to his or her remains. This is not just about supporting one's own claims, though; this is also about disproving the claims of other, rival religious sites. The motivation of these editors is competition for pilgrims and the relative status of particular churches. What is at stake in the reworking and invention of traditions is status, power, prestige, and pilgrims. Early Christians were willing to rewrite the truth in order to acquire them.

The Growth of Polemic in the Martyrdom Tradition

IT IS CERTAINLY TRUE that there were social practices that fostered the sudden production of martyrdom literature. Martyrs were popular, powerful, and persuasive; they attracted pilgrims and bolstered the reputation of bishops and urban centers. At the same time, we should consider the somewhat troubling possibility that early Christians liked hearing about persecution and death. In the previous chapter we saw that Christians saw martyrs as soldiers in the battle between good and evil. This view of the world led them to portray the Roman government and their jailers, judges, torturers, and executioners as agents of Satan. Christians were at war with a world possessed by Satan, and the martyrs could not yield a rhetorical inch. Ultimately, this is the worldview of apocalyptic, a form of writing and mode of thinking concerned with the supernatural, divine revelations, visions, eschatological salvation, and cosmic battle.[45]

Many scholars have found this polemical and apocalyptic view of the world faintly embarrassing.[46] Since the nineteenth century, biblical scholars have dismissed visions of the afterlife and discussions of the proximity of the devil as some of the more "lowbrow" aspects of early Christianity. It is generally assumed that apocalyptic literature emerges out of contexts of suffering.[47] It is only under extreme psychological stress and under threat of destruction that Christians would write like this. Without it, scholars seem to assume, early Christians would have been philosophers and homilists. To take just one scholarly statement as an example, Scott Lewis describes apocalyptic as "primarily sectarian in nature. As Christianity became less of a sect and finally a state religion, the very conditions which gave rise to apocalyptic—persecution and alienation—began to disappear."[48]

In this way, the explanation that "Christians were persecuted" is used to account for many aspects of early Christian martyrdom literature: the violence, the preoccupation with gruesome tortures, and the obsession with eschatological reward and punishment. We can empathize with the early Christians because they were under pressure, and if they viewed the world as a battlefield between good and evil, then surely this was because the oppression they suffered forced them into it. Surely it is not their fault, so the argument goes, that later generations of Christians appropriated this view of the world. The misuse or misappropriation of Christian scripture, rhetoric, and history is a widespread issue and can hardly be laid at the feet of those in the early church struggling for survival. The purpose of this argument is, in essence, to explain away the violence of Christian martyrdom. For modern readers, unsavory elements of Christianity are more palatable if they were responses to crisis. Accepting this explanation allows us to overlook the dark side of early Christianity.

This kind of apology for the violence of Christian martyrdom and its presence in Christianity rests on two assumptions: first, that Christians really were persecuted, and second, that it was during periods of persecution that these stories were composed and this apocalyptic worldview dominated. We've already seen that persecution was much less severe than Christians imagined it to be—imperially initiated legislation affecting Christians under Decius, Valerian, and Diocletian lasted no more than twelve years over a period of almost three hundred years—but even if Christians only perceived themselves to be persecuted, this could account for the polemical tone of the martyr's battle with Satan. More problematic for this argument is the assumption it makes about the historical contexts in which apocalyptic martyrdom stories were written. If Lewis is right, the apocalyptic elements of martyrdom stories, perhaps martyrdom stories themselves, should have disappeared with the Christianization of the Roman Empire.

When we look at the evidence, a very different picture emerges. Curiously, references to Satan and the work of evil are very rare in the earliest Greek martyrdom stories. The *Acts of Ptolemy and Lucius* and the *Acts of Justin and Companions* are philosophical. The *Martyrdom of Polycarp* makes reference to Satan at the opening and conclusion of the work, but these references serve more to explain why Christians don't have relics than why they are in the arena. By and large, with the exception of the *Martyrs of Lyons*, there are virtually no references to Satan, demons, or the role of evil. In Latin martyrdom accounts from the early third century on, however, there is a much more pronounced interest in the devil. We already saw this in the *Passion of Perpetua and Felicity*, in which Perpetua gets into a wrestling contest with Satan. The same was true in the case of stories influenced by Perpetua. Apparently Christians in the Latin West—North Africa and Gaul—were very interested in the devil and had an appetite for demonic torture.

In the post-Constantinian period, furthermore, many of the early Greek martyrdom stories were edited to feature the devil *more* prominently. For example, in the earliest version of the *Acts of Justin and Companions* there is no mention of Satan at all. The opening of the account merely designates the decrees to sacrifice to the emperor as "wicked." The idea is still not present in the second version, which was produced perhaps in the third century. The third and final recension, however, is quite different. We know that the text was composed after the reign of Constantine, because it concludes with a liturgical prayer asking that God grant victories to the emperor.[49] The most striking change in the text is the sudden appearance of the devil. The account now opens in this way:

> While the wicked Antoninus wielded the scepter of the Roman empire, Rusticus happened to be the despicable prefect at Rome, a terrible man, a plague, and filled with all impiety. Once while he was sitting at the tribunal, a group of the saints was brought before him as prisoners, seven in number. For this was

eagerly sought after by the ministers of Satan, to arrest them, afflict them with cruel torments, and thus to deliver them to death by the sword.[50]

The hostility toward the Romans escalates throughout the three versions of the story, but it is only here, in the latest edition, that Satan is explicitly named as the source of the attacks. In opening the account in this way, the editor has changed the *Acts of Justin* from a philosophically styled courtroom debate to a battle with the devil.

This isn't the case just with the *Acts of Justin;* as other Greek martyrdom accounts were translated into Latin, their translators often supplemented their sources with references to the devil. For instance, although the devil is nowhere to be found in the Greek version of the *Acts of Phileas,* he becomes a central character in the Latin version.[51] In the same way, the fifth-century liturgical editor of the beautifully philosophical *Acts of Apollonius* describes the day of Apollonius's martyrdom as his victory over the evil one.[52] According to the story, Apollonius was a levelheaded rhetorician and philosopher who was willing at his trial to consider the possibility that heaven did not exist. If this is an accurate depiction of an actual person, we can imagine him being absolutely appalled by this revision of his legend.

We cannot dismiss this contest between good and evil as merely the product of a church under stress. The explosion of apocalyptic martyrdom stories and of martyrdom stories in general demonstrates that Christians wanted to hear about the devil, torture, and death regardless of whether they themselves were persecuted. It's not necessary to judge ancient Christians for this interest. Lots of people find martyrdom stories interesting and inspirational. It's important to note, though, that the idea of Christian martyrs at odds with Satan and the world was just as, if not more, popular in periods of peacetime.

The reason this growth of apocalyptic in martyrdom stories matters is that it amplifies a polarized, polemical view of the world. If Eusebius subtly pits orthodoxy against heresy, martyrdom stories beat us over the head with the battle between good and evil. The invention of the idea of a persecuted church that must rise up against an evil enemy became popular after the "age of persecution" had drawn to a close. It was in periods of peace that Christians expanded the stories about the devil pursuing Christians and subjecting them to brutal torture. This is because ancient audiences enjoyed hearing this kind of material in the same way that modern moviegoers enjoy horror movies. The idea of the persecuted church at odds with Satan has more to do with literary tastes than with any historical reality. The problem is that subsequent generations of Christians haven't treated stories about martyrs as inspirational fiction; they have treated them as accurate descriptions of the world.

Although we can understand how people who were part of a widely disliked minority group might think that they were assailed by the devil, the idea is still dangerous. We should be worried by a powerful church that sees its dissenters as inspired by Satan. The Christians who lived during the reign of the emperor Constantine and later did not extend to pagans the toleration *they* had asked for generations before. They destroyed pagan shrines and temples, and stories of Christian mobs attacking Roman prefects and swarming around pagan religious centers are surprisingly common. With the legalization of Christianity, Christians turned—in the words of historian Hal Drake—from lambs into lions.[53] Their violence was legitimized by the fact that they were Christian and in a martyr-led war against Satan. There was, for some, no difference between dying as a martyr under Decius and dying while trying to destroy a pagan temple. In the words of the fifth-century monk Shenoute, "There is no crime for those who have Christ."[54]

Conclusion

THE IDEA OF A persecuted church comes predominantly from authors who were writing after the reign of Constantine had begun and in some cases centuries after his death. Although there were other historians and church thinkers, Eusebius has uniquely shaped the way that people tell the story of Christianity. Eusebius helped to make the history of Christianity the history of persecution. The historical evidence suggests that the majority of texts about martyrs were either written down or heavily edited during this period of relative peace and quiet. These stories were composed because a martyr's opinion, as a holy person prepared to die in defense of Christ, had great authority in the eyes of readers. When it came to matters of truth, there was no better authority than a saint.

At the same time that Eusebius was editing his *Church History*, other Christians began to edit and compose their own stories about persecution and suffering. As competition between religious centers and towns grew, there was a greater motivation for longer, more ornate martyrdom stories. It was important to demonstrate concrete links between the remains and the story of a saint over and against the claims of nearby religious centers. More broadly, Christians enjoyed hearing martyrdom stories. They relished the horrifying tortures, delighted in the battle between good and evil, and cheered the martyr's final triumph. As time went on, the stories about early Christians were edited and changed in order to address later doctrinal issues and cater to evolving liturgical and literary tastes.

The result is that we are farther and farther removed from the historical martyrs. What remains is a narrative of persecution and suffering developed to justify and support the institutions of orthodoxy. We can see how Eusebius and the editors of Christian stories are using martyrs, and we can admire the edifice of Eusebius's history of the church, but the idea of the persecuted church is almost entirely the invention of the fourth century and later.

What is striking about the emergence of this myth of a persecuted church in the writings of Eusebius and others is just how polarized it is. With peace the rhetoric grew more polemical, not less. This is the conflict between truth and error, God and the devil, orthodoxy and heresy. Sides have to be chosen here. Even though Eusebius seems to see himself as living in a new era of peace, he still has a sense that the church is under threat. This "new persecution" is the threat posed by schismatics and heretics to the existence of orthodoxy. The proper response, according to Eusebius, is to avoid and reject these heretics. This is the behavior that is modeled by the martyrs in the *Church History*. Already in the fourth century, then, persecution and martyrdom have become polarizing rhetorical tools. Claims of being persecuted are used in order to exclude and suppress other groups, to identify them with demonic forces, and to legitimize rhetorical and perhaps also literal violence against them. From the very beginning Christian claims to membership in a historically persecuted group and the formation of the myth of persecution were strategic. This myth of persecution was, paradoxically enough, a way to marginalize others. Ironically, if modern Christians are the heirs of early church traditions about martyrs, it is this myth that they have preserved. Just like Christian writers in late antiquity, we continue to use the claimed experience of persecution to justify our attacks on others and legitimize our opinions.

CHAPTER EIGHT

The Dangerous Legacy of a Martyrdom Complex

ON JANUARY 11, 2012, A news report emerged of France's president, Nicolas Sarkozy, touring the village of Domrémy-la-Pucelle.[1] Sarkozy was no ordinary tourist, and it was no accident that he was touring this particular village four months before his country's presidential election. Domrémy-la-Pucelle is the birthplace of Joan of Arc, the patron saint of France, and Nicolas Sarkozy was there to curry the favor of the saints, or at least the favor that the saint could bring with her.

According to legend, Joan was born into a peasant family in 1412. This was a bleak period in France's history. Still recovering from the devastating effects of the Black Death, the French were engaged in a series of protracted conflicts with the English known as the Hundred Years' War. A vision of Sts. Michael, Catherine, and Margaret that Joan had when she was twelve years old instructed her to drive the English out of France and to bring the dauphin to the city of Rheims for his coronation. The experience so greatly moved Joan that, even though she was just an illiterate farm girl, she set about trying to turn the predictions into reality. She dressed as a boy and journeyed through the treacherous Burgundian territory in order to secure an audience with Charles VII at the royal court. After several attempts and a thorough investigation by religious authorities, Charles agreed to put Joan to the test.

Joan traveled to Orléans, where she usurped the power of the local duke and, despite being wounded several times in battle, led the French armies to a succession of victories over the English. Eventually, though, she was captured by the Burgundians and sold to the English, who put her on trial for heresy. The result was that on May 30, 1431, at the age of nineteen, Joan of Arc was tied to a pillar in the old market at Rouen and burned alive. The English, fearing that her body might be collected for veneration, burned it twice more before unceremoniously dumping her remains into the Seine.

After her death the Catholic Church declared Joan of Arc innocent of heresy, and she was eventually canonized as a saint in 1920. Her popularity, however, preceded her elevation to sainthood for, in the centuries after her death, Joan of Arc became a legendary figure. In particular, since the Napoleonic Wars, she has morphed into a political champion and an icon of French resistance and patriotism. Soldiers prayed to her in the trenches during World War I and remembered the brave virgin patriot who drove the English out of France. Interestingly, her appeal is not limited to one political party or position; she has been invoked by monarchists, republicans, conservatives, and liberals alike. During World War II she was claimed by both the French resistance leaders, who saw themselves as retracing her footsteps, and the pro-Nazi Vichy government. The Vichy government portrayed the allied English forces, which at the time were engaged in a bombing campaign against France, as continuing the legacy of Joan of Arc's executioners.

Again in 2012, Sarkozy was trying to capture some of Joan of Arc's magic. The move was strategic: the political right in France has claimed Joan of Arc as its political icon for years, and so in his visit to Domrémy-la-Pucelle the comparatively liberal Sarkozy attempted to wrest control of Joan of Arc's memory from his political opponents. In the speech he gave during his visit, Sarkozy said, "Joan doesn't belong to any party, faction, or clan. Joan belongs to France."[2] His actions sought to preempt the right-wing National Front's annual celebration of Joan of Arc, during which its members rally around her golden statue. For the National Front, the new English invaders who must be driven out of France are immigrants. Sarkozy has been criticized for allowing the "Islamicization" of France. By visiting Joan of Arc's birthplace, Sarkozy wanted to show that he too is a patriot. With every step through the village, with every interested expression and choreographed gesticulation, Sarkozy allied himself with the saint and attempted to claim her memory for centrist politics.

Joan of Arc was always a political saint. But her constant moonlighting in modern politics demonstrates that, even if martyrs are long dead, their political and cultural power is not. Her invocation in a twenty-first-century political dispute about immigration, Islam, the economy, and the role of France in the European Union has brought her a long way from her roots in rural medieval Europe. That so many conflicting and feuding groups have claimed her as a heroine for their cause demonstrates just how malleable the memories and persons of martyrs can be. Joan of Arc is shaped and reshaped into the image of later French generations. No matter what our individual politics are, we are sure to empathize with some of her devotees, even as we would be outraged by others. Any French group can claim Joan of Arc, because Joan of Arc's story can be subtly altered and reconfigured so that she can speak to any issue or political stance. What she represents is constantly changing, because in the modern world martyrs are sources of political and rhetorical power.

Persecution and Politics

THE MALLEABILITY OF MARTYRS is even more acute when they are treated en masse as part of the persecuted history of Christianity. Just as many French political organizations have selected Joan of Arc, members of any Christian group can claim to be persecuted as long as they feel opposed. The cultural power that drives these claims, the oil in the machine, so to speak, is the idea that Christians have *always* been persecuted. In Christian terms, if you're being persecuted, you must be doing something right. It's a rather easy trick: if anyone can claim to stand in continuity with the martyrs and be victims of persecution, and if being persecuted authenticates one's religious message, then anyone can claim to be right.

It's for this reason that the modern media is filled with advocacy groups and political pundits claiming that they are being persecuted. This tendency is clearest in, but not limited to, the work of right-wing organizations acting in defense of Christianity. A series of Democracy Corps focus-group studies conducted in 2009 revealed that Republican voters viewed themselves as a maligned minority.[3] According to the report, they felt that they were a persecuted group "whose values are mocked and attacked by a liberal media and class of elites" who were "actively working to advance the downfall of the things that matter most to them in their lives—their faith, their families, their country, and their freedom." Some of the participants in the focus groups were concerned that their ideological hero, political commentator Glenn Beck, was in physical danger. Like any good martyr, though, Beck's "willingness to face this danger head on only adds to his legend."[4] Bubbling just barely beneath the surface of this discussion are very Christian ideas about persecution and martyrdom. Both the fear of martyrdom and the view that Beck is somehow a better person because of the risk are part of the ideology of Christian martyrdom. Beck is a modern-day confessor: because he is believed to be at risk of death, his words have greater power.

But it is not just Glenn Beck. When, in 2012, Newt Gingrich was asked about how his religious beliefs would affect his conduct should he become president, the Republican nominee hopeful answered, "One of the reasons I am running is there has been an increasingly aggressive war against religion and in particular against Christianity" in the United States.[5] For a potential president to state that he sees himself as a wartime candidate who will defend his party against *other citizens* is astonishing. There is not even a pretense here of "united states." Gingrich is clear that he would lead one portion of a nation at war with itself, a nation that he sees as divided under God, a nation engaged in a religious civil war. Gingrich's rhetoric, which is propped up by the idea that Christians are under attack, can work only to polarize people even further.

Were it not for the myth of Christian martyrdom, none of these claims would make sense.

Persecution and the Modern Church

ON A TUESDAY IN the spring of 2011, I attended Mass with one of my colleagues from the history department at the University of Notre Dame. Neither of us knew that on that particular day the liturgy would be a celebration of the work of the pro-life advocates at Notre Dame. The former bishop, John Michael D'Arcy, who had been a strong supporter of the pro-life movement, was there to celebrate the Mass.

The reading for that day was taken from the Acts of the Apostles. When Bishop D'Arcy began his homily, he compared the apostles and their struggles against "the world" in the first century, struggles that led to their eventual martyrdom, to the struggles of advocates of the pro-life movement. The implication was that pro-lifers are modern-day martyrs and victims of persecution. I vividly recall turning to my friend and raising my eyebrows.

Abortion is a hot-button issue for Roman Catholics living in the twenty-first century. It is for many Catholics the preeminent issue facing the church. Advocates for the pro-life movement often frame their comments using the rhetoric of martyrdom and persecution. And yet, even in specific incidents in which pro-life advocates are marginalized and penalized, is the rhetoric of persecution helpful? The problem with using persecution as the template for the modern world is that it becomes prescriptive. It determines the kinds of conversations that we can have. As I listened to Bishop D'Arcy, I couldn't help but wonder, if the pro-life advocates are the ill-treated and persecuted apostles, who is everyone else? Is the rest of the world full of persecutors and aggressors? Is the rest of the world acting for Satan? Once the world is divided into the persecuted and the persecutors, it is difficult to escape this conclusion.

At the same time, Bishop D'Arcy's homily reminded me of a day in 2009 when I was walking across an American college campus behind two female undergraduates. They were discussing a recent news case involving a nine-year-old girl in Brazil who had become pregnant with twins after being raped by her stepfather. Even apart from the terrible emotional damage suffered by this girl, she was in immediate physical danger. Standing just four feet tall and weighing fewer than eighty pounds, her doctors informed the girl's mother that if the pregnancy was not terminated, she would die. In the interests of saving her child, the mother proceeded with the termination, and when the case hit the media, she and the child's doctor were excommunicated by their bishop. It was and is a gut-wrenching case.

I listened to these two young women, who may well have had siblings the same age as the rape victim, condemn the medical staff and the girl's mother. And I found myself horrified. Not so much by their assessment of the correct response to this situation, which I could doctrinally and intellectually comprehend, but by their coldness. There was no note of compassion in their voices. "They" should have made her carry the babies to term, "they" had committed great sins, "they" weren't really Catholic, "relativism" was at work here, and "we" needed to stand up and fight it. One of them repeated the argument of Archbishop Sobrinho, the bishop responsible for excommunicating those involved, that although rape is bad, abortion is worse. She added that she couldn't feel sorry for a rape victim who committed murder. She *couldn't*. One of them mentioned Gianna Molla, a twentieth-century Catholic saint canonized for dying after having refused an abortion and hysterectomy despite knowing she could die.[6] If the Brazilian girl were to die, one of the girls seemed to intimate, she could be a martyr too.[7]

At no point in their conversation did these young, educated, and privileged women express the anguish, profound sadness, or protective anger that this situation so obviously called for. They were so clear in their own minds that this was an example of evil secularism infecting the church that they lost sight of the horror of the situation. Their focus shifted from empathizing with the victims to a defense of a church under attack. Why did they not feel sorry for the girl, a mere child? Why couldn't there be more than one victim? A defensive insensitivity that refuses to acknowledge the sufferings of those with whom we disagree is far too often where this obsession with persecution leads us.

When politically secure Christians claim to be persecuted, they polarize the world around them. This isn't just something that Catholics do. In his evangelical Protestant commentary on Acts, John Stott ruminates on how the devil attacked the early church using "persecution, moral compromise, and distraction."[8] Moreover, he says, the devil continues to act in the same way in the modern world:

> Now I claim no very close or intimate familiarity with the devil. But I am persuaded that he exists, and that he is utterly unscrupulous. Something else I have learned about him is that he is peculiarly lacking in imagination. Over the years he has changed neither his strategy, nor his tactics, nor his weapons: he is still in the same old rut. So a study of his campaign against the early church should alert us to his probable strategy today. If we are taken by surprise, we shall have no excuse.[9]

Stott assumes that the devil acts in the present the way he always has. He assumes Luke's view of a world in which the apostles were persecuted by Satan. It is the same viewpoint of the early church, of John Foxe, and of a whole host of Christians. The church was always persecuted and being Christian means being persecuted. In the words of Bishop Jenky, "It has never been easy to be a Christian, and it's not supposed to be easy!"

254 | THE MYTH OF PERSECUTION

The myth of persecution is theologically grounded in the division of the world into two parties, one backed by God and the other by Satan. And everyone knows that you cannot reason with the devil. Even when the devil is not explicitly invoked, the rhetoric of persecution suggests that the persecutors are irrational and immoral and the persecuted are innocent and brave. In a world filled with persecution, efforts to negotiate or even reason with one's persecutors are interpreted as collaboration and moral compromise. We should not attempt to understand the other party, because to do so would be to cede ground to injustice and hatred.

The Problem with Persecution

THIS, THEN, IS THE problem with defining oneself as part of a persecuted group. Persecution is not about disagreement and is not about dialogue. The response to being "under attack" and "persecuted" is to fight and resist. You cannot collaborate with someone who is persecuting you. You have to defend yourself. When modern political and religious debates morph into rhetorical holy war, the same thing happens: we have to fight those who disagree with us. There can be no compromise and no common ground. This isn't just because one's persecutors act in the stead of evil. It is because persecution is, by definition, unjust. It is not about disagreement; it is about an irrational and unjustified hatred. Why would you even try to reason with those who are persecuting you?

Prior to the rise of Christianity, being persecuted, oppressed, or marginalized was not something that in a debate could be used to one's rhetorical or political advantage. Prior to Christianity, being persecuted was a sign either of one's own moral failings or that one's deity was weak, angry, or indifferent. Although the success of one's group still serves in some quarters to legitimize all sorts of actions, persecution has now become a marker of moral righteousness. And because of this, the claim that one experiences persecution actually becomes a way of acquiring political and cultural power. Even once we move out of explicitly Christian conversations about how society should be run, we still run into Christian principles. Every time a political organization or group claims that it represents the "last persecuted group" in society or the "only group that is unfairly discriminated against," it is invoking the fundamentally Christian idea that persecuted groups have the moral high ground.

All of these claims, this worldview, and this set of values are grounded in a myth about martyrdom and persecution. They are connected to a series of inaccurate beliefs about Christian history: that only Christians are martyred, that being Christian means being persecuted, and that the experience of persecution is a sign both that one is right and that one is good. Yet, as we have seen, early Christians were rarely the targets of sustained and organized persecution. Very few Christians died, and when they did die, it was often because they were seen as politically subversive.

But the impact of this rhetorical celebration of persecution goes even further. During the 2012 election season, in a radio show in which he questioned whether African Americans have been persecuted, Rush Limbaugh said, "Defeating these people [African American voters] is what's paramount, not getting along with them and not trying to find common areas of agreement."[10] Here common ground and agreement would actually get in the way of what is important—defeating one's political opponents in an election year. Similarly, in her review of David Limbaugh's book *Persecution*, Ann Coulter writes, "There is no surer proof of Christ's divinity than that he is still so hated some 2,000 years after his death."[11] Somehow, and quite perversely, hatred has become a witness not just to truth, but to the Truth. No longer are reasoned argument, good judgment, or logic able to win the day, because failing to convince others of one's opinions would be a better sign that one's opinions were correct. Framed by the myth that we are persecuted, dialogue is not only impossible, it is *undesirable*. We revel in the outrage and scandal that our words and opinions elicit. We don't want to be understood by our opponents.

We will fan the flames of hatred and bask in the knowledge that we are right and their criticism proves it.

Heaven help us if this worldview, which pervades political commentary and activism as well as religion, wins the day. The myth of Christian martyrdom and persecution needs to be corrected, because it has left us with a dangerous legacy that poisons the well of public discourse. This affects not just Christians, but *everyone*. We cannot use the mere fact that we feel persecuted as evidence that our cause is just or as the grounds for rhetorical or actual war. We cannot use the supposed moral superiority of our ancient martyrs to demonstrate the intrinsic superiority of our modern religious beliefs or ideological positions. Once we recognize that feeling persecuted is not proof of anything, then we have to engage in serious intellectual and moral debate about the actual issues at hand.

How to Do Without Persecution

THROUGHOUT THIS BOOK I'VE argued that the view of the church as continually and unrelentingly persecuted throughout history is a myth, a myth that was solidified after the conversion of the emperor Constantine for the purposes of retelling the history of Christianity, supporting the authority of bishops, financing religious buildings, and marginalizing the views of heretics. The myth of Christian persecution is not only inaccurate; it has contributed to great violence and continues to support a view of the world in which we are under attack from our fellow human beings.

What I would like to suggest instead is that we abandon the conspiratorial assumption that the world is out to get us and that Christians are always persecuted and instead ask how Christians would fare differently without this narrative of persecution. How would the church look different if we put aside the idea that we are, by definition, persecuted?

In the political and religious arenas, it would allow us to find common ground in debates that are currently sharply polarized. Rather than demonizing our opponents, we could try to find points of agreement and work together. This is not a book about abortion, and I am not an ethicist, but I find it hard to believe that anyone would truly like to see more abortions. Given that a resolution to this issue does not seem to be immediately forthcoming, bipartisan collaboration on the underlying causes of so many pregnancy terminations—limited access to health care and maternity leave, poverty, lack of education, and sexual violence—would seem to be one such step in the right direction. Refusing to work together to achieve common goals because we do not agree on all points with our dialogue partners is akin to cutting off our nose to spite our face.

Even in situations where it is easier to demonize our opponents, putting away polemic would force us to empathize with the economic, political, and social realities that engender real violence against Christians. It is certainly the case that Christians continue to die in many parts of the world. Their deaths are tragedies, and the risk to these individuals is not mitigated by the fact that elsewhere Christians are a powerful majority.[12] Violence against fellow human beings is, to my mind, always a crime, but that doesn't mean that we should stop trying to understand why it happens. If we are willing to attempt to understand the mind-set of those ancient Romans who sentenced Christians to die or the worldview that permitted Christian Crusaders to attack Jerusalem, then we should—in fact, we must—be willing to do the same for those who attack us. The reasons for violence are rarely unambiguous, but the rhetoric of persecution effectively enables us to dismiss the grievances of those who harm us.

Many Christians do live in situations that are oppressive and in which they are persecuted. To give but one recent example, on April 22, 2012, nineteen Christians were killed and twenty-two injured as they gathered to worship on the grounds of Bayero University in Kano, Nigeria.[13] The unidentified attackers hurled explosives into the crowd and opened fire on those who tried to escape. Given that the attackers are unidentified, it would be premature to state categorically that this is a clear-cut example of *persecution*, but it is certainly an example of injustice and violence against Christians.[14] Examples like this are not highlighted by the constant refrain that Christians are persecuted; they are overshadowed. The impact that they should have is lost. Amid the shrill rhetoric of persecution, the plight of those who fight actual violence and experience systematic injustice is forgotten. We are so desensitized to claims of the "persecuted" and the warnings of "crusades" that we no longer take seriously or even notice real violence.

In North Korea, China, Vietnam, Russia, Saudi Arabia, Nigeria, Syria, Egypt, and Iran—to name but a few countries—Christians face real violence, danger, and even death. The situation in these places is dire and, studies have shown, only grows worse. These are flagrant human rights violations and their experiences demand our attention and action.

At the same time, we need to exercise good judgment and moderation in the identification of persecution. Not every Christian who dies tragically and violently in a foreign country is the victim of persecution. And it is not necessary to set every tragedy in the apocalyptic framework of the struggle between good and evil. Nor should we allow a particular interest in Christians to obscure the broader historical context of these events. The persecution of Christians in China is less one front in a "global war" than it is one facet of the Chinese government's censorship of religion in general. Failing to adequately contextualize such incidents means that the plight of other groups, in this case the Falun Gong, is obscured by the claim that Christians have it the worst. If we want to help Christians in China, we should recognize that this situation is caused by the specifically Chinese mistreatment of religious organizations of any type, not by a global war on Christianity.

Is it reasonable to imply that the situation facing Catholics in North America is anything like that facing Christians in China? Is it even sensible to define persecution today as being ridiculed, as the Apostolic Nuncio to the United States Archbishop Carlo Maria Viganò did in a speech in November 2012, when Christians in other parts of the world face real violence?

I would argue that it is not. To give but one example, on January 26, 2012, the day that Newt Gingrich stated in a debate that he had entered the race for the Republican nomination in order to fight the "war against Christianity," a report emerged of thirty-five thousand Christians being forced to flee their homes in Nigeria.[15] The Christians were forced to leave, it was reported, by the Islamic group Boko Haram. In media reports the mass exodus of thousands of people in Nigeria received considerably less attention than Gingrich's reference to the war on Christianity. This is in part the result of the American media's (and people's) interest in national affairs, but at the same time it demonstrates the extent to which the rhetoric has trumped reality.

This example illustrates that the description of Christianity's encounters with political views, secularism, or competing ideas about governance and education as "persecution" does not draw attention to the struggles of those facing real violence. It cannibalizes them. When the political and ideological disagreements experienced by Christians in America are understood as part of a global war on Christianity, then the dramatic differences between these relatively benign challenges and the authentic human suffering of Christians in other parts of the world are too easily conflated. The suffering of Christians in Tehran is not the same as the "War on Christmas" here in America. This easy shift from foreign, to global, to domestic persecution effectively colonizes the experiences of people in other parts of the world. The heavy mantle of persecution hangs as lightly on the indignant shoulders of Western Christians as the emperor's new clothes. But we should worry that these are garments manufactured at high cost and out of sight by uncredited workers.

Moreover, in spinning this grand narrative of persecution, we forget to look for the causes of violence, and we buy into a polarized view of the world in which our opponents are evil. In the early church,

Christian apologists such as Justin Martyr and Tertullian wrote letters to the authorities explaining and defending the cause of Christians. They used the rhetoric and ideals of the Roman Empire to make their case that Christians should be tolerated. They drew on Roman myths and Greek icons to argue that Christians and Romans shared much in common. Justin and Tertullian lived during the so-called Age of the Martyrs, but even as they refused to give up Christianity, they were still open to conversation and actively involved in trying to find common ground. Perhaps, if we are to appeal to the history of persecution in the early church, this should be our model.

What to Do with Martyrs?

WHAT WE DO HAVE to give up is a binary view that only our martyrs are good and true. Many stories about Christian martyrs are troublesome and worrying. In this case the truth about the authenticity of ancient martyrdom stories themselves can be of some help. Despite the dubious historicity of these stories, we know that they were preserved for entertainment, for moral instruction, and to encourage people. The story of Josaphat, the Buddhist saint, was tremendously popular. Josaphat was never a Christian, but he did embody Christian virtues, and surely those virtues are things that we can continue to admire. The danger comes in the way we use the examples of the saints. Perhaps Hippolyte Delehaye said it best when he remarked, "Fictions of this type are not without a certain danger. As long as they continue to be read in the spirit in which they were written, all goes well. But a moment comes, and in some cases comes very quickly, when people no longer recall the original intention of the story."[16] If we want to use these stories, we need to be aware of their limitations.

Even though Christians were never the subjects of sustained persecution, the *idea* that suffering for Christ could be valuable and meaningful was a pervasive one in antiquity and continues to be influential today. Stories about martyrs have inspired generations of

Christians to liberate themselves from slavery, to resist tyranny, to live lives in the service of others and in the pursuit of justice, to find courage despite adversity, and to seek out a life full of purpose. These are good things, surely. For Christians who are sick, the example of the martyrs can be a consolation. Martyrs can motivate those who *are* oppressed to stand up against political tyranny and social injustice. They can inspire understanding and forgiveness. It is not my intention to deny people the right to read martyrdom stories, to identify their personal sufferings with those of their religious heroes, or to feel inspired by the courage, endurance, and beliefs of their protagonists.

More often than not, though, when Christian martyrs enter the public arena in the modern world, they are invoked as evidence of Christian superiority and to support the idea that Christians are at odds with the world and other people in it. The church needs opposition, and Christians, in order to be authentically Christian, need enemies. When Christians are invested in the history of martyrdom, they see themselves as persecuted, make their opponents into enemies, and equate disagreement with demonic activity. This story of Christian martyrdom is a myth that leads Christians to claim the rhetorical high ground, but a myth that makes collaboration and even compassion impossible. The recognition that this idea is based in myth and rhetoric, rather than history and truth, reveals that Christians are committed to conflict and opposition, but also that they don't have to be. We can choose to embrace the virtues that martyrs embody without embracing the false history of persecution and polemic that has grown up around them.

ACKNOWLEDGMENTS

As someone who has spent the past decade working on scholarly publications that highlight the importance of ideas about martyrdom for early Christians, I know that it comes as a great surprise to many of my colleagues to find that I would choose to write a book dismantling commonly held modern perceptions about persecution in the early church. But just because early Christians cherished the idea of suffering like Christ does not mean that Christians were constantly persecuted, and I am enormously thankful for those friends and colleagues who have supported me as I have labored to explain the difference. Among many others, Mary Rose D'Angelo, Blake Leyerle, Michael Peppard, Charles Camosy, and Timothy and Christine Luckritz Marquis especially stand out as sources of support and encouragement. I might not have had the courage to see this book through to completion, were it not for the friendship of Dan Myers, who directed me to various relevant news items, encouraged me to stand my ground, and assured me that I wouldn't be fired.

Ideas expressed in this book were presented at conferences and as invited lectures at Columbia University, Yale Divinity School, Duke University, the University of Kentucky, the University of Manchester, Oxford University, and Chicago Divinity School. I am grateful to the organizers and participants of these events for the careful and gracious feedback. Chapter 7, "The Invention of the Persecuted Church," was greatly influenced by the work of Professor Kate Cooper, of the University of Manchester, who has never failed to share her ideas and passion with others. David Devore was especially helpful, supplying a copious bibliography and corrections to my reading of Eusebius. A number of nonspecialist friends were kind enough to read chapters for me. I am grateful to Alex Coccia, Micah Corning-Myers, Genna McCabe, and Mark Mannucci for their encouragement and direction.

Despite our differences of opinion, Brad Gregory read sections of the book and gave me invaluable suggestions about how to articulate my ideas. Meghan Henning could not have been more of a personal cheerleader as she commented on the introduction and final chapter. Joel Baden, of Yale Divinity School, read every word of this book, as he does with everything I write. I remain in awe of his talents and utterly indebted to him for his generosity and graciousness.

Finally, I am grateful to everyone at HarperOne who worked on my book. Mark Tauber, Claudia Boutote, and Julie Burton have set the bar perilously high for publishing experiences in the future. Above all I am thankful to my editor, Roger Freet. His warm honesty, unfailing humor, and remarkable dedication have made him more of a partner in crime than an editor. I will be grateful for his work long after *The Myth of Persecution* has been remaindered.

NOTES

Introduction

1. Mariam's story captured public attention and appeared in newspapers and on websites throughout the world. The text used here comes from Fouad Ajami, "Pity the Christian Arabs," *Newsweek*, January 16, 2011; http://www.newsweek.com/2011/01/16/pity-the-christian-arabs.html.

2. This figure was given in a study by Italian scholar Antonio Socci in his book *I Nuovi Perseguitati: Indagine sulla Intolleranza Anticristiana nel Nuovo Secolo del Martirio* (Alexandria: Piemme, 2002). Of these seventy million, Socci estimates that approximately 65 percent died in the twentieth century. Socci takes a much broader view of persecution than we will in this book.

3. To ancient spectators Jesus's overturning of the tables in the Jerusalem Temple would have been understood as a symbolic destruction of the Temple. In other words, it was an act of sedition. See E. P. Sanders, *The Historical Figure of Jesus* (New York: Penguin, 1993), 259–60.

4. The story about the Great Fire of Rome is found in the writings of the Roman historian Tacitus. According to Tacitus, Nero punished the Christians because they were a handy scapegoat (*Annals* 15.44). This wasn't, strictly speaking, religious persecution. Moreover, as we will see later it may not have happened.

5. Tertullian, *Apology* 50.

6. The full, rather lengthy title of John Foxe's work is *Actes and Monuments of these latter and perillous Dayes, touching matters of the Church, wherein ar comprehended and described the great persecu-*

tions and horrible troubles, that have bene wrought and practised by the Romishe Prelates, speciallye in this Realme of England and Scotlande, from the yeare of our Lorde a thousande unto the tyme nowe present. Gathered and collected according to the true copies and wrytinges certificatorie, as wel of the parties themselves that suffered, as also out of the Bishops Registers, which wer the doers thereof (London: John Day, 1563). Foxe's book was reprinted in 1570, 1576, 1583, 1596, 1610, 1632, 1641, and 1684.

7. The virulently anti-Catholic tone of Foxe's tome cast long shadows over English history, as it has shaped English Protestant identity ever since. When it was reread in the seventeenth century, it contributed to what historians call the "Catholic myth": the belief that the Catholics were engaged in a worldwide conspiracy to overthrow the government and enslave the people. The popularity of the "Catholic myth" contributed to the marginalization of Catholics and even to the outbreak of the English Civil War. The influence of Foxe's writing on anti-Catholicism in England is discussed by Owen Chadwick in *The Reformation*, vol. 3 (New York: Penguin, 1990), 128. Foxe's appropriation of the history of martyrdom and his demonization of Catholics only led to and endorsed further violence and oppression. In the words of Elizabeth Evenden and Thomas S. Freeman: "Well into the nineteenth, if not the twentieth century, Foxe's woodcuts would keep the memory of the Marian persecution green and rub salt into the wounds of sectarian hatred" (*Religion and the Book in Early Modern England: The Making of Foxe's "Book of Martyrs"* [Cambridge: Cambridge Univ. Press, 2011], 229).

8. Jonathan Mann, "Will Satan Stop Rick Santorum?" *CNN*, February 24, 2012; http://articles.cnn.com/2012-02-24/politics/politics_mann-santorum-satan_1_rick-santorum-satan-latest-poll?_S=PM:POLITICS. Santorum's speech was delivered at Ave Maria University. He went on to say that Satan used the "vices of pride, vanity, and sensuality" to attack America, and he described the state of affairs as "spiritual war." These remarks resurfaced in his 2012 bid for the Republican presidential nomination.

9. Rick Perry, in "Strong," presidential campaign video (www.rickperry.org), released December 2011.

10. All Jenky quotes are taken from the transcript of his sermon provided by *The Catholic Post*; http://www.thecatholicpost.com/post/PostArticle.aspx?ID=2440.

11. David Limbaugh, *Persecution: How Liberals Are Waging War Against Christianity* (Washington, DC: Regnery, 2003).

12. The remarks were made on Friday, August 26, 2011, at a campaign lunch in Spartanburg, South Carolina, and were widely reported in the national press.

13. Maureen Dowd, "Is Pleasure a Sin?"; http://www.nytimes.com/2012/06/06/opinion/dowd-is-pleasure-a-sin.html? (accessed June 10, 2012).

14. It might be argued that it is not only the myth of persecution, but also apocalyptic literature that fosters this worldview. As many scholars have demonstrated, whether or not the authors of apocalyptic texts were persecuted, they claim to experience persecution and often warn their audiences of impending arrests and executions. Persecution and apocalypticism are, thus, entangled with one another. In a study of Revelation, for instance, Adela Collins has argued that, although the author of Revelation was not actually persecuted, he believed that he was. See Adela Yarbro Collins, *Crisis and Catharsis: The Power of the Apocalypse* (Louisville, KY: Westminster John Knox, 1984).

15. Justin Martyr, *Second Apology* 2. It is really an accident of preservation that Justin is known in lay circles as "Justin Martyr," while, for example, Cyprian is known just as "Cyprian."

16. In the *Passion of Perpetua and Felicity*, the martyr Saturus says to the crowd, "Note our faces diligently, so that you may recognize them on that day of judgment!" The implication here is that the martyrs will watch their opponents condemned.

17. Peter Brown, *The Cult of the Saints: Its Rise and Function in Latin Christianity* (Chicago: Univ. of Chicago Press, 1981), 4, 78–79.

Chapter 1: Martyrdom Before Christianity

1. Justin Martyr, *First Apology* 4.1–4.

2. Glen W. Bowersock, *Martyrdom and Rome* (Cambridge: Cambridge Univ. Press, 1995), 5.

3. H. G. Liddell and R. Scott, *A Greek-English Lexicon*, s.v. *martys*.

4. Norbert Brox, *Zeuge und Märtyrer: Untersuchungen zur frühchristlichen Zeugnis-Terminologie*, Studien zum Alten und Neuen Testament 5 (Munich: Kösel, 1961).

5. Homer, *Iliad*, trans. Robert Fitzgerald (New York: Farrar, Straus, and Giroux, 2004), 21.122–23.

6. Homer, *Iliad* 7.95.

7. Homer, *Iliad* 9.410.

8. The standard work on literacy is William V. Harris, *Ancient Literacy* (Cambridge, MA: Harvard Univ. Press, 1989), which suggests that literacy rates in Attica (Greece) were about 5 percent and below 15 percent in Italy. The literacy rate depends on both geographical location and how we define "literate." People might have been able to read their names or a simple inscription but unable to compose a short letter.

9. Euripides, *Iphigenia at Aulis* 1374–99. Translation adapted from James Diggle, *Euripidis Fabulae*, vol. 3 (Oxford: Clarendon, 1994).

10. The influence of Pericles's funeral oration on nineteenth-century American politics is discussed in Garry Wills, *Lincoln at Gettysburg: The Words That Remade America* (New York: Simon & Schuster, 1992).

11. Demonsthenes, *Funeral Oration* 60.27, from *Martyrdom and Noble Death: Selected Texts from Graeco-Roman, Jewish, and Christian Antiquity*, trans. Jan Willem van Henten and Friederich Avemarie (London: Routledge, 2002).

12. Epictetus, *Discourses* 4.1.165.

13. Diogenes Laertius, *Lives of the Philosophers* 2.18–47.

14. Plato, *Phaedo* 64A.

15. Plato, *Phaedo* 58D, 98E–99A.

16. Plato, *Phaedo* 60A, 117E.

17. Plato, *Phaedo* 117B–C, 118.

18. Socrates says in the *Phaedo*, "So long as we have the body, and the soul is contaminated by such an evil, we shall never attain completely what we desire, that is, the truth" (66B).

19. Plato, *Crito* 48B.

20. Plato, *Phaedo* 107B–115C.

21. Plato, *Phaedo* 114E.

22. Diogenes Laertius, *Lives of the Philosophers* 9.58–59. The translation of this passage is based on H. S. Long, *Diogenis Laertii: Vitae Philosophorum*, vol. 2 (Oxford: Clarendon, 1964). The famous saying crops up in a number of other ancient texts. Other treatments of Anaxarchus's death are found in Valerius Maximus 3.3.4 and Plutarch, *On Moral Virtue* 10.

23. Dying Matters Coalition Survey, ComRes, May 16, 2011; www.comres.co.uk/polls/Dying_Matters_16_May_2011.pdf.

24. Charles Leadbeater and Jake Garber, "Dying for Change," pub-

lished by Demos, November 2010; http://www.demos.co.uk/files/
Dying_for_change_-_web_-_final_1_.pdf.

25. Ovid, *On Festivals* 2.8.47.

26. This argument has been made by Jan Willem van Henten in *The Maccabean Martyrs as Saviours of the Jewish People: A Study of 2 and 4 Maccabees*, Supplements to the Journal for the Study of Judaism 57 (Leiden: Brill, 1997), 271–94.

Chapter 2: Christian Borrowing of Jewish and Pagan Martyrdom Traditions

1. Ignatius of Antioch, *Letter to the Romans* 6.3.

2. Albert Schweitzer, *The Quest of the Historical Jesus: A Critical Study of Its Progress from Reimarus to Wrede*, trans. W. Montgomery (London: Black, 1911), 370–71.

3. Celsus's words are preserved only in the response of Origen, a Christian writer who lived in the third century, who quotes Celsus and then responds to his criticisms. Origen, *Contra Celsum* 6.10.

4. Greg Sterling offers a very insightful analysis of Jesus as philosopher in his article "*Mors Philosophi:* The Death of Jesus in Luke," *Harvard Theological Review* 94 (2001): 383–402.

5. I have excluded vv. 43–44 from this passage, which read: "Then an angel from heaven appeared to him and gave him strength. In his anguish he prayed more earnestly, and his sweat became like great drops of blood falling down on the ground." The reason for this is that these verses in which Jesus sweats drops of blood are omitted in a number of ancient widely diverse manuscripts. The fact that these verses are not included in earlier manuscripts leads many scholars to believe that they were added later. For this reason the New Revised Standard Version of the Bible places these verses in square brackets to signify that they are a later addition. Even if they were original to the text, Jesus's anguish in the garden is explained with reference to his prayer and bloody sweat. It's his fervent prayer, not fear, that leads to his anguish, and although they aren't bullets, he is sweating blood. For a discussion of the textual problems here, see Bruce M. Metzger, *A Textual Commentary on the Greek New Testament*, 2d ed. (New York: United Bible Societies, 1993), 151.

6. Sterling, "*Mors Philosophi*," 395–400.

7. Seneca, *Epistle* 104.28, 21. Cited in Sterling, "*Mors Philosophi*," 397.

8. *Acts of Apollonius* 1.41.

9. For a discussion of the dating of this text and the possibility that it was based on an earlier, now lost, story, see Victor Saxer, "Martyrium Apollonii Romani: Analyse structurelle et problèms d'authenticité," *Rendiconti della Pontifica Accademia Romana di Archeologia* 55–56 (1983–84): 265–98.

10. A more in-depth analysis of the *Martyrdom of Polycarp* together with a summary of the copious literature on this important story can be found in my "On the Dating of Polycarp: Rethinking the Place of the *Martyrdom of Polycarp* in the History of Christianity," *Early Christianity* 1, no. 4 (2010): 539–74.

11. Details of Polycarp's biography are provided by Irenaeus in his *Against the Heresies* 3.3.4. A piece of the correspondence between Ignatius and Polycarp is preserved in Ignatius, *Letter to Polycarp*. See the discussion in my article "On the Dating of Polycarp."

12. *Martyrdom of Polycarp* 1.2; 5.2; 6.2; 7.1–2; 8.1; 12.2–13.1; 9.3–11.2; 9.1; 21.1; 16.1.

13. Plato, *Euthyphro* 3B; *Martyrdom of Polycarp* 12.2. Polycarp is called noble only as part of a description of all the martyrs.

14. Plato, *Apology* 35D; *Martyrdom of Polycarp* 10.2.

15. Plato, *Phaedo* 116D.

16. *Martyrdom of Polycarp* 13.2–3.

17. Plato, *Phaedo* 117C; *Martyrdom of Polycarp* 14.1–3.

18. Plato, *Phaedo* 118A; *Martyrdom of Polycarp* 14.1.

19. Plato, *Apology* 17D; *Crito* 52E; *Martyrdom of Polycarp* 9.3.

20. Plato, *Phaedo* 115C; *Martyrdom of Polycarp* 1.2; 19.1.

21. Tacitus, *Annals* 34–35; Cassius Dio, *Roman History* 62.26.4. Once again it is unclear whether this was truly how the senators died, but their biographers, at least, chose to present them as philosophers.

22. *Martyrdom of Polycarp* 13.3.

23. This interpretation was raised by L. Stephanie Cobb in "*Imitatio Socratis*: The Martyrdom of Polycarp and the Noble Death Tradition," paper presented at the Annual Meeting of the Society of Biblical Literature, November 2009, New Orleans. For a discussion of this theory and other early Christian and scholarly views of this scene see Candida R. Moss, "Nailing Down and Tying Up: Intertextual Impossibilities in the *Martyrdom of Polycarp*," *Vigilae Christianae* 66 (2012): 1–20.

24. Justin Martyr, *Second Apology* 1.2.

25. *Martyrs of Lyons* 5.1.9.

26. *Martyrs of Lyons* 5.1.29.
27. *Martyrs of Lyons* 5.1.55–56.
28. This point is eloquently made by L. Stephanie Cobb in her book *Dying to Be Men: Gender and Language in Early Christian Martyr Texts*, Gender, Theory, and Religion (New York: Columbia Univ. Press, 2008). On female martyrs in general, see Gail Corrington Streete, *Redeemed Bodies: Women Martyrs in Early Christianity* (Louisville, KY: Westminster John Knox, 2009); Kate Cooper, *The Virgin and the Bride: Idealized Womanhood in Late Antiquity* (Cambridge, MA: Harvard Univ. Press, 1996); and Virginia Burrus, *Saving Shame: Martyrs, Saints, and Other Abject Subjects* (Philadelphia: Univ. of Pennsylvania Press, 2008).
29. *Martyrdom of Marian and James* 13.1.
30. *Martyrdom of Montanus and Lucius* 16.4.
31. *Martyrs of Lyons* 5.1.41.
32. Euripides, *Hecuba* 568–70. This aspect of the *Passion of Perpetua and Felicity* is discussed in Jan N. Bremmer's "Myth and Ritual in Greek Human Sacrifice: Lykaon, Polyxena and the Case of the Rhodian Criminal," in *The Strange World of Human Sacrifice*, ed. Jan N. Bremmer (Leuven: Peeters, 2007), 55–79.
33. Even a quick glance at the Gospel of Mark reveals that the final week of Jesus's life takes up a much larger proportion of the Gospel than one might expect. This observation led to the hypothesis that the passion narrative was composed first and circulated separately. Detlev Dormeyer suggests that the genre of this pre-Markan passion narrative was a kind of early martyrdom story. See Detlev Dormeyer, *Die Passion Jesu als Verhaltensmodell: Literarische und theologische Analyse der Traditions- und Redaktionsgeschichte der Markuspassion*, Neutestamentliche Abhandlungen 11 (Münster: Aschendorff, 1974), 238–58. For the argument that the passion narratives are themselves martyrdom accounts or protomartyrdom accounts dependent on a preexisting genre, see Jan Willem van Henten, "Jewish Martyrdom and Jesus's Death," in *Deutungen des Todes Jesu im Neuen Testament*, ed. Jörg Frey and Jens Schröter (Tübingen: Mohr Siebeck, 2005), 157–68; Donald W. Riddle, "The Martyr Motif in the Gospel According to Mark," *Journal of Religion* 4, no. 4 (1924): 397–410; and M. E. Vines, "The 'Trial Scene' Chronotype in Mark and the Jewish Novel," in *The Trial and Death of Jesus: Essays on the Passion Narrative in Mark*, ed. G. van Oyen and T. Shepherd (Leuven: Peeters, 2006), 189–203.

34. Edgar J. Goodspeed, *A History of Early Christian Literature*, rev. Robert M. Grant (Chicago: Univ. of Chicago Press, 1966), 25.
35. *Acts of Appianus* col. i 40.
36. English translations of these stories can be found in B. P. Reardon, *Collected Ancient Greek Novels* (Berkeley: Univ. of California Press, 1989).
37. Similarities between the apocryphal acts and the Greek romance have been noted by scholars since the 1920s. For a classic treatment, see Stevan L. Davies, *The Revolt of the Widows: The Social World of the Apocryphal Acts* (Carbondale: Southern Illinois Univ. Press, 1980).
38. For this view, see Judith Perkins, *The Suffering Self: Pain and Narrative Representation in the Early Christian Era* (London: Routledge, 1995); and Kate Cooper, *The Virgin and the Bride*.

Chapter 3: Inventing Martyrs in Early Christianity

1. Roland H. Bainton, *Here I Stand: A Life of Martin Luther* (New York: Meridian, 1995), 231.
2. In Christian tradition the story was attributed to John of Damascus, an important church writer who lived in the eighth century. No doubt the association with a famous saint boosted the reputation of the legend, but scholarly investigation into the story has shown this tradition to be false.
3. A companion of Marco Polo, Diego de Couto, noticed the similarities too and argued in his continuation of the *Décadas* (5.54.6.2) that the Buddhist legend was dependent on the Christian one. I cannot help but admire his optimism. All scholars since have recognized that it is the Christian story that is derivative. Hippolyte Delehaye encapsulates the prevailing view when he writes, "And which of us today is unaware that the life of the saints Barlaam and Josaphat is merely an adaptation of the Buddha legend?" (*The Legends of the Saints* [Notre Dame, IN: Univ. of Notre Dame Press, 1961], 63).
4. Max Müller, a scholar of "oriental religions" and one of the first to explore the parallels between Buddha and Josaphat, tries to argue for the retention of Josaphat alongside other "not always more saintly saints" in *Last Essays by the Right Hon. Professor F. Max Müller, First Series* (London: Longmans, Green, 1901), 277.

It's difficult not to admire Professor Müller for his honesty and ecumenical spirit.

5. This point is made by Alexander Robertson in *The Roman Catholic Church in Italy*, 5th ed. (London: Morgan and Scott, 1905), 194. Robertson did not have high hopes for Catholicism. He further notes, "One need not wonder, for even if the Church gets hold of a truth, it never rests till it builds a pyramid of falsehoods above it. One need not wonder that pagans and fictitious beings are adored as saints, when mules, mice, dogs, pigs, deer, sheep, lambs, and donkeys have all been exalted into the blessed category" (194).

6. The full title of this work is *Fasti sanctorum quorum vitae in belgicis bibliothecis manuscriptae* (Antwerp, 1607). Rosweyde referred only to manuscripts contained in Belgian libraries. His successor, John Bolland, was more of a delegator and sent out inquiries to contacts at monasteries and libraries all over Europe. A fuller treatment of the fascinating history of the Bollandists can be found in Hippolyte Delehaye, *The Work of the Bollandists Through Three Centuries: 1615–1915* (Princeton, NJ: Princeton Univ. Press, 1922); or Robert Godding et al., *Bollandistes, saints et légendes: Quatre siècles de recherche* (Brussels: Société des Bollandistes, 2007).

7. Aurelio Palmieri, "The Bollandists," *Catholic Historical Review* 9, no. 3 (1923): 341–57 [342].

8. Aurelio Palmieri, "The Bollandists: The Period of Trial," *Catholic Historical Review* 9, no. 4 (1924): 517–29 [517].

9. This much was acknowledged by Papebroch. See Delehaye, *Work of the Bollandists*, 126.

10. On St. Christopher medals, Christopher is pictured as a giant holding a staff and carrying a child on his shoulders. Christopher was in all probability an unknown martyr from Asia Minor who *perhaps* died during the reign of Diocletian. The story of a cannibalistic monster and Christopher the giant ferryman-hermit is a medieval legend. His feast day was removed from the Catholic calendar of saints by Pope Paul VI in 1969.

11. See, for example, the *Acts of Tarachus, Probus, and Andronicus*, which all scholars recognize as a forgery despite the formal courtroom style. See Timothy D. Barnes, *Early Christian Hagiography and Roman History* (Tübingen: Mohr Siebeck, 2010), 58.

12. The arguments for dating and influence discussed in this chapter are laid out in greater depth in my books *The Other Christs:*

Imitating Jesus in Ancient Christian Ideologies of Martyrdom (New York: Oxford Univ. Press, 2010) and *Ancient Christian Martyrdom: Diverse Practices, Theologies, and Traditions*, Yale Anchor Reference Library (New Haven, CT: Yale Univ. Press, 2012).

13. The number of other trustworthy martyrdom stories is hotly contested. Some of the more reliable stories can be found in Herbert Musurillo's *The Acts of the Christian Martyrs* (Oxford: Clarendon, 1972). Even these stories betray evidence of later editing, interpolated speeches, and anachronistic details. Similarly, Christian authors like Tertullian, Origen, Eusebius, and Augustine refer to the deaths of other Christians or groups of Christians, often in improbably large numbers. Without more information, however, it is impossible to reconstruct the circumstances in which these Christians died, if, in fact, they existed.

14. An alternate view has been put forward by Elizabeth Castelli, who has argued that it is memorialization, not historical details, that secures the martyr's position. This may be true and certainly *has* been the case, as the vast number of inauthentic stories shows us, but to many people it is important that a martyr actually died for Christ. If we are going to use these stories to make claims about the historical reality of persecution and martyrdom across time, especially claims that relate to our present situation, then we need to evaluate the evidence. See Elizabeth A. Castelli, *Martyrdom and Memory: Early Christian Culture Making*, Gender, Theory, and Religion (New York: Columbia Univ. Press, 2004).

15. Dan Luzadder and Kevin Vaughan, "Biggest Question of All," *Rocky Mountain News*, December 14, 1999; http://therocky.com/news/1999/dec/14/inside-columbine-investigation-part-3-biggest-ques/.

16. A fuller treatment of the dating of the *Martyrdom of Polycarp* can be found in my article "On the Dating of Polycarp."

17. In actual fact we have very little evidence to suggest that anyone read the *Martyrdom of Polycarp* until the middle of the third century. This means that regardless of the date of the account, it was not especially important. See my "Polycarphilia and the Origins of Martyrdom," in *The Rise and Expansion of Christianity in the First Three Centuries C.E.*, Wissenschaftliche Untersuchungen zum Neuen Testament, ed. Jens Schröter and Clare K. Rothschild (Tübingen: Mohr Siebeck, 2012).

18. *Martyrdom of Polycarp* 1.1.

19. *Martyrdom of Polycarp* 9.1.
20. *Martyrdom of Polycarp* 15.1–2.
21. *Martyrdom of Polycarp* 3.2.
22. *Martyrdom of Polycarp* 13.1.
23. Joseph Barber Lightfoot, *The Apostolic Fathers* (London: Macmillan, 1889).
24. *Martyrdom of Polycarp* 1.1; 1.2.
25. This problem was recognized by Edgar Goodspeed, an American papyrologist who examined the fragments of the martyrdom story when visiting Jerusalem in 1900. See Edgar J. Goodspeed, "A Martyrological Fragment from Jerusalem," *American Journal of Philology* 23, no. 1 (1902): 68–74. Other examples of historically suspect martyrdom stories that imitate the phraseology of official legislation can be found in Delehaye, *Legends of the Saints*, 93.
26. *Martyrdom of Polycarp* 4.1.
27. *Martyrdom of Polycarp* 4.1.
28. In actual fact and as we will see in later chapters, the *Martyrdom of Polycarp* is in the minority; most Christians did not see offering themselves for martyrdom as problematic.
29. Clement, *Miscellanies* 4.16–17.
30. *Martyrdom of Polycarp* 17.2.
31. *Martyrdom of Polycarp* 17.3.
32. *Martyrdom of Polycarp* 18.2.
33. *Passion of Perpetua and Felicity* 21; Cyprian, *Epistle* 76.2; *Acts of Cyprian* 5.
34. This suggestion was made by the great early Christian historian Adolf von Harnack in *Analecta* 3–5. He has been followed by R. M. Grant, who not only identifies Ptolemy with the Valentinian Ptolemy, but the unnamed woman as Flora, the addressee of Ptolemy's *Letter to Flora*. See R. M. Grant, "A Woman of Rome: The Matron in Justin, *2 Apology* 2.1–9," *Church History* 54 (1985): 461–72. More recent scholars have seen this argument as unnecessary, arguing that it is possible that there were two Christian Ptolemys in Rome at the same time. See, for example, Paul Parvis, "Justin, Philosopher and Martyr: The Posthumous Creation of the *Second Apology*," in *Justin Martyr and His Worlds*, ed. Sara Parvis and Paul Foster (Minneapolis, MN: Fortress, 2007), 22–37.
35. See Karen L. King, *What Is Gnosticism?* (Cambridge, MA: Harvard Univ. Press, 2003). For a recent, considered approach to Gnosti-

cism, see David Brakke, *The Gnostics: Myth, Ritual, and Diversity in Early Christianity* (Cambridge, MA: Harvard Univ. Press, 2011).

36. Pagels's classic treatment of Gnosticism is found in Elaine Pagels, *The Gnostic Gospels* (New York: Random House, 1979). Her discussion of the *Gospel of Judas*'s antagonistic take on martyrdom is found in Elaine Pagels and Karen L. King, *Reading Judas: The Gospel of Judas and the Shaping of Christianity* (New York: Viking, 2007).

37. Justin, *Second Apology* 2.16.

38. Justin, *Second Apology* 2.16.

39. Justin, *First Apology* 2.1. This point is noted in the excellent translation and commentary by Denis Minns and Paul Parvis, *Justin, Philosopher and Martyr: Apologies*, Oxford Early Christian Texts (Oxford: Oxford Univ. Press, 2009), 279, n. 4. Minns and Parvis argue that the *Second Apology* was put together after Justin's death by some of his students. In this case it would have been Justin's students who copied a section of the *First Apology* into the *Second Apology*. In either case the effect is the same. Lucius did not say these words; someone else did.

40. Eusebius, *Church History* 4.16.8.

41. Barnes, *Early Christian Hagiography*, 63.

42. Gary A. Bisbee, *Pre-Decian Acts of Martyrs and Commentarii*, Harvard Dissertations in Religion 22, ed. Margaret R. Miles and Bernadette J. Brooten (Philadelphia: Fortress, 1988); and "The Acts of Justin Martyr: A Form-Critical Study," *Second Century* 3, no. 3 (1983): 129–57.

43. Bisbee, *Pre-Decian Acts*, 117.

44. Barnes, *Early Christian Hagiography*.

45. *Acts of Justin* A5.6.

46. For this usage, see Pliny, *Letters* 10.96.3. For Barnes's argument, see *Early Christian Hagiography*, 63–64.

47. Justin, *Second Apology* 2.15.

48. This theory is developed in Parvis, "Justin, Philosopher and Martyr," 22–37.

49. See Moss, *Ancient Christian Martyrdom*, 89–90.

50. Eusebius, *Church History* 5.1.3.

51. Eusebius, *Church History* 5.1.1–5.3.4.

52. *Martyrs of Lyons* 5.1.7–9.

53. *Martyrs of Lyons* 5.1.45.

54. Methodius, *Symposium* 3.8.

55. *Martyrs of Lyons* 5.1.1; *Martyrs of Palestine* 2.28; *Church History* 3.4.4.

56. *Church History* 3.24.1.

57. There are in fact two versions of the text: a long and short version. The short version, which is judged by most scholars to be the earlier of the two texts, is extant in both Greek and Latin. Ordinarily we might suppose that the Greek version preceded the Latin version, but in fact this was shown by J. Armitage Robinson not to be the case. To my knowledge no scholars today doubt that the shorter Latin version is the earlier of the texts. The arguments for the priority of the shorter Latin version can be found in Robinson, *The Passion of S. Perpetua*, Texts and Studies 1 (Cambridge: Cambridge Univ. Press, 1891), appendix.

58. Musurillo, *Acts*, 86–89.

59. This observation is made by David L. Eastman in his book *Paul the Martyr: The Cult of the Apostle in the Latin West* (Atlanta: Society of Biblical Literature, 2011). Eastman follows the critical edition of Bastiaensen; I have altered the chiasmus to reflect my own judgment on the original form of the account.

60. The best overview of this subject is found in Jan N. Bremmer and Marco Formisano, *Perpetua's Passions* (New York: Oxford Univ. Press, 2012), introduction.

61. This reading of Perpetua's diary apart from the agenda of the editor is undertaken in Kate Cooper, "A Father, a Daughter, and a Procurator: Authority and Resistance in the Prison Memoir of Perpetua of Carthage," *Gender and History* 23 (2011): 685–702.

62. *Passion of Perpetua and Felicity* 11.1.

63. Tertullian, *On the Soul* 55.4–5.

64. For a discussion of the parallels, see Jan N. Bremmer, "Magic, Martyrdom, and Women's Liberation," in *The Apocryphal Acts of Paul and Thecla*, ed. Jan N. Bremmer (Kampen, Netherlands: Kok Pharos, 1996), 36–59.

65. *Passion of Perpetua and Felicity* 21.2–3.

66. *Passion of Perpetua and Felicity* 7.4–8.

67. *Passion of Perpetua and Felicity* 8.1.

68. *Acts of Paul and Thecla* 29.

69. Tertullian, *On Baptism* 17.5.

70. Bremmer, "Magic," 44; and Moss, *Ancient Christian Martyrdom*, 141–43.

Chapter 4: How Persecuted Were the Early Christians?

1. Justin, *First Apology* 4.4. He is adamant, in fact, that "with respect both to our name and to our behavior, we are found to do no wrong" (4.2). Justin's *First Apology* goes on to offer a full and detailed defense of Christians that appeals to their Jewish heritage and draws on comparisons with Greek and Roman religion. Even though it offers reasons for the innocence of Christians, it's uncertain that this letter was even intended to reach the emperor. Some scholars have argued it is a carefully crafted piece of Christian literature designed to foster and forge Christian identity. All the same, Justin gives us some insight into why Christians *thought* they were being targeted by the Romans, namely, just for being Christian.

2. Tertullian, *Apology* 20.

3. The dating of the "Great Persecution" depends a great deal on the extent to which we are willing to give credence to the evidence provided by later Christian authors. The final piece of the legislation against Christians was enacted in 304 (Eusebius, *Martyrs of Palestine* 3.1). In theory the persecutions continued in certain regions as late as 313, when Maximinus Daia—the last great persecutor—issued an edict restoring the privileges and property of the Christians. The rights of Christians had already been restored in Gaul, Spain, Britain, Italy, and Africa in 306 and in Macedonia and Greece in 311. The extent to which there was active persecution of Christians after the fourth edict in 304 is open for debate. See the discussion under "The Great Persecution" (p. 154) and in G. E. M. de Ste. Croix, "Aspects of the 'Great' Persecution," in *Christian Persecution, Martyrdom, and Orthodoxy* (New York: Oxford Univ. Press, 2006), 35–78.

4. There was a brief period in 362, during the short reign of the emperor Julian "the Apostate," when paganism was revived and wealthy and powerful Christians were driven out of the governing classes, but this is not, by and large, included in studies of persecution. Peter Brown compares the program of pagan renewal under Julian with the suppression of Buddhism during a period of Confucian revival in thirteenth-century China. See Peter Brown, *The World of Late Antiquity: AD 150–750* (New York: Norton, 1989), 93.

5. G. E. M. de Ste. Croix, "Why Were the Early Christians Persecuted?" *Past and Present* 26 (1963): 6–38, reprinted in de Ste. Croix, *Christian Persecution, Martyrdom, and Orthodoxy*, 105–52 [106].

6. It's historically improbable that even the disciples knew what was said at the crucifixion. Although in Luke the disciples are described as being present at the crucifixion, Mark, the earliest Gospel, only notes the presence of the women who had followed Jesus (15:40).

7. It might be argued that Jewish followers of Jesus were attempting to distance themselves from non–Jesus-believing Jews. For example, in the Gospel of John the followers of Jesus are repeatedly pitted against "the Jews." The Gospel of John, however, is estimated by scholars to have been written sometime after 90 CE. Moreover, the antagonism expressed by the fourth Gospel toward the Jews seems to be the result of a schism at the time between the community for whom the Gospel was written and synagogue-going Jews.

8. The question of when Jesus followers began to think of and call themselves Christians is a huge one. Regardless of when this process began, it seems clear that the "parting of the ways" was a lengthy process. Early Christian thinking about martyrdom seems to have played a role in this process and the formation of Christian identity. For the role of theories about martyrdom in the development of Christian identity with respect to Jews, see Judith M. Lieu, *Image and Reality: The Jews in the World of the Christians in the Second Century* (Edinburgh: Clark, 1996); and Daniel Boyarin, *Dying for God: Martyrdom and the Making of Christianity and Judaism* (Stanford, CA: Stanford Univ. Press, 1999). The moment at which the title "Christian," or *christianos*, began to be used is similarly controversial and in part rests on the dating of the Acts of the Apostles. It seems to have emerged at the end of the first century and become common usage by the beginning of the second. For more information on the development of the term, see David G. Horrell, "The Label Χριστιανος: 1 Peter 4:16 and the Formation of Christian Identity," *Journal of Biblical Literature* 126, no. 2 (2007): 361–81.

9. An excellent bibliography and introduction to these important stories can be found in Hans-Josef Klauck, *The Apocryphal Acts of the Apostles: An Introduction*, trans. Brian McNeil (Waco, TX: Baylor Univ. Press, 2008).

10. So Jan N. Bremmer, "Aspects of the *Acts of Peter*: Women, Magic, Place, and Date," in *The Apocryphal Acts of Peter: Magic, Miracles, and Gnosticism*, ed. Jan N. Bremmer (Leuven: Peeters, 1998), 1–20; and Christine M. Thomas, *The "Acts of Peter," Gospel Lit-*

erature, and the Ancient Novel: Rewriting the Past (New York: Oxford Univ. Press, 2003).

11. *1 Clement* 5:1–7.

12. Tacitus, *Annals* 15.44.

13. Some scholars have attempted to argue that from the time of Nero Christianity was illegal across the empire. This argument suffers from a number of problems, most notably: (1) our evidence for Nero's treatment of Christians comes from the second century and does not mention a law of any kind; and (2) if Christianity was illegal, then why does Pliny need to ask Trajan (ca. 112) about how to treat Christians?

14. Pliny, *Letters* 10.13, 4.

15. Recent scholarship on the correspondence between Pliny and Trajan has argued that these letters are not solely about imperial business; they were also a way for Pliny to put his "best foot forward" and construct a public image of himself as an intimate friend of the emperor. For this argument, see Carlos F. Noreña, "The Social Economy of Pliny's Correspondence with Trajan," *American Journal of Philology* 128, no. 2 (2007): 239–77.

16. Pliny, *Letters* 10.25–28.

17. Pliny, *Letters* 10.96; www.fordham.edu/halsall/source/pliny1.asp.

18. The legal grounds for Pliny's treatment of the Christians have long been the subject of interest. The standard scholarly articles on the subject are still de Ste. Croix, "Why Were the Early Christians Persecuted?"; the response by A. N. Sherwin-White, "Why Were the Early Christians Persecuted?—An Amendment," *Past and Present* 27 (1964): 23–27; and de Ste. Croix's response, "Why Were the Early Christians Persecuted?—A Rejoinder," *Past and Present* 27 (1964): 28–33. One problem that emerges in this scholarly exchange is that the evidence from the martyrdom stories does not match up with the Pliny–Trajan correspondence. The charges of obstinacy and defiance are not mentioned in the martyrdom stories. Moreover, Pliny administers the sacrifice test only to those who deny Christ, but some judges give the Christians time to think over the matter and sacrifice to the emperor *even after they have admitted to being Christian*. My own opinions are laid out in the introduction to *Ancient Christian Martyrdom*, 9–12.

19. Pliny, *Letters* 10.97; www.fordham.edu/halsall/source/pliny1.asp.

20. The situation with the Pliny–Trajan correspondence might be considered similar to the treatment of polygamy in the United

States today. Polygamy is illegal in all fifty states, but most polygamists are not prosecuted. The situation in which a polygamist would be most likely to find him- or herself prosecuted would be if a formal complaint were made to legal authorities or if he or she were suspected of related crimes.

21. Here Eusebius is beholden to his sources Melito of Sardis (*Church History* 4.26) and Tertullian (*Apology* 5) cited in *Church History* 2.2.25; 3.20; 5.5.

22. James B. Rives, "The Piety of a Persecutor," *Journal of Early Christian Studies* 4, no. 1 (1996): 1–25.

23. The historicity of this story is also difficult to assess. In the first place its source, Tertullian, is writing in North Africa, some distance away from Asia Minor. Moreover, many scholars think that letters like these from Christians to Roman emperors or governors were actually written for Christian audiences. So instead of sending an actual letter to the governor, Tertullian is using the genre of a formal letter to instruct other Christians.

24. Because it has not survived, there is some debate about the precise date of the decree. The date is inferred from a variety of potential occasions upon which Decius *might* have demanded a universal sacrifice from the people. January 3, 250, was the date when Roman officials would have offered their annual sacrifices and oaths for the health and safety of the emperor (*pro salute imperatoris*). Thus G. W. Clarke has argued that this was the occasion for the edict's implementation (see "Persecution of Decius," in *Cambridge Ancient History* vol. 12, ed. Alan Bowman, Averil Cameron, and Peter Garnsey [New York: Cambridge Univ. Press, 2005], 625–34). David Potter, who points out the exceptionality of the edict, dates the edict immediately following Philip I's death in November 249 (*Prophecy and History in the Crisis of the Roman Empire: A Historical Commentary on the* Thirteenth Sibylline Oracle [Oxford: Clarendon, 1990], 261). Others date the edict to the day on which the Roman Senate officially recognized Decius's accession (A. Alföldi, "Zu den Christenverfolgungen in der Mitte des 3. Jahrhunderts," *Klio* 31 [1938]: 323–48).

25. This text is a translation of P.Mich. III 158, which was found at Theadelphia. Transcriptions and translations of the *libelli* are found in J. Knipfing, "The *Libelli* of the Decian Persecution," *Harvard Theological Review* 16 (1923): 345–90. Three more *libelli*

were discovered after Knipfing's article (PSI vii.78; SB vi.9084; P.Oxy. xli.2990).

26. The facts that the decree is lost and that there are scant references to it from antiquity have led scholars to compile various theories about the number of and character of the decree(s). All we have are the *libelli* and references in early Christian literature. The discovery of the *libelli* led a number of scholars to the conclusion that there was a single general edict directed against everyone in the empire. In an effort to maintain the anti-Christian nature of the Decian edict, other scholars argued that there were two edicts or other legislation (also lost) that specifically targeted Christians. For an exhaustive overview of the scholarly arguments together with his own view that the Decian edict functioned as an act of apotropaic supplication (a supplication to the gods to avert harm) intended to achieve the *pax deorum* ("peace of the gods"), see Allen Brent, *Cyprian and Roman Carthage* (Cambridge: Cambridge Univ. Press, 2010), 117–249.

27. Cyprian refers to *libelli* obtained by bribery in his *On the Lapsed* 27 and *Letters* 55.13.2.

28. Cyprian, *On the Lapsed* 3.

29. Decius's edict would have been difficult, but not impossible, to implement. It might have been possible to use census registers assembled for the purposes of taxation in order to identify and document those who had failed to appear for the sacrifice. Scholars are divided about how much of an administrative nightmare the edict would have been. In either case, whether there were "well-established bureaucratic procedures" (James B. Rives, "The Decree of Decius and the Religion of Empire," *Journal of Roman Studies* 89 [1999]: 135–54 [150]) or not (Robin Lane Fox, *Pagans and Christians* [New York: Knopf, 1987], 455–56), it does not appear that the Romans hunted down those who had played truant.

30. There is some disagreement about the cause of the nineteen-year-old Gordian's death and the reliability of the various sources, all of which were composed some time after his death. For a discussion of the four main theories, see Xavier Loriot, "Les premières années de la grand crise du IIIe siècle: De l'avènement de Maximin de Thrace (235) à la mort de Gordien III (244)," in Hildegard Temporini and Wolfgang Haase, *Aufstieg und Niedergang der römischen Welt* II.2 (Berlin: De Gruyter, 1975), 770–72.

31. Although Decius had advised his predecessor, Philip I—whom he

ultimately usurped—that rebellions often sprang up and fizzled of their own accord, once he became emperor these challenges to his power and authority likely seemed more serious. During his short reign he faced challenges from two would-be emperors—Jotapianus, who rebelled either in Syria (Aurelius Victor 29) or in Cappadocia (Zosimus, *New History* 1.20.5), and Julius Valens Licinianus, a Roman senator who claimed the imperial purple for himself while Decius was away at war (Aurelius Victor 29.5). The fact that Decius himself seized power from Philip may cast some doubts on Decius's sincerity in his statement to Philip.

32. See J. Molthagen, *Der Römische Staat und die Christen im zweiten und dritten Jahrhundert,* Hypomnemata 28 (Göttingen: Vandenhoeck & Ruprecht, 1970), 73–74. Molthagen sees Decius's edict as motivated by a desire to reinforce political unity in danger of collapse.

33. On the popularity of Trajan, see Julian Bennett, *Trajan: Optimus Princeps* (London: Routledge, 2000).

34. Even church historian Eusebius admits this when he says that Decius "persecuted" the Christians because his rival Philip I was a secret Christian (*Church History* 6.29). Eusebius seems to be stretching the truth here.

35. This argument is persuasively made by Rives in "Decree of Decius."

36. Rives, "Decree of Decius," 151.

37. It is not even clear how long the effects of the decree were felt. Once the decree arrived in a particular location, it would have had to have been enforced, but the enforcement of the sacrifice would have taken place in a relatively short time period and with as much efficiency as the Roman administrators could muster. Thus, the actual period in which citizens were expected to present themselves and participate in the ritual might have lasted only a few months.

38. Cyprian, *Letter* 80.2.

39. The prohibition is rooted in the Bill of Rights of 1689 and the Act of Settlement of 1701 and emerged out of the events of civil war in England and the century that followed, but it still remained on the books until the end of 2011. At that time in England's history, Protestants felt that it was not in the best interests of a Protestant country to have a monarch who might be unduly influenced by a Catholic spouse.

40. According to the American Humanist Society, this information is current as of May 2012; http://www.americanhumanist .org/HNN/details/2012-05-unelectable-atheists-us-states-that -prohibit-godless.

41. Timothy Barnes believes that the *Acts of Cyprian* was not based on a court report but was instead composed by eyewitnesses as a composite of two separate trials. He states that, given the openness of the trial, it was not necessary for anyone to seek to obtain an official court transcript (*Early Christian Hagiography*, 81–82). This kind of explanation, which Barnes supplies in a number of cases, seems determined to preserve the authenticity of these reports. The fact of the matter is this. The *Acts of Cyprian* looks like a court report, and yet, as Barnes and I agree, it is not a court report. Why a hypothetical eyewitness, recording the events that he had witnessed, would feel compelled to write a document ex nihilo in the style of a court report is beyond me. Nothing about the account suggests that it is an eyewitness report. It is not composed in the first person. It seems more likely that the author wants to give the account the feel of an official trial.

42. Lactantius, *On the Deaths of the Persecutors* 5.

43. On political turbulence in the third century, see Peter Garnsey and Caroline Humfress, *The Evolution of the Late Antique World* (Cambridge: Orchard Academic, 2001), 9–24.

44. The extent of economic instability is debated. For a discussion of the Diocletian persecution, see D. Vincent Twomey and Mark Humphries, *The Great Persecution: The Proceedings of the Fifth Patristic Conference, Maynooth, 2003* (Dublin: Four Courts, 2009).

45. This legislation against the Manichaeans also blended political, social, and religious concerns.

46. As with all episodes of so-called persecution, scholars have debated the precise motivations of the Diocletian persecution. The literature on this question is vast, and much of the bibliography can be found in Mark Humphries, "The Mind of the Persecutors," in Twomey and Humphries, *Great Persecution*, 11–32. For a more recent bibliography and the argument that the underpinnings of the persecution can be found in debates about philosophy and piety, see Elizabeth DePalma Digeser, *A Threat to Public Piety: Christians, Platonists, and the Great Persecution* (Ithaca, NY: Cornell Univ. Press, 2012).

47. Books were rare and expensive, but the statement that many Christians did not attend church may surprise people. I follow here the argument of Ramsay MacMullen, who argues that only 5 percent of the Christian population actually attended church services. See Ramsay MacMullen, *The Second Church: Popular Christianity A.D. 200–400*, Writings from the Greco-Roman World Supplements (Atlanta: Society of Biblical Literature, 2009).

48. P.Oxy. xxxi 2601. This example is provided by Barnes in *Early Christian Hagiography*, 111, n. 27.

49. Lactantius, *On the Deaths of the Persecutors* 11.8.

50. Lactantius, *On the Deaths of the Persecutors* 15.7. Eusebius, *Church History* 8.13.13. Eusebius does, however, list Gaul as an area afflicted by persecutions in his *Martyrs of Palestine* 13.12. This has to be judged next to the claim of a group of bishops that Gaul was "immune" to persecution (Optatus 1.22, cited in Graeme Clarke, "Third Century Christianity," *CAM* 12: 589–671 [651, n. 149].

51. Lactantius, *On the Deaths of the Persecutors* 24.7.

52. On this and other aspects of the Great Persecution, see Stephen Williams, *Diocletian and the Roman Recovery* (London: Routledge, 1996), 173–85.

53. Eusebius, *Church History* 8.2.5.

54. Eusebius, *Church History* 8.6.8–9; *Martyrs of Palestine*, Praef. 2.

55. The suggestion was occasionally made. When, at the conclusion of his trial, Socrates suggested that the city provide him with free meals as punishment for his crimes, the Athenian jury responded to his joke by sentencing him to death.

56. Eusebius, *Church History* 8.2.5; 6.10.

57. Some scholars have hypothesized that Diocletian wanted to secure good publicity for his persecution and that he issued this edict in the hopes that clergy would apostatize. So Roger Rees, *Diocletian and the Tetrarchy* (Edinburgh: Edinburgh Univ. Press, 2004), 64.

58. Eusebius, *Martyrs of Palestine* 1.5.

59. Eusebius, *Martyrs of Palestine* 3.1; Lactantius, *On the Deaths of the Persecutors* 15.4.

60. De Ste. Croix, "Aspects of the Great Persecution," 65.

61. De Ste. Croix, "Aspects of the Great Persecution," 42.

62. Lactantius, *Divine Institutes* 5.11.13.

Chapter 5: Why Did the Romans Dislike Christians?

1. Of course cruelty is largely in the eyes of the beholder, and the Romans were not as kind as their propaganda or their admiring nineteenth-century classicists would have us believe. The Assyrians had a reputation for impaling their enemies on sticks, but crucifixion also involved the public hanging of enemies. For readers of German, a recent volume examines the extreme forms of torture used in antiquity: Martin Zimmermann, *Extreme Formen von Gewalt in Bild und Text des Altertums*, Münchner Studien zur Alten Welt (Munich: Herbert Utz, 2009).

2. For those interested in this question more broadly, a valuable resource is Robert L. Wilken, *The Christians as the Romans Saw Them* (New Haven, CT: Yale Univ. Press, 1984).

3. Peter Garnsey, "Religious Toleration in Classical Antiquity," *Studies in Church History* 21 (1984): 9.

4. Clifford Ando, "The Ontology of Religious Institutions," *History of Religions* 50, no. 1 (2010): 54–79.

5. Julius Caesar, *Gallic War* 6.16; Strabo, *Geography* 4.4.5.

6. Pliny, *Natural History* 20.12; Tacitus, *Annals* 14.30.

7. Tacitus, *Annals* 14.29.

8. Livy, *History of Rome* 39.8.

9. Tertullian, *Apology* 40.

10. Clifford Ando, "The Ontology of Religious Institutions."

11. Compare, for example, *Martyrdom of Pionius* 4:24.

12. It has commonly been argued that the Jews were exempt from participation in the imperial cult. Recent work has questioned this thesis. Archaeological data suggest that although they did not participate in imperial processions, the Jews would accord the emperor certain honors, inscriptions dedicated to the well-being of the emperor, for instance. For recent studies on Jewish participation in the imperial cult, see Monika Bernett, "Roman Imperial Cult in the Galilee: Structures, Functions, and Dynamics," in *Religion, Ethnicity, and Identity in Ancient Galilee*, ed. Jürgen Zangenber, Harold W. Attridge, and Dale B. Martin, Wissenschaftliche Untersuchungen zum Neuen Testament 1.270 (Tübingen: Mohr Siebeck, 2007), 337–56; and Justin K. Hardin, *Galatians and the Imperial Cult*, Wissenschaftliche Untersuchungen zum Neuen Testament 2.237 (Tübingen: Mohr Siebeck, 2008). Both authors suggest that Jewish involvement in the cult should be understood

not as part of an official exemption, but rather as carefully moderated involvement. It should be noted that if the Jews were *not* exempt, then the arguments and conduct of Christians would have appeared even more outlandish to Roman authorities. The fact that records of Romans prosecuting Jews and stories of these trials do not survive would be further evidence that later Christian authors have tightly controlled our evidence about "persecution" during this period.

13. A. N. Sherwin-White, "The Early Persecutions and Roman Law Again," *Journal of Theological Studies* 3, no. 2 (1952): 199–213.

14. Pliny, *Letters* 10.96.3.

15. G. E. M. de Ste. Croix, "Why Were the Early Christians Persecuted?—A Rejoinder."

16. See Dale B. Martin, *Inventing Superstition: From the Hippocratics to the Christians* (Cambridge, MA: Harvard Univ. Press, 2004).

17. This point is made by Clifford Ando in *The Matter of the Gods: Religion and the Roman Empire* (Berkeley: Univ. of California Press, 2008). The Romans acquired their knowledge about the gods through observation. It was empirical and factual. The Christians spoke about "trust" and "belief." Why anyone would want to die for something as flimsy as a belief must have seemed quite curious to an ancient Roman.

18. Pliny, *Letters* 10.96.

19. Tertullian, *To the Nations* 1.

20. Athenagoras, *Embassy for Christians* 3. Thyestes was part of the House of Atreus, a family plagued by cannibalism. He inadvertently ate his own sons at a banquet hosted by his vengeful brother. Oedipus, made famous by Sigmund Freud, became king of Thebes after unknowingly marrying his mother.

21. Minucius Felix, *Octavius* 9.5, in *Religions of Rome*, vol. 2: *A Sourcebook*, ed. Mary Beard, John North, and Simon Price (Cambridge: Cambridge Univ. Press, 1998), 281.

22. Justin, *First Apology* 66.

23. Ignatius of Antioch refers to the *agape* meal, or love feast, in his *Letter to the Smyrneans* 8.2. The idea of the *agape* meal is sometimes inferred from 1 Corinthians, but even here Paul does not explicitly call the meal he describes in 1 Cor. 11:20–34 an *agape* meal. There is considerable scholarly debate about whether these *agape* meals are eucharistic meals.

24. Suetonius, *Lives of the Twelve Caesars*, Caligula 24. See also Cassius Dio, *Roman History* 59.11, 22.

25. *Martyrs of Lyons* 5.1.14.

Chapter 6: Myths About Martyrs

1. For the classic treatment of the Circumcellions, see W. H. C. Frend, *The Donatist Church* (Oxford: Clarendon, 1952); "The *Cellae* of the African Circumcellions," *Journal of Theological Studies* 3 (1952): 87–89; "Circumcellions and Monks," *Journal of Theological Studies* 20 (1969): 542–49; and "The Donatist Church—Forty Years On," in *Windows on Origins: Essays on the Early Church in Honour of J. A. A. A. Stoop*, ed. C. Landman and D. P. Whitelaw (Pretoria: Unisa, 1985), 70–84. For a recent reappraisal of the Circumcellion question, see Brent D. Shaw, "Who Were the Circumcellions?," in *Vandals, Romans, and Berbers: New Perspectives on Late Antique North Africa*, ed. A. H. Merrills (Aldershot: Ashgate, 2004), 227–58.

2. Isiodore, *Encyclopedia* 8.5.51.

3. One difficulty with the Circumcellions is that almost all our evidence about them comes from the works of their opponents, especially those of Augustine, Philastrius, and Isiodore.

4. For a fuller discussion of voluntary martyrdom in early Christianity, see my "The Discourse of Voluntary Martyrdom: Ancient and Modern," *Church History* 81, no. 3 (2012): 531–51.

5. While suicide is still regarded as objectively wrong, with the rise of psychology the position of the Catholic Church toward those who have committed suicide has warmed. Those who have taken their own lives are now often provided with funerals, and it was always the case that funeral masses were dedicated to those who had committed suicide (*Catechism* 2282).

6. For a survey of ancient views of suicide and its relationship to martyrdom see Arthur J. Droge and James D. Tabor, *A Noble Death: Suicide and Martyrdom Among Christians and Jews in Antiquity* (San Francisco: HarperSanFrancisco, 1992).

7. Clement, *Miscellanies* 4.16–17.

8. See, for example, Timothy D. Barnes, *Tertullian: A Historical and Literary Study* (New York: Oxford Univ. Press, 1985), 177–78; Ronald A. Knox, *Enthusiasm: A Chapter in the History of Religion* (Oxford: Clarendon, 1950), 49; A. R. Birley, "Persecutors and Martyrs in Tertullian's Africa," in *The Later Roman Empire Today*,

ed. Dido Clark (London: Institute of Archaeology, 1993), 37–86 [47]; and William Tabbernee, *Fake Prophecy and Polluted Sacraments: Ecclesiastical and Imperial Reactions to Montanism*, Supplements to Vigiliae Christianae 84 (Leiden: Brill, 2007), 201.

9. William Tabbernee's work in this area cannot be highly enough recommended. See particularly "Christian Inscriptions from Phrygia," in *New Documents Illustrating Early Christianity*, ed. G. H. R. Horsley and S. R. Llewelyn (Grand Rapids, MI: Eerdmans, 1978), 3:128–39; "Early Montanism and Voluntary Martyrdom," *Colloquium* 17 (1985): 33–44; and *Fake Prophecy and Polluted Sacraments*, 201–42. Tabbernee demonstrates that there was really no difference between Montanists and "Catholics" when it comes to voluntary martyrdom.

10. Augustine, *City of God* 1.20. Lactantius makes the same claims in *Divine Institutes* 3.18.

11. This story is found in an Egyptian martyrdom account called the *Acts of Shenoufe and His Brethren*, preserved in the Pierpont Morgan Codices. See E. A. E. Reymond and J. W. B. Barns, *Four Martyrdoms from the Pierpont Morgan Coptic Codices* (Oxford: Clarendon, 1973). There are some ambiguities in the story about who kills whom. It is possible that Eusebius grabs the sword only to kill himself.

12. *Acts of the Abitinian Martyrs* 18, 16. Cf. *Martyrdom of Maximian and Isaac* 7: "But the devil was not permitted to overpower the second martyr, because it was not right that the victory of Christ which burned bright should cede to anyone in any way"; and *Martyrdom of Marculus* 5: "The enemy was conquered and subdued in battle."

13. *Martyrs of Lyons* 5.1.23.

14. *Martyrs of Lyons* 5.1.42.

15. For a discussion of Blandina see Perkins, *Suffering Self*, 113–15; and Burrus, *Saving Shame*.

16. Standard histories of the Crusades have likened them to colonialism, barbarian invasion, and other forms of aggressive conquest. The appropriateness of the label "colonialism" has been challenged by those who see its application as overestimating the resources of medieval Europe, anachronistic, and generated by late-twentieth-century political movements.

17. See Rodney Stark, *God's Battalions: The Case for the Crusades* (San Francisco: HarperOne, 2009), in which it is argued that the Crusades were a military response to Muslim aggression.

18. Jeremy Cohen, *Sanctifying the Name of God: Jewish Martyrs and Jewish Memories of the First Crusade*, Jewish Culture and Contexts (Philadelphia: Univ. of Pennsylvania Press, 2004).

19. See J. Riley-Smith, "Death on the First Crusade," in *The End of Strife: Death, Reconciliation, and Expressions of Christian Spirituality*, papers selected from the proceedings of the Colloquium of the Commission Internationale d'Histoire Ecclésiastique Comparée, held at the University of Durham, 2 to 9 September 1981, ed. D. Loades (Edinburgh: Clark, 1984), 14–31; Jean Flori, "Mort et martyre des guerriers vers 1100: L'exemple de la première croisade," *Cahiers de Civilisation Médiévale* 34 (1991): 121–39; Colin Morris, "Martyrs on the Field of Battle Before and During the First Crusade," in *Martyrs and Martyrologies*, papers read at the 1992 Summer Meeting and the 1993 Winter Meeting of the Ecclesiastical History Society, Studies in Church History 30, ed. D. Wood (Oxford: Blackwell, 1993), 93–104; and Marek Tamm, "Martyrs and Miracles: Depicting Death in the Chronicle of Henry of Livonia," in *Crusading and Chronicle Writing on the Medieval Baltic Frontier*, ed. Marek Tamm, Linda Kaljundi, and Carsten Selch Jensen (Farnham: Ashgate, 2011), 135–56.

20. According to Guibert of Nogent, *Gesta Dei per Francos* 2.4, cited in Tamm, "Martyrs and Miracles," 149.

21. *Martyrdom of Polycarp* 17.3.

22. The "moral exemplar" model of salvation is traced back to the work of medieval theologian Peter Abelard, who described Jesus as providing a moral example of love, humility, and obedience. The theory is extrapolated from Abelard's appendix to his commentary on Rom. 3:19–26, in which he intimates that those who imitate Christ's love win freedom from sin and redemption through Jesus.

23. An evolutionary psychologist might argue that parents' willingness to lay down their lives for their children is actually tied to a desire to see the continuation of their genetic lineage. That said, even in modern society, the notion of maternal love is couched in religious, not reproductive terms. The way we *think* about these actions is using implicitly Christian notions of what it means to love a person. It is not at all clear that, without New Testament passages about laying down one's life for one's friends (e.g., John 15:13), we would have a concept of love that is so intricately bound up with notions of sacrifice.

24. Delores S. Williams, *Sisters in the Wilderness: The Challenge of*

Womanist God-Talk (Maryknoll, NY: Orbis Books, 1993), 166; and "Black Women's Surrogacy Experience and the Christian Notion of Redemption," in *Cross Examinations: Readings on the Meaning of the Cross Today*, ed. Marit Trelstad (Minneapolis, MN: Fortress, 2006), 19–22. Other criticisms can be found in Rita Nakashima Brock and Rebecca Ann Parker, *Proverbs of Ashes: Violence, Redemptive Suffering, and the Search for What Saves Us* (Boston: Beacon, 2001).

25. Archbishops' Council, *Responding to Domestic Abuse: Guidelines for Those with Pastoral Responsibility* (London: Church House, 2006). This particular study was initiated in 2004 by the Church of England.

26. Archbishops' Council, *Responding to Domestic Abuse*, 20.

27. *Martyrdom of Maximian and Isaac* 18.

28. *Martyrdom of Marian and James* 12.8

29. *Martyrdom of Marian and James* 31.

30. For a positive use of martyrs as models of resistance, see the work of liberation theologian Gustavo Gutiérrez.

31. *Passion of Perpetua and Felicity* 17.2.

32. Tertullian, *On Spectacles* 30.

33. Friedrich Nietzsche, *On the Genealogy of Morality: A Polemic*, trans. Carol Diethe (Cambridge: Cambridge Univ. Press, 2000), 19.

34. We have good reason for thinking that Jesus actually said this. By the time the Gospel of Mark was written, the disciples had already started to die. There would have been no reason to preserve the saying if it weren't a part of the pre-Gospel oral tradition.

35. *Acts of the Scillitan Martyrs* 15.

36. *Martyrdom of Polycarp* 14.2.

37. *Martyrdom of Pionius* 21.4.

38. I argued in my book *The Other Christs* that it is possible that some Christians thought that martyrs shared the status of Christ in heaven (149–72).

39. *Martyrdom of Marian and James* 8.11.

40. *Acts of Apollonius* 1.42.

Chapter 7: The Invention of the Persecuted Church

1. William Bramley-Moore, *The Book of the Martyrs by John Foxe* (London: Cassell, Petter & Galpin, 1867), 2.

2. Ironically, Eusebius wanted to preserve the reputations of some good emperors. At the beginning of *Church History* 5 he used the

name "Antoninus Verus" for Marcus Aurelius because it could be easily confused with the coemperor Lucius Verus. Marcus Aurelius was well regarded in the fourth century, and Eusebius wanted to deflect blame onto his less remarkable coemperor. See H. A. Drake, *Constantine and the Bishops: The Politics of Intolerance* (Baltimore: Johns Hopkins Univ. Press, 2000), 386-87.

3. By the nineteenth-century historian Jacob Burckhardt, cited in Drake, *Constantine and the Bishops*, 365-66.

4. On the peace that preceded the Great Persecution, see Eusebius, *Church History* 8.1.

5. Although many scholars assume that Eusebius was a bishop when he wrote the first edition of the *Church History*, we only know that he was a bishop in 315 when he addressed Paulinus of Tyre as an equal in *Church History* 10.1, 4. I am grateful to David Devore, of UC Berkeley, for this observation.

6. There is considerable debate about the chronology of Eusebius's writings in regard to his status as a bishop and his relationship to Constantine.

7. That Eusebius composed his own collections of martyrdom stories demonstrates for us just how interested he was in martyrs. We are dealing with a man who was a devotee of the martyrs, who understood their allure, and was himself interested in preserving their stories.

8. So Timothy D. Barnes, *Constantine and Eusebius* (Cambridge, MA: Harvard Univ. Press, 2006), 148.

9. This story is relayed in Epiphanius, *Panarion* 68.8.3 and referred to in Raymond Van Dam, *The Roman Revolution of Constantine* (Cambridge: Cambridge Univ. Press, 2007).

10. *Martyrdom of Polycarp* 17.

11. Eusebius, *Church History* 8.6.7.

12. Eusebius, *Church History* 1.1.

13. Eusebius, *Church History* 5, Pref. 3-4.

14. In *Church History* 4.7.1, Eusebius says that Satan is behind the persecutions.

15. Eusebius, *Church History* 4.14.7.

16. Eusebius, *Church History* 4.14.6.

17. Eusebius, *Church History* 5.20.6.

18. W. H. C. Frend, *Martyrdom and Persecution in the Early Church: A Study of Conflict from the Maccabees to Donatus* (Oxford: Blackwell, 1965), 291-92, 361; Barnes, *Tertullian*, 177-78.

19. So Jan den Boeft and Jan Bremmer, "Notiunculae Martyrologicae V," *Vigiliae Christianae* 49 (1995): 146–64 [148].

20. Eusebius, *Church History* 2.25.6; 4.27.1; 5.16.1; 5.18.1.

21. Eusebius, *Church History* 4.15.6.

22. Eusebius, *Church History* 5.3.4.

23. This argument is anticipated in the writings of Irenaeus, who uses animalistic language to portray heretics as wild beasts in the arena. Looking even farther back in time, a similar strategy is employed by Paul, who uses his claim that he is persecuted like Jesus to counteract those opposing his message in the communities he founded, and by Ignatius of Antioch, who used his status as imprisoned sufferer-like-Christ to institute order in the churches in Asia Minor. It is Eusebius, however, who writes this idea into history and creates the bridge so that heretics, schismatics, and insubordinates can be treated as persecutors. For a discussion of persecution rhetoric in Paul, see James A. Kelhoffer, *Persecution, Persuasion, and Power: Readiness to Withstand Hardship as a Corroboration of Legitimacy in the New Testament*, Wissenschaftliche Untersuchungen zum Neuen Testament 1.270 (Tübingen: Mohr Siebeck, 2010). Kelhoffer's work builds upon Elizabeth A. Castelli, *Imitating Paul: A Discourse of Power* (Louisville, KY: Westminster John Knox, 1991), 21–34.

24. On the archaeological material, see MacMullen, *The Second Church*; and Kim Bowes, *Private Worship, Public Values, and Religious Change in Late Antiquity* (Cambridge: Cambridge Univ. Press, 2008).

25. Eusebius's agenda drew upon already established rhetorical moves. Ignatius of Antioch, one of the most famous of the early Christian martyrs, had already issued thinly veiled threats to his addressees that they "must regard the bishop as the Lord himself" (*Letter to the Ephesians* 6.1). Ignatius had instructed his audience that should anyone disagree with him or any other bishop, then that person would be cut off: "If any hold to alien views, they dissociate themselves from the passion" (*Letter to the Philadelphians* 3.3, translation here is that of Michael Holmes, *Apostolic Fathers: Greek Texts and English Translations* [Grand Rapids, MI: Baker, 2007]). Conformity to the image of Christ is a happy ideal, but for Ignatius the bishop was Christ's representative in the church. Practically speaking, Ignatius is telling his addressees to obey their bishops and conform to the views of the community. See discussion in Perkins, *Suffering Self*, 191.

26. Eusebius, *Church History* (*Martyrs of Lyons*) 5.4.1–2.

27. Eusebius, *Church History* (*Martyrs of Lyons*) 5.5.8–9.

28. Tertullian, *Against the Heretics* 22; *On Modesty* 21.

29. On the relationships between bishops and monks, see Claudia Rapp, *Holy Bishops in Late Antiquity: The Nature of Christian Leadership in an Age of Transition* (Berkeley: Univ. of California Press, 2005).

30. Eusebius, *Church History* 6.44.19.

31. For more on this topic see Brad S. Gregory, *Salvation at Stake: Christian Martyrdom in Early Modern Europe* (Cambridge, MA: Harvard Univ. Press, 1999).

32. Delehaye, *Legends of the Saints*, 104.

33. Delehaye, *Legends of the Saints*, 104.

34. Pio Franchi De Cavalieri, *Santa Agnese nella tradizione e nella leggenda*, Römische Quartalschrift, Supplementheft 13 (Rome, 1899), 20.

35. The phenomenon in general was remarked upon in the nineteenth century. For a discussion with respect to the fourth century, see Delehaye, *Legends of the Saints*, 94–95. As time progressed, things only grew worse. Medieval hagiographers filled the lives of saints with extracts from the lives of *other* saints. The lives of St. Hubert, St. Arnold of Metz, and St. Lambert share certain sections, for instance, and the life of St. Vincent Madelgarus is an exercise in "spot the early Christian source," as transcriptions of no fewer than six different Christian texts about *other* martyrs are included! (Delehaye, *Legends of the Saints*, 101–2).

36. The best book on the cult of the saints is still, to my mind, Peter Brown's classic *The Cult of the Saints*. This particular point is emphasized in the first chapter.

37. For more on this phenomenon see Sabine G. MacCormack, *Art and Ceremony in Late Antiquity* (Berkeley: Univ. of California Press, 1981).

38. Archaeological digs yield treasure troves of this kind of material. See, for example, the photographs of Thecla lamps in Stephen J. Davis, *The Cult of Saint Thecla: A Tradition of Women's Piety in Late Antiquity* (Oxford: Oxford Univ. Press, 2001).

39. Hippolyte Delehaye, "La passion de S. Théodote d'Ancyre," *Analecta Bollandiana* 22 (1903): 320–28.

40. See the well-received article by Stephen Mitchell, "The Life of Saint Theodotus of Ancyra" (*Anatolian Studies* 32 [1982]: 93–113),

which dates the account itself to the 360s. This excellent article uses archaeology to ascertain that the author of the account had a very detailed knowledge of the topography of Malos. It further argues, against Delehaye, that the connection between Theodotus and the seven virgins was not accidental and that they were all members of the New Prophecy movement. This argument, although popular, seems to me to be based on now outdated views of voluntary martyrdom in the early church (see my "Discourse of Voluntary Martyrdom Ancient and Modern," *Church History* 81.3 [2012]: 531–51). Furthermore, the knowledge of local topography only demonstrates that the author was familiar with the region. As the text appears to me to have been written to support the martyr cult in that area, this familiarity is expected.

41. On wealthy women and private worship, see Nicola Frances Denzey, *The Bone Gatherers: The Lost Worlds of Early Christian Women* (Boston: Beacon, 2008); and Bowes, *Private Worship, Public Values, and Religious Change*.

42. *Passion of Saint Sebastian* 88.

43. The first two options are considered in Denzey, *Bone Gatherers*, xv–xvi. The notion that Lucina is fictional is found in Kate Cooper, "The Martyr, the *Matrona*, and the Bishop: The Matron Lucina and the Politics of Martyr Cult in Fifth- and Sixth-Century Rome," *Early Medieval Europe* 8, no. 3 (1999): 297–317. She has been followed by others, including David L. Eastman in *Paul the Martyr*, 107.

44. See Cooper, "The Martyr, the *Matrona*, and the Bishop," in which Cooper examines the collections of texts in which Lucina appears in light of church politics at the turn of the sixth century.

45. For the traditional definition of apocalyptic literature and its attendant worldview, see John J. Collins, "Introduction: Toward the Morphology of a Genre," in *Apocalypse: The Morphology of a Genre*, Semeia 14, ed. John J. Collins (Atlanta: Society of Biblical Literature, 1979), 9; and Christopher Rowland, *The Open Heaven: A Study of Apocalyptic in Judaism and Early Christianity* (New York: Crossroad, 1982).

46. See, for example, Donald W. Riddle, "The Physical Basis of Apocalypticism," *Journal of Religion* 4, no. 2 (1924): 174–91.

47. See the introduction to John Joseph Collins, Bernard McGinn, and Stephen J. Stein, eds., *The Encyclopedia of Apocalypticism* (New York: Continuum, 1999), x.

48. Scott M. Lewis, *So That God May Be in All: The Apocalyptic Message of 1 Corinthians 15, 12–34* (Rome: Gregorian Press, 1998), 211.
49. *Acts of Justin* C 6.3.
50. *Acts of Justin* C 1.1.
51. *Acts of Phileas*, Latin 9.1.
52. *Acts of Apollonius*, 47.
53. Hal A. Drake, "Lambs into Lions: Explaining Early Christian Intolerance," *Past and Present* 153 (1996): 3–36; and "Intolerance, Religious Violence, and Political Legitimacy in Late Antiquity," *Journal of the American Academy of Religion* 79, no. 1 (2011): 193–235.
54. This shocking proclamation was the title of Michael Gaddis's excellent exploration of Christian violence in late antiquity. His thesis, alluded to here, was that martyrdom and the idea that Christians were engaged in a spiritual war with Satan fostered violence against pagans. See Michael Gaddis, *There Is No Crime for Those Who Have Christ: Religious Violence in the Christian Roman Empire* (Berkeley: Univ. of California Press, 2005); and Thomas Sizgorich, *Violence and Belief in Late Antiquity: Militant Devotion in Christianity and Islam* (Philadelphia: Univ. of Pennsylvania Press, 2008).

Chapter 8: The Dangerous Legacy of a Martyrdom Complex

1. My attention was drawn to this particular news report by my friend Dan Myers, Professor of Sociology at the University of Notre Dame.
2. Translation by Eleanor Beardsley, National Public Radio, Paris, January 11, 2012.
3. Stan Greenberg, James Carville, Karl Agne, and Jim Gerstein, "The Very Separate World of Conservative Republicans," *Democracy Corps*, October 16, 2009; http://big.assets.huffingtonpost .com/TheVerySeparateWorld.pdf. All the examples cited here are taken from Michael Wolraich, *Blowing Smoke: Why the Right Keeps Serving Up Whack-Job Fantasies About the Plot to Euthanize Grandma, Outlaw Christmas, and Turn Junior into a Raging Homosexual* (Cambridge, MA: Da Capo, 2010), 19.
4. Cited in Wolraich, *Blowing Smoke*, 19.
5. CNN Florida Republican Presidential Debate, January 26, 2012.
6. Gianna Molla had refused an abortion or a hysterectomy and had

instead opted for a less invasive procedure in the hopes of saving her child. She was canonized by John Paul II in 2004.

7. Neither woman seemed aware of the sentiment expressed by Vatican bioethicist Archbishop Rino Fisichella, in which he acknowledged that in this case the teachings of the church appeared to many "to be insensitive, incomprehensible, and lacking mercy" (cited in Alexei Barrionuevo, "Amid Abuse in Brazil, Abortion Debate Flares," *New York Times*, March 27, 2009).

8. John Stott, *The Spirit, the Church, and the World: The Message of Acts* (Downers Grove, IL: InterVarsity, 1990), 89–90.

9. Stott, *Spirit, Church, and World*, 105.

10. *The Rush Limbaugh Show*, May 29, 2012.

11. Ann Coulter, "Persecution in the USA?" October 2, 2003; www.anncoulter.com.

12. On this point I agree with John Allen in his article, "Five Myths About Anti-Christian Persecution," *National Catholic Reporter Online;* http://ncronline.org/blogs/all-things-catholic/five-myths-about-anti-christian-persecution (accessed January 29, 2012).

13. Mark Lobel, "Deadly Attack on Nigeria's Bayero University in Kano," BBC, April 30, 2012; www.bbc.co.uk/news/world-africa-17886143.

14. Sadly, similar examples can be adduced from Indonesia, Egypt, and Iran. In many parts of the world Christians continue to be the victims of religiously motivated violence.

15. "Panicked Catholics Flee Violence in Northern Nigeria," Catholic News Agency, January 26, 2012; www.catholicnewsagency.com/news/panicked-catholics-flee-violence-in-northern-nigeria.

16. Delehaye, *Legends of the Saints*, 64.

INDEX